Literary Pathways

Literary Pathways
Selecting Books
to Support New Readers

Barbara Peterson

HEINEMANN
Portsmouth, NH

Heinemann
A division of Reed Elsevier Inc.
361 Hanover Street
Portsmouth, NH 03801–3912
www.heinemann.com

Offices and agents throughout the world

The author and publisher wish to thank those who have generously given permission to reprint borrowed material:

Excerpt from *The Ghost* (Story Box) by Joy Cowley. Copyright © 1983 by The Wright Group. Used by permission of The Wright Group, 19201 120th Avenue NE, Bothell, WA 98011. Telephone: (800) 523-2371.

Excerpt from *The Carrot Seed* by Ruth Krauss. Text copyright © 1945 by Ruth Krauss. Used by permission of HarperCollins Publishers.

Excerpt from *Look for Me* (Story Box) by June Melser. Copyright © 1982 by The Wright Group. Used by permission of The Wright Group, 19201 120th Avenue NE, Bothell, WA 98011. Telephone: (800) 523-2371.

Material from *Saturday Morning* is reproduced by permission of the publishers Learning Media Limited on behalf of Ministry of Education, PO Box 3293, Wellington, New Zealand, © Crown, 1983.

(Credits continue on page 218)

Library of Congress Cataloging-in-Publication Data
Peterson, Barbara
    Literary pathways : selecting books to support new readers / Barbara Peterson.
        p.   cm.
    Includes bibliographical references and index.
    ISBN 0-325-00164-2 (alk. paper)
        1. Children—Books and reading.   2. Reading (Elementary).   3. Children's
    literature—Bibliography.   I. Title.

Z1037.A1 P47 2001
028.5′5—dc21

                                                                    2001047223

Editor: Danny Miller
Production service: Colophon Production Service
Production coordinator: Sonja S. Chapman
Cover design: Jenny Jensen Greenleaf
Manufacturing: Steve Bernier
Cover photo: Barbara Peterson

Printed in the United States of America on acid-free paper
05   04   03   02   01   VP   1   2   3   4   5

For Charlotte,
           who has inspired me to keep exploring

And, especially for Jim,
           who has made all the difference

Contents

Foreword

CHARLOTTE S. HUCK

D r. Barbara Peterson is uniquely qualified to write a book on *Literary Pathways: Selecting Books to Support New Readers* for she has been trained as both a children's librarian and as a Reading Recovery teacher. Her dissertation at The Ohio State University was based on the research that she did on determining the difficulty of texts for beginning readers. I wish every school librarian had Barbara's knowledge of how children take on the reading process, and I wish every teacher had Barbara's knowledge of the wide range of books that will enable a child to become successful in learning to read. We have quantities of texts about the teaching of reading, many texts about the field of children's literature, but few texts written about ways to identify the characteristics of books that support children in becoming readers.

In this text, Barbara Peterson gives us a personal view of her work as the children's librarian at the Tully Magnet School in Tucson, Arizona. She tells us about Cassandra, who so wanted to be seen as a reader, she checked out many books from the library, but could not read any of them. Barbara recognized this and quietly gave her Reading Recovery lessons during her lunch hour, bringing her up to a level of reading that allowed her to enjoy reading books rather than just carrying them home. Barbara shares her delight when a beginning reader discovers "his book," one that he can read easily, over and over again, until he becomes a fluent reader. She elicited children's responses to books by forming a Reading Explorers group to discuss their preferences for particular books. She states, "Almost every book I write about in *Literary Pathways* is one I know through the eyes of children by way of teaching, book discussions, and informal conversations."

For years the motto of every librarian has been, "To find the right book for the right child at the right time." But how do you do that for the new reader? Publishers of reading series have tried to create texts which will guarantee success for all beginning readers, regardless of background. They have created non-stories with controlled vocabularies, controlled sounds, and two-word sentences, thereby eliminating story and real meaning. Other publishers have produced a flood of "little books," some of which are written in the same style as the decodable texts, but others are written as real stories, by real authors, and in ways that support children in their efforts to become readers. This text discusses ways to identify these books and to evaluate them for both their appeal to children and their ease of reading.

Some children who have very literate parents will have been read stories since infancy and do not need so-called easy texts. They already know about concepts of print and how a story works. They know where to begin on a page, and that we read from left to right. They have a sense of story and how to predict action, how particular characters such as a princess or an evil stepmother will behave. They are accustomed to joining in on such refrains as "not by the hair of my chinny chin-chin" or the cumulative refrain of "I know an old lady who swallowed a fly—perhaps she'll die." They expect stories to be meaningful and enjoyable. For many children, all they have to do is attach words to the stories they already know, and they do it easily.

But some children have never heard a story until they come to school. They are being introduced to the idea of a story at the same time they are beginning to learn to read. They need quantities of simple stories, such as Brian Wildsmith's *Cat On The Mat* or *All Fall Down,* with his beautiful colorful pictures, or the wonderfully funny tale of *Mrs. Wishy-Washy,* who is involved in the unending task of trying to keep her animals clean. These little books have repetitious language patterns that support children's reading, at the same time that their stories delight them.

Many factors influence the choice of a level of difficulty for a particular book, including content in relation to children's personal experiences, language patterns, vocabulary, illustrations, and the narrative style that supports the meaning of the text. But two things are major in helping a child persist in the difficult task of learning to read: the desire to read a real story and the joy of being successful in the reading of it.

This text helps teachers to identify those books that will provide success for the new reader and at the same time, put him on the pathway to becoming a reader; one who knows how to read and discovers the pleasure of reading for a lifetime.

Acknowledgments

The roots of *Literary Pathways* are far reaching, for it is a book I could never have written without the nurturing of many people throughout my life. My parents and grandparents gave me books, and read to me often. Reading was an important part of family life when my children, Amy and George, were small. When they were eight and ten, they entered the informal education program at Barrington Elementary in Upper Arlington, Ohio. I was astounded by the richness of the school's literature program, and I expressed surprise that their classrooms were filled with an abundance of wonderful books I had only seen in the public library, where I had previously worked.

"Charlotte Huck," I was told, over and over again. Thus began a journey that transformed my professional life, for eventually, I met Charlotte and began the doctoral program in children's literature at Ohio State under her guidance. While at Ohio State, I had the good fortune to be mentored by a group of amazing women, of whom Charlotte was the first. Charlotte's passion for children's literature is legendary, but what endeared her to me was her commitment to making children's literature the essence of reading in classrooms. My own children were beneficiaries of her vision, and school became a wonderful, exciting place for them.

Through Charlotte, I met Martha King. I took several courses in language and writing development from Martha, and I began to learn about the importance of language to teaching and learning. Janet Hickman's research on children's response to literature led me to think more deeply about what it means to be a reader. From Marie Clay, I learned how to observe young readers, and the importance of focusing on what children know and can do, not on what they are lacking. Lastly, while I was still at Ohio State, I was fortunate to meet Margaret Meek, whose work with readers and texts helped me to consider more closely the interactions between them.

The voices of children are important to me, and many are woven throughout the pages of this book. They are some of the children I have taught, and who have taught me, during my eight years as the teacher–librarian at Tully Elementary Accelerated Magnet School in Tucson. I am grateful to Lynda

Brady for helping establish the Reading Explorers program with her second-grade students. Seeing books through the eyes of the children for whom they were written is quite different from reading them with adult eyes. Thank you, Reading Explorers, for your enthusiasm!

First-year Reading Explorers were Nikki, Dylan, Isaiah, José, Nolan, Angie, Joel, Salina, Jacob, Danielle, Mariah, Kosmos, Raul, Joseph, Sonia, Ana, Nicholas, Chris, and Andrea. Second-year Reading Explorers were Alberto, Celina, Calvin, Tori, Tonie, Danielle, Jimmie, Ruben, Brian, Rachel, Michelle, Kathleen, Chelsea, Savannah, Nico, Frankie, Davi, Casarah, Antonio, Saundra, and Victor. The Poetry Stars were a small group of second-grade students from another class who read and laughed their way through many poetry books. Thank you to Flor, Laylana, Yarimeth, Esperanza, Mark, Gabriel, and Bryana. (I have used other names for all of them in the book.) Thank you also to my grandson Andrew for letting me include his kindergarten writing on *Nate the Great*, and to my grandson Dominic for listening to many stories about *The Three Bears*.

I am so fortunate to have many friends and colleagues who share a passion for teaching, and I am extremely grateful that many of them were willing to read the manuscript for this book. Marilyn Carpenter, Janet Hickman, and Cornelia Carlson read early drafts of several chapters when they were still very rough and hardly resembled a book. Their encouragement and advice helped give shape to my thoughts and kept me going. Others read the first five chapters and gave useful suggestions for everything from smoothing out quirky syntax to clarifying clouded thoughts. They are true friends, for who else would accept a "gift" of an unedited 200-page manuscript the day before winter vacation! Special thanks to: Kathleen Holland, Dan Woolsey, Carol Cribbet-Bell, Gudrun Godare, Randall Smith, Joanne Robinson, Craig Sooy, Gloria Carrington, Kathy Marshall, Lynn Trepicchio, Rosaisela Moreno, Belén Córdova, and Elaine Noble.

I have also been fortunate to have two editors at Heinemann to help with the enormous process of turning years of work into a coherent book. Amy Cohn brought up the idea long after I given up trying to figure out a way to do it. Through several months of correspondence she nudged, listened, and helped me to see the possibilities. Danny Miller edited the entire manuscript, encouraging me with his enthusiasm and making me laugh with his wry commentary on an assortment of topics. His suggestions for revisions were always on target, and I could count on him to help me find a way to transform my cluttered thoughts into linear prose.

I have also made the acquaintance of another team of wonderful people at Heinemann and at Colophon Production Services. Peggy Wishart provided wise guidance that helped me find my way through a maze of permissions procedures. Maura Sullivan planned and implemented a strategy for connecting this book with its potential audience. Sonja Chapman coordinated all aspects of production that transformed a stack of computer files into the finished book. Peg Latham managed the day-to-day production matters, ever ready to offer gentle reassurance along the way. Julie de Silva's thoughtful and meticulous copyediting ensured that stumbling phrases were made lucid.

While writing this book, I used resources from three fine libraries. I found many books to include in this one by browsing the shelves of the Bear Canyon Branch of the Tucson Pima Public Library. The Educational Materials Center of the Tucson Unified School District has a superb professional collection, and many of my professional references were found there. A special thanks to librarian Jan Strell, who answered my e-mail pleas for journal citations as I was preparing the bibliographies for this book. The library at Tully Elementary is a very busy place, and I am immensely thankful for the friendship and dedicated work of Gail Mattix, my library assistant when I began writing, and Angela Agellon, my library assistant when I finished this book. And, with my writing deadline rapidly approaching, Alicia Basemann came to my rescue by typing several bibliographies.

The incomparable Bill Morris, Director of Library Promotions for HarperCollins Children's Books, has been a friend to me, and to countless other teachers and librarians, for many years. I treasure the many lively conversations we have had about books for young readers.

Without a doubt, my husband Jim is the most important person behind this book, for he has encouraged me, cooked dinner, proofed pages, and never complained when writing interfered with our hiking plans.

Literary Pathways

1

Literature, Readers, and Text Complexity— An Inseparable Trio

Literary Pathways is a book to guide teachers and librarians in understanding what makes a text easy or challenging for a reader. It is also a book about choosing literature to meet and extend the interests of all readers. Most importantly, it is a book threaded with the voices of children discovering that the books they *can* read are also books they *like* reading. *Literary Pathways* is not a book about how to teach reading; rather, it is a book designed to support teachers and librarians in their unique, but overlapping roles, as they strive to provide each child with the right book at the right time. In the words of Charlotte Huck, eminent teacher of children's literature and author of many children's books:

> We must do more than just teach our students to read. We must help them become readers who are completely absorbed in their books and look forward to a lifetime of pleasure in reading good books (1990, 12).

The readers I have in mind range from those just learning to recognize a word or two in print to those capable of reading the very short chapter books that are often referred to as "easy readers." When children first learn how to read, they eagerly and willingly read all they are asked to read. Soon, however, they develop very definite ideas about what is a good book. Some do not hesitate to try something new, but others need help pushing the boundaries of their interests. By thoughtfully providing them with a range of literature in many styles of writing, both fiction and nonfiction, we can help them learn how to explore and enjoy a wide variety of books they might not discover on their own.

Twenty-five years ago, when I became a children's librarian, I read most of the books in the children's department of our public library collection. I

1

also learned something about the authors, illustrators, and publishers of those books. Parents and children came to me and the other librarians for guidance in selecting books that were the right reading level, met the readers' interests, and extended their range of reading, both by topic and difficulty. Matching readers with books was the most enjoyable part of my job, especially when they returned and talked eagerly about how much they liked a particular book. Making the right match seemed intuitive and easy at the time.

Several years later, as a doctoral student in children's literature and early literacy at The Ohio State University, I discovered that making the match was not as easy with children who were struggling with learning to read. While there, I became a Reading Recovery teacher and teacher leader. Developed in New Zealand by Marie Clay (1993b), Reading Recovery provides intensive, short-term instruction for first-grade students having difficulty learning to read. As a Reading Recovery teacher, I found that most of the books I knew and loved were far too difficult for our students, and through my work with students and other Reading Recovery teachers, I learned what kinds of texts were best for their instruction. This work led to my dissertation research in which I studied books used in Reading Recovery and described characteristics of text and illustration that made them easy or difficult for readers (Peterson 1988).

Now, as the librarian in an elementary school, I have developed a broader understanding of the challenges teachers face in matching readers to books. One part of my job is to acquire materials in English and Spanish to support the wide range of instructional programs and the recreational reading needs of our school community. Occasionally, we have students who enter kindergarten reading fluently, and sometimes we have third and fourth graders come to us able to read only simple caption books. Another part of my job is to work in collaboration with teachers to plan and co-teach research, reading, literature, and writing to their students (Peterson 1998; Giorgis and Peterson 1996). I have also taught a few children how to read and a few others how to become better readers. As a result of my work, I have had abundant opportunities to observe children as readers, and I have done a lot of thinking about the books that have supported their learning and excited them as readers.

My knowledge of literature and text complexity influences how I work with children, who, in turn, have taught me much of what I know about selecting books to support new readers. By knowing more about the inseparable trio of literature, readers, and text complexity, teachers and librarians can work together to create powerful, richly textured reading instruction for all children. While instructional level books are the focus of *Literary Pathways,* it is important to keep in mind that such texts comprise only one component of an effective reading and literature program. Three questions have guided my writing.

1. How can teachers and librarians provide books that each of their students *can* read and *want* to read?

2. How can teachers and librarians select materials appropriate for reading instruction that will introduce their students to many styles of writing?

3. How can teachers and librarians gently guide their students in finding books for recreational reading that will support and extend their developing knowledge, interests, and abilities as readers?

Literary Pathways

The title for this book grew out of an experience I had a few years ago with a group of fourth-grade students who met with me every morning in the library to read and discuss books. In our first sessions together, we talked about what kind of stories they might like to read and I showed them several books I thought they would enjoy. The first book they selected was *The Green Book* by Jill Paton Walsh. They were intrigued by the opening line of the story—"Father said, 'We can take very little with us.'" It is the story of several families preparing to leave Earth to settle a new planet. *The Green Book* is a small book of fewer than seventy pages, and one that I have known other fourth graders to read. My students, however, despite their enthusiasm and hard work, just could not understand the plot of the story.

We finally decided to move on to another book, one that proved to be a much better choice for this group. There are so many wonderful books for children that I have never considered any single title to be a "must read," and I was happy to see these students find a book that held their attention. However, I continued to be perplexed about why they had so much difficulty with *The Green Book*. Each member of the group was a capable reader, and each was genuinely interested in the story. Gradually, I came to realize that the problem lay in the way the plot develops. It is the kind of story where the writer does not immediately reveal everything the reader needs to know to completely understand the unfolding narrative. Thus, readers of *The Green Book* can read and understand the story sentence by sentence, or even paragraph by paragraph, but still not be quite sure of the meaning of what they are reading. It is not until the last two sentences of the book that the whole story begins to fall into place, at which point, many readers want to read the whole book again.

Once I realized that my students were confused by the structure of the book, the phrase "literary pathways" began echoing in my mind. What experiences with literature, both through independent reading and class read alouds, might have prepared them to read *The Green Book*? I do not have the answer, but the question has remained with me as I work with younger children. Certainly, I do not believe there is one set of books everyone must read. Literary pathways are not curriculum guides or prescribed bibliographies. Becoming a reader is a lifelong journey that can take many pathways. Teaching children *how* to read is an important part of our job, and we do that daily. However, I believe we can choose books carefully from the cauldron of literary styles so that our students learn the many ways in which a writer can tell a story or convey information.

Literature

Many teachers who work with developing readers are fortunate to have access to thousands of wonderful stories and informational books that are just right for helping their students grow as readers. When children are learning to read, they are not just learning how to decode the written word well enough so they can understand whatever we ask them to read. They are also discovering through reading that they can read to learn something new, learn more about a favorite subject, and enter the universe of imagination to meet engaging characters who have exciting adventures. One way that teachers and librarians can facilitate this journey is by carefully putting books in children's hands that will not only support learning *how* to read, but also help them learn *through* their reading.

Imagine going to an art museum and seeing several paintings hanging together—a Degas ballerina next to a Diego Rivera mural next to a Rembrandt portrait next to an O'Keeffe calla lily, and so on. If you are familiar with these artists and their work, you might be puzzled by this haphazard grouping, because museums typically arrange displays to feature the work of a particular artist or style of art. Nevertheless, your prior knowledge would allow you to focus on each individual piece and mentally visualize other paintings by the artist. You might even amuse yourself with trying to figure out if the paintings were hung randomly or if there was a master plan you just could not see. On the other hand, if you entered this exhibit as someone with little knowledge about painting, you could easily be overwhelmed by the extreme diversity in the artists, styles, and subjects in front of you.

Similarly, new readers can be easily overwhelmed by the vast number of books they see before them. By thoughtfully grouping books for children that have something in common, such as the same writer or illustrator; a particular kind of character; a similar plot; or the same subject, we can provide them with additional layers of support for learning more about literature. Teachers who use reading textbooks as the foundation of their instructional program can help children become better readers. Teachers can help children become *eager* readers by providing them with many kinds of books for making connections to the literary pathways leading to the wider world of literature.

Margaret Meek, in *How Texts Teach What Readers Learn,* a small gem of a book, emphasizes that there are many lessons children learn from texts that are not taught explicitly by their teachers. She makes a distinction between recognizing words on a page and learning to read a book, saying that "a young reader has to become both the teller (picking up the author's view and voice) and the told (the recipient of the story, the interpreter)." She goes on to say that this "symbolic interaction is learned early," and "rarely, if ever, taught . . ." (1988, 10).

This was demonstrated to me in a powerful way by Michael, a Reading Recovery student I taught many years ago. He was reading *The Chick and the Duckling* written by Mirra Ginsburg and illustrated by Jose Aruego and Ariane Dewey, a story about a chick who tries to do everything a duckling can do. All goes well until the duckling takes a swim and the chick follows suit, almost drowning until rescued by the duckling. A double-page spread illustration shows this action, but there are no words to describe the scene. Michael's reading of the text was accurate and fluent. When he turned to the drowning scene, he studied the picture, then looked up at me and softly said, "This is the sad part."

Not only was he reading the words and following the action; his words and the tone of his voice suggested to me that he had connected with the story in a powerful way. Literary theorist Louise Rosenblatt describes this involvement between reader and text as a transaction, in which the reader pays attention not only to the words on a page, but also "to the images, feelings, attitudes, associations, and ideas that the words and their referents evoked in him" (1978, 10). Consequently, readers are "immersed in a creative process that goes on largely below the threshold of awareness" (1978, 52).

Rosenblatt's discussion of the interplay between reader and text also draws attention to the fact that readers read for different purposes. They may read to quickly find out needed facts, such as first-aid procedures. In such cases, readers seek clearly written information, and are not looking for artistic design or clever prose. This kind of reading Rosenblatt calls "efferent," taken from the Latin word that means "to carry away" (1978, 24). At other times, a reader's goal may be to "get lost" in a book, and to become a part of the author's created world. When this happens, a reader's own experiences and reflections will mingle with the author's words and ideas. Rosenblatt calls this kind of lived-through experience "aesthetic" reading (1978, 25).

Readers can, and often do, read a text from both an aesthetic and efferent stance. Kathleen Holland and Leslie Shaw call this move "dances between stances."

Within the context of one book, children can also shift in and out of the efferent stance, where they focus on acquiring information, and the aesthetic stance, where they focus on what they are experiencing, thinking, and feeling" (1993, 114).

Michael's response to *The Chick and the Duckling* demonstrated that he understood the facts (efferent), but also that he had entered the world of these two characters in an aesthetic way. Rosenblatt believes that, too often, schools present literature only as texts for developing reading skills, and neglect the pleasurable aspects of reading. While skills may be enhanced and worthy moral and social values communicated, ". . . literary works often fail to emerge at all if the texts are offered as the means for the demonstrations of reading skills" (1993, 18).

Text Complexity or Readability

Researchers have long attempted to explain what makes a text easy or hard to read. Vocabulary, word repetition, sentence length, reader interest and background, sentence structure, print size, placement of print, illustrations, repetition of language patterns, and familiar story structures are some of the features that play a part in readability. Some researchers have devised readability formulas to help teachers decide where a book falls along a continuum of easy to hard, while others have developed rubrics describing features of texts along a sequence of levels. There is no foolproof way to organize—or level—a group of books into a series of readability levels to suit every need.

Trying to sort out and understand the various numbers and letters publishers use to indicate a reading level for their books can be confusing. Many publishers currently use a three- or four-level or stage system to advise readers about which books are easier or harder than others. Others use descriptive words, such as *emerging, developing,* and *transitional.* However, each system of leveling texts generally leads to a group of books being organized along an approximate gradient of easier to more difficult. These categories can be a useful starting point, but ultimately, the best way to level books is to read them and observe children reading them.

Knowing how to evaluate a variety of books and sort them along a gradient of difficulty can be enormously helpful for teachers and librarians. Teachers using basal readers as the foundation of their reading program will find that understanding text difficulty can be useful for identifying additional books their students can read along with their basal stories. Teachers who build their reading programs from a variety of trade books and "little books" written for new readers will find this knowledge helpful for organizing the hundreds of books that form the core of their reading instruction.

Most classrooms typically have students reading at several levels, so it is essential for teachers to know how to find the "just-right" book for each child. Sometimes, students do not grow as readers because they are given texts that are too difficult for them; in contrast, some students do not grow as readers because they are not given texts that interest or challenge them. Furthermore, those "just-right" books change continually, as children become better readers.

While it is useful to have textbooks, a collection of books organized into a series of levels by a publisher, or someone else's reading list, instruction will take place more smoothly when teachers can rely on their own knowledge and judgment to level books. For example, Sharon Taberski (2000) provides numerous examples of how she uses her knowledge of children's literature to select books appropriate for each one of her students and their differing needs and interests in her book *On Solid Ground: Strategies for Teaching Reading K-3.*

Seven Blind Mice

Each readability-organizing framework provides useful information, but figuring out how they overlap or fit together can be a puzzle. Trying to understand the big picture is somewhat like having the perspective of a mouse in Ed Young's picture book *Seven Blind Mice.* Similar to the traditional Indian fable of *The Blind Men and the Elephant,* it is the story of seven blind mice who encounter something strange. Each day, one mouse tries to figure out what it is. The first touches its leg and calls it a pillar. The second touches the trunk and declares it a snake. The third feels the tusk and is certain it is a spear. Climbing across its head, the fourth mouse says he has found a cliff. To the fifth, the shape of the ear tells him it must be a fan. The sixth mouse knows that the tail is a rope. Each has good reason for his guess, but it is the seventh mouse who grasps the nature of the whole being and calls it by its correct name—elephant.

My goal in this book is to help readers learn to think like the seventh mouse. Whenever I have read *Seven Blind Mice* aloud to a group of kindergartners or first graders, they are quick to tell me that the mice are looking at the elephant's leg, trunk, tusk, head, ear, and tail. They recognize that those parts comprise important parts of the whole, but in order to make an elephant, everything must work together. Similarly, texts are composed of many parts—*words, sentences, paragraphs,* and *chapters* are a few of the labels used to describe their surface structure of "something" that altogether is a book. While texts are considerably more complex and varied than this portrait of an elephant, I think the story will serve as a helpful reminder to always keep the whole in sight, even when considering its parts.

There are other important reasons why *Seven Blind Mice* is a fitting metaphor for *Literary Pathways.* First, the roots of the story come from an ancient storytelling tradition, and is one known by adults and children alike. Second, Ed Young is an acclaimed artist whose memorable art has brought to life other stories, including *Yeh-Shen: A Cinderella Story from China* (Louie 1982) and *Lon-Po-Po: A Red-Riding Hood Story from China*. These are books that forever enrich the lives of those who read them. In addition to knowing how to describe a book by a readability level, it is essential that we know how to select books with the potential of making a difference in our students' lives. Any book can be assigned a level, but merely knowing a level for a book or creating a massive booklist in which hundreds of books are leveled will not serve as a useful guide for carefully selecting the right book for the right child at the right time. Nor can such a booklist guide teachers to develop literary pathways for children to explore to encourage a lifetime of reading.

Reflections and Points to Ponder

From my own professional experiences, I must sadly agree with Rosenblatt that literature is all too often lost in the rush of trying to cover the curriculum. I confess, also, to being part of the problem with our newer readers—trying to give them books they *can* read without giving too much thought to how those choices will help them grow as readers, to deepen their love of literature. Yes, I tell them about *Frog and Toad, Little Bear,* and the many adventures of *Henry and Mudge.* I have many copies of *Amelia Bedelia*'s misadventures, the antics of *Fox* and his friends, and easy-to-read poetry anthologies, such as *Surprises* and *Weather,* compiled by Lee Bennett Hopkins. I have science books by Franklyn Branley, the inimitable *Magic School Bus* books by Joanna Cole and Bruce Degen, and many other information books they can read.

However, until recently, I hadn't taken time to know books written especially for new readers as literature in the same way I know about picture books or chapter books for intermediate grade children. I looked at them as "on the way to something else books." As I began to read more books like these, I discovered wonderful literature. I found small fictional stories that are not only enjoyable to read, but that also give children the opportunity to encounter many styles of writing in formats they can easily manage. I also discovered nonfiction books that give readers information they are looking for, and also provide "untaught" lessons about the language and organization of nonfiction.

At first, I assumed that my only reason for having these new insights would be to make better recommendations to new readers. In the back of my mind, though, are larger, more troubling concerns. I often see fourth- and fifth-grade students who are capable readers, but who do not risk reading anything that will challenge them. I worry, too, that our society has become so obsessed with test scores that teachers are being put in the position of choosing between nurturing readers and spending large blocks of time teaching them how to take tests. While there is much I know about literature and reading, I still have many questions, some of which propel me as I write.

1. How can we guide our students' early reading to prepare them to navigate and comprehend literary language, complex plots, and character development?

2. How can we support them in learning how to read to gather information for research they will be expected to do throughout their academic lives?

3. How can we help them develop the literary pathways that will support their growing into readers who have the ability and interest to read more complex literature?

Charlotte Huck, Susan Hepler, Janet Hickman, and Barbara Kiefer (2000), co-authors of *Children's Literature in the Elementary School,* the quintessential textbook for using literature in the classroom, consider discovering delight and learning to connect literature to one's life to be the most important purposes for a school literature program. They emphasize, however, that the experience of literature itself, not the study of literary criticism, is most important for children. Through wide reading, they believe, children will gradually develop literary awareness of traditional elements such as genre, plot, characterization, theme, style, setting, point of view, and literary allusion. I concur wholeheartedly, and while I use some of these terms when writing about books, it is with the purpose of looking more closely at them from an adult perspective so we may more wisely select literature for all of our children.

A Vexing Problem

Now, it is time to return to a vexing problem—how to address matters of text difficulty within the context of a literature program. Many professionals who work with children and their literature are uncomfortable trying to assign a grade level or age to a book because they know the potential of using books in different ways to reach various audiences. On the other hand, there are many teachers and librarians who need guidance in knowing what kinds of texts are best for the changing needs of their new readers. Marie Clay has aptly described this dilemma:

> Gradients of difficulty are essential for teachers making good decisions about materials they select for children to read but all gradients are inevitably fallible. They cannot be right for individual children and yet a program cannot work efficiently without them (1991, 201).

There is an inevitable tension between teachers who fear that attention to readability will limit children's experiences with quality literature and those who need more precise information about text difficulty to help them do their job of teaching children how to read. My goal in this book is to bring balance to the discussion and to shed light on how to consider books for their literary values along with knowing when to give them to individual readers. Any discussion of text complexity, however, must be firmly grounded in our goals for children as readers of literature.

Summary

The purpose of this book is twofold: (1) to write about the features of texts that influence how easy or hard a book will be for readers; (2) to support children in their growth as lifelong readers of quality literature by calling attention to many wonderful books available for reading instruction and recreational reading. I think of it as a trail guide for turning new readers into eager readers. When my husband and I go hiking, we read the trail guides for the area to help us decide which trail to take. Trail guides use descriptors, such as *easy, moderate, moderate to difficult,* and *difficult* to indicate the amount of challenge hikers will encounter. Those terms are relative, however, depending on whether the hiker is a novice or a well-conditioned athlete.

Some trail guides, such as the one from the Chiricahua National Monument in southeastern Arizona, help hikers with more descriptive information about the rating system. An easy (Grade A) hike, for example, has "fairly level terrain with very little change in elevation." In contrast, a difficult hike (Grade D) is one that "most people can hike one to three miles per hour . . . elevation changes of approximately 500 to 1000 feet." Trail guides compiled by experienced hikers can provide helpful information, but they are not a substitute for thoughtful decision making. Hikers must factor in variables like personal stamina, the amount of time available for a hike, and weather conditions.

Like a trail guide, this book will help readers learn more about the factors that make one book easier or more difficult than another, but that information will be useful only to someone with wide knowledge of books and readers. Like hikers, who sometimes disagree with the level someone else has assigned to a trail, readers of this book will sometimes disagree with a level I suggest for a book. Trail guides cannot possibly account for all possible conditions of trails and hikers. Similarly, there is no formula or system of leveling books that can take into account the knowledge and experience of all children who read them. Hikers would never pick a trail solely on difficulty, nor should teachers use difficulty as the prime consideration in selecting books for readers. Adventure and beauty come in many forms, and readers, like hikers, are enriched by each new journey connecting scenic and literary pathways.

Each chapter of this book focuses on a different aspect of literature for new readers. Chapter 2 addresses matters related to readability, predictability, and text leveling. Chapter 3 looks at a broad sweep of fiction books with surprise endings and nonfiction books about frogs in a style I call a "conversational dance." Chapter 4 discusses books with predictable, repeated language patterns for emergent readers. Chapter 5 explores longer, more detailed stories with predictable events for transitional readers who are ready for small, easy-to-read chapter books. Chapter 6 discusses books with moderately complex plots and literary language for more advanced readers who have well-developed reading vocabularies.

Closing Points

- Becoming a reader is a lifelong journey that can take many pathways.
- By providing children with a range of literature in many styles of writing, teachers and librarians can help them to discover books they might not find on their own.
- Grouping books that have something in common—a particular kind of character, a similar plot, the same author or illustrator, or the same—subject will connect children to the wider world of literature.
- It is essential that we know how to select books with the potential of making a difference in our students' lives.
- There is no formula or system of leveling books that can take into account the knowledge and experience of all children who read them.

Bibliography

Children's Books

1. *The Green Book* by Jill Paton Walsh. Farrar, Straus and Giroux, 1982.
2. *The Chick and the Duckling* by Mirra Ginsburg. Illus. by Jose Aruego and Ariane Dewey. Simon & Schuster, 1972.
3. *Seven Blind Mice* by Ed Young. Philomel, 1992.
4. *Yeh-Shen: A Cinderella Story from China* by Ai-Ling Louie. Illus. by Ed Young. Philomel, 1982.
5. *Lon-Po-Po: A Red-Riding Hood Story from China* by Ed Young. Philomel, 1989.
6. *Frog and Toad* books by Arnold Lobel. HarperCollins.

7. *Little Bear* books by Else Holmelund Minarik. Illus. by Maurice Sendak. HarperCollins.

8. *Henry and Mudge* books by Cynthia Rylant. Illus. by Suçie Stevenson. Simon & Schuster.

9. *Amelia Bedelia* books by Peggy Parish. Illus. by Fritz Siebel and Wallace Tripp. HarperCollins.

10. *Fox* books by James Marshall. Puffin.

11. *Surprises* by Lee Bennett Hopkins. Illus. by Megan Lloyd. HarperTrophy, 1986.

12. *Weather: Poems for All Seasons* by Lee Bennett Hopkins. Illus. by Melanie Hall. HarperTrophy, 1995.

13. *Magic School Bus* books by Joanna Cole. Illus. by Bruce Degen. Scholastic.

2

Understanding Text Complexity
in Books for New Readers

In the previous chapter, I compared the story of the *Seven Blind Mice* and their attempts to identify the creature they were exploring to the challenge of understanding how features of texts, such as words, sentences, and paragraphs, fit together to create a whole text. Similarly, I think of the process of describing how the many components of texts work together to create a work of literature as "mapping the elephant," because explaining text complexity and creating a map of an elephant present similar challenges. Where do you begin? How much detail do you include? What are the defining characteristics of the beast? And, when you have finished, will anyone else recognize what you have just described? Furthermore, is the map a useful one? A map, after all, is a two-dimensional artifact showing surface features; a map of an elephant would not be helpful for understanding the mammal's physiology, social behavior, and dietary needs.

Texts are no simpler to describe. Do you begin with the words, size of the print, or sentence lengths? What about the illustrations or the physical layout of a book? If it is a work of fiction, what is its genre? Are the characters well-developed or unchanging? Does the plot emerge in a linear fashion, or are there twists and turns to confuse the reader? If the purpose of the book is to communicate factual information, does it present a richly detailed close-up of a subject, or does it provide a broader, less detailed perspective? Most importantly, how can such descriptions or maps of books assist teachers and librarians in supporting their children's development as readers? What makes a book comprehensible and enjoyable for some readers and not others?

Whether talking about elephants or texts, you can quickly see that the possibilities for debate are endless. No wonder many of us have looked to formulas or levels of one kind or another to help us choose the right book for each reader—they seem so simple, so clear, and so helpful. Many times I have used such indicators as guides in initially selecting books, and I do consider them useful in a limited way. While any book can be assigned a level indicating its approximate position along a text gradient, that alone is not sufficient information for making choices about which books to purchase or recommend for readers, let alone for developing a meaningful literature program for children.

Readable Texts / Predictable Texts

When I began my dissertation research in the mid 1980s, most children received their first reading instruction from basal readers with controlled vocabularies and short sentence lengths. Not only were most of these texts leveled by readability formulas; some publishers inappropriately used readability formulas to produce textbooks to match a specified grade level. Ironically, most of these texts were difficult for children to read because they were written in a style that did not reflect children's natural spoken language nor the literary language found in picture books. Researchers who compared children's readings of basal reader stories with children's readings of picture books with rich, interesting language and repeated, predictable language patterns, found that the students were able to read and comprehend the literature stories with greater success, even though the picture books had higher readability levels than the basal stories (Rhodes 1979; Gourley 1984; Bussis et al. 1985).

My own interest in text complexity grew out of my experiences in Reading Recovery, because, at the time, the current research in readable texts or predictable texts was not adequate for understanding what made books easy or difficult for Reading Recovery students. The literature books used in the predictability studies were much too difficult for beginning Reading Recovery students to read. Historically, the research in readability cast a wide net, looking at an array of factors that influence text difficulty, including vocabulary, sentences, subject matter, ideas, concepts, text organization, abstractness, appeal, format, and illustrations. Two factors, however, vocabulary and sentence length, are the foundations of most readability formulas because research has shown them to be most closely associated with comprehensibility of texts (Chall and Dale 1995). Readability formulas, however, are inadequate for evaluating difficulty of the easy texts written for children who are just learning how to read. For example, according to the Dale-Chall readability formula, *Frog and Toad Together* by Arnold Lobel has a readability level of 1, the lowest level on that scale, indicating an easy text (Chall and Dale, 145). Teachers and librarians who work with beginning readers know that a child capable of reading the *Frog and Toad* books independently is well beyond needing beginning reading instruction.

The concept of predictability is a useful one to consider when selecting books for beginning readers because it encourages teachers to think about texts in relation to the knowledge their students bring to the reading. Predictability, however, should not be confused with endless repetition. Keep in mind that our ability to predict helps us to make sense of the world in an efficient manner, whether we are driving across town, eating a meal at our favorite restaurant, or looking for the latest bestseller at the local library. We rely on the organization and routines of traffic, restaurants, and libraries to help us take care of our needs as smoothly as possible. Furthermore, the knowledge and experience we accumulate over time in familiar environments provides a framework for helping us to make sense of new places and situations.

With respect to readers, predictability needs to be thought of as a relationship between readers and texts that changes over time as readers become more proficient. A text can be predictable for a reader who is just discovering how to read a short sentence from left to right and match each spoken word to a printed word. A text can also be predictable for an experienced reader, who knows what to expect, including the unexpected when reading a mystery, for example. Consequently, it is important to qualify discussions of predictability by pointing out which characteristics of a particular text are predictable and understand how those characteristics support a particular reader at a particular time in their development. A book like Bill Martin's and Eric Carle's *Brown Bear, Brown Bear, What Do You See?* has a lively, repetitive text with bright, bold illustrations and has inspired countless children to become readers, and it has long been a favorite read aloud book for parents, teachers, and children. However, the long sentences and small print make it too challenging for independent reading for a child who only knows a few words in print.

Texts that do not have repetitive sentence patterns can also be predictable, but in different ways from books like *Brown Bear, Brown Bear, What Do You See?* The plot of the story *Titch* by Pat Hutchins is predictable to readers because all through the book, Titch, the smallest child, has the smallest toy, while Mary, his older sister, has the medium-sized toy, and Pete, the oldest, has the largest toy. Even the ending, in which Titch's small seeds grow larger than anything his siblings have, is predictable to experienced readers who are familiar with stories in which the youngest, smallest character triumphs over the oldest, strongest characters. Another predictable element of this story is the cycle of events happening in groups of three, just as they do in many tales of European origin, such as *The Three Billy Goats Gruff* (Galdone 1979; Stevens 1990).

Furthermore, once children have read *Titch* and know about his relation to Mary and Pete, they can make useful predictions about the direction of the plots in *You'll Soon Grow Into Them, Titch* and *Tidy Titch*.

A book like *Whose Mouse Are You?* by Robert Kraus, illustrated by Jose Aruego, is predictable because it is written in a question/answer format, so readers know that a question ("Whose mouse are you?") is always followed by an answer ("Nobody's mouse."). Merle Peek's picture book version of *Mary Wore Her Red Dress, Henry Wore His Green Sneakers* is predictable in two ways. First, readers know that each new page will feature a new character wearing a colorful item of clothing. Second, they learn the refrain "all day long," and know that each page will end with those words.

Longer books have predictable elements as well. The story of *Amelia Bedelia*, written by Peggy Parish and illustrated by Fritz Siebel, develops around the comical way in which Amelia Bedelia misinterprets instructions that are given to her. On her first day of work as the maid at the Rogers' house, she follows her list of written instructions in a most unusual way. For example, when she reads "Dust the furniture," she thinks it a silly thing to do because "at my house we undust the furniture." She solves the problem by finding a box of dusting powder in the bathroom and shaking it over the furniture. Thus, what makes this story predictable is that as Amelia Bedelia reads through the list, she puts her own unique twist on the meaning of the instructions and the actions she must take to complete her jobs. Furthermore, the plot of each of the more than ten books about Amelia Bedelia develops around her "mix-ups," so her fans begin reading with useful predictions about the kind of language that will follow.

Research in Emergent Literacy

Research in readability and predictability influenced how I thought about what makes texts easy or difficult, but it was not adequate for describing the small changes between levels of texts used in Reading Recovery. Research in emergent literacy led me to consider how the life experiences of children prior to entering school might be related to the kinds of texts that supported them as beginning readers. Few teachers believe that children start school knowing nothing, yet it took pioneering work on the part of many researchers to lead the teaching profession to a better understanding of how children's preschool experiences with language support early school learning. Yetta Goodman (1996) calls these the "roots of literacy," and I strongly recommend her article of the same name for a more thorough discussion of these concepts. *Literacy Before Schooling* (1982) is a report of Emilia Ferreiro and Ana Teberosky's seminal work in how children construct their own hypotheses about print. Another excellent source of information is *Emerging Literacy: Young Children Learn to Read and Write* (1989), edited by Dorothy Strickland and Lesley Mandel Morrow. The articles in this book were written to assist and support classroom teachers, but readers who are interested in the academic roots of the underlying research will find abundant references to this research.

I will briefly describe some of the major themes of the work on emergent literacy, because they had a profound impact on my thinking about readability and complexity in books for beginning readers. First and foremost, children have been participants in the world of language and communication since birth. By the time they enter school, they know how to carry on conversations, talk about themselves, ask questions, tell imaginative stories, and use language for a multitude of other purposes. Without instruction, they have learned to speak in the grammar of their language and use a host of words to express concepts they are familiar with. For the most part, they do this by talking in phrases and sentences they construct from their own thinking, not by copying or repeating the precise words they hear spoken by others. They draw pictures, make letters or letter-like forms, and most know the difference between writing and drawing. Immersed in a world of print, they learn to recognize some words in print, such as the names of family members or favorite foods. Many can write their names and write down some of the sounds they hear in words. Some know that print contains a message and is read from left to right (in some languages). They observe adults using print for a variety of purposes, such as checking schedules, writing messages, getting directions, and reading for pleasure. They learn the language of stories from books, movies, and family story-telling traditions. They also know quite a bit about the people and places around them.

Moreover, children who come to school after having countless books read aloud to them and exploring these books on their own have additional resources to help them with the prediction that supports reading. They encounter different styles of language sometimes referred to as literary or book language. For example, when my own children were young, one of their favorite books for me to read aloud to them was Virginia Kahl's *The Duchess Bakes a Cake,* a lively story in verse about a duchess who sends the cook off for a day so she can make a "lovely light luscious delectable cake." This memorable phrase appears several times in the story and became a part of our conversational repertoire, so that whenever we made a cake together, it was always a "lovely light luscious delectable cake."

My favorite example of a child internalizing book language comes from my grandson Andrew at the end of his kindergarten year. He had been trying to read the *Nate the Great* books we had given his older brother, but he had already heard them being read aloud many times by his parents and brother. They are a series of 48-page mystery books written by Marjorie Weinman Sharmat and illustrated by Marc Simont. The title of each one begins with *Nate the Great* and ends with a phrase describing the case facing Nate the Great, such as *Nate the Great and the Sticky Case.* They are written as first-person narratives in the voice of Nate, and several times throughout each story, he refers to himself as "I, Nate the Great." He says those words fourteen times in *Nate the Great and the Sticky Case.* Here are two examples of how the phrase is used.

> I, Nate the Great,
> was drying off
> from the rain. (7)

> "Good thinking," I said.
> "I, Nate the Great,
> will go to your house
> and look at your table." (12)

Andrew was writing about *Nate the Great* in the computer lab at school, and this is what he wrote. Notice how he refers to them as the *I, Nate the Great* books, an indication of how the stories worked their magic on him. One of the books is called *Nate the Great and the Halloween Hunt,* which might have inspired Andrew to write about being Nate the Great for Halloween.

> i lik to ryd *i naet the grat* books the oru not that esy the begiten of the book is esy i sum tims i ned hlup sum pagis i dot ned hlp but most pagis i ned hlup ryden pajis bekus the oru ordto ryd books i emu gowin to peu *i naet the grat* frou haluwen.

> (I like to read *I Nate the Great* books. They are not that easy. The beginning of the book is easy. I sometimes need help. Some pages, I don't need help, but most pages I need help reading pages because they are hard-to-read books. I am going to be *I Nate the Great* for Halloween.)

Children who have heard books read aloud over and over also know that stories unfold in certain ways, and that some characters behave in predictable ways. They also learn to look for surprises at the end. When children listen over and over to books about subjects they are interested in, they hear how writers present information, and the framework and organization of a descriptive text becomes familiar to them. They learn, also, to pay attention to the illustrations, both for pleasure and for their role in telling the story or conveying important information. Thus, by the time they start to read independently, most children have had five or six years of experience with language and stories that support and contribute to the success of their new endeavor.

Emergent Literacy and Books for Beginning Readers

How does this information help us think more closely about books that support beginning readers? Children use the grammar of their language and expect a message to make sense; thus, a good beginning reading text will tell a meaningful story or convey interesting facts in language commonly used by a five- or six-year-old. Children have had many life experiences and use the vocabulary of those places and events; thus, a good beginning text will make connections with real-life experiences, even when it is an imaginative story (for example, books about childhood nighttime fears, such as Mercer Mayer's *There's a Nightmare in My Closet*). Children are watchers and observers of their environment; thus, a good beginning text will provide clear illustrations to assist readers in interpreting the written message. Children have learned something about print from their own writing and observing others write, but they may not realize that going from left to right is essential or that there are spaces between words in print, which are often different from the spaces between spoken words. For example, when speaking, many people say "gonna," not "going to," and "an apple" often sounds like one word in speech—"anapple." A good beginning text will have the print set in the same place, using a clear type face and large print to help readers learn about the conventions of print.

Characteristics of Texts for Beginning Readers

Books in Reading Recovery are organized into twenty reading levels to guide teachers in introducing children gradually to a variety of stories and features of print. The easiest texts in this range are books such as Eric Carle's *Have You Seen My Cat?*, composed of two brief sentence patterns repeated alternately from start to finish, and the most challenging books in this range are books such as Arnold Lobel's *Frog and Toad* stories. This hierarchy was developed in New Zealand based on teachers' observations of their students' progression through the *Ready to Read* books, a graded series of little books read by all beginning readers in New Zealand. Thus, these books came to serve as benchmarks for comparison in assessing levels for new books. Reading Recovery teachers in the United States used this twenty-level framework, but had many questions about the criteria used to assign a level to a book.

These questions, plus my own curiosity about why some books were easier or harder for readers, led to the research for my dissertation, *Characteristics of Texts That Support Beginning Readers* (1988). There were two phases to this study—the first phase focused on books and the second on students' reading of some of those books. First, I selected 88 of the approximately 400 books in use at the time for Reading Recovery and evaluated them with respect to six categories: text and illustration layout; sentence length and text length; content and theme; illustrations; narrative form; and language patterns.

Once I completed that process, I focused on how students read 22 of those books by studying running records (Clay 1993a 2000) of their readings taken during Reading Recovery lessons. A running record is like a map of a reading, showing accurate reading, errors or miscues, self-corrections, and other reading behaviors. By analyzing miscues and self-corrections, teachers can see evidence of how a reader is using visual information from print, the structure or syntax of the language, and the meaning of the story to make sense of the text. An accuracy rate between 90 and 94 percent is considered an instructional level text for a particular student, while an accuracy rate between 95 and 100 percent is considered an easy level text for that student (Clay 1993a, 23).

After spending countless hours reading and examining all aspects of those texts, I decided it was impossible to write a description that would clearly define the characteristics of each level of text. However, it was possible to describe shifts in text complexity along the continuum of twenty levels, and to describe features common to groups of levels. I used the phrase "sources of predictability" to describe the shifts across levels. The easiest books, those in levels 1–4, have vocabulary and syntax that is very similar to young children's spoken language, as well as repetition of sentences with only one or two words changed. Books in levels 5–8 are similar to those in lower levels, but with less repetition of phrases and a gradual introduction of literary, or book language. Books in levels 9–12 exhibit a great deal of variation in sentence patterns, and a literary style of language becomes more prominent. Books in levels 13–15 contain a greater variety of words or a more specialized vocabulary than easier books. In the highest group of levels, 16–20, narratives are developed in greater detail. These categories will be more fully explained in the following chapters.

Words About Words

You might wonder why I did not establish a separate category for words. There were two reasons. First, writers and publishers who create books for beginning readers generally use words that are part of young children's vocabularies. Second, and more important, observations of my own Reading Recovery lessons and those of others demonstrated to me many times that words that look easy are sometimes difficult, and words that look challenging are sometimes easy for readers. Consequently, I considered words within the context of language patterns and content and theme. Words do not work alone, but in combination with other words to form ideas, descriptions, and actions.

In all of my years as a librarian and a teacher, I have never heard a child or an adult say they like books made up of words they know how to read. Even children who are just learning how to read will tell me they like books about dinosaurs or fairy tales or the *Magic School Bus* books, written by Joanna Cole and illustrated by Bruce Degen. Yet, words are the part of language that most often come to mind when adults think about texts for newer readers. Having a large core of known words and being able to decode and analyze patterns in words in order to solve unfamiliar words is certainly an important part of reading, but understanding the meaning of a text is a more complex process than identifying all of the words in the text.

To illustrate, I will give an example from my own reading. Recently I came across the phrase "Sailor Plots the Revenge of the Tomatoes." Although I know the definitions of each of those words and can read the phrase accurately and fluently, I was baffled as to its meaning. Gradually I was able to figure it out. The phrase was a headline in a *New York Times* article (May 2, 1999) that appeared in the Sports section under the subheading of "The Boating Report." Below the text is a photo of a lone sailboat in rough seas. From those context clues, I surmised that "revenge" must have something to do with a competition the sailor lost.

The first paragraph of the article was also composed of words I know, but other than confirming my guess that the article was about racing, I was still confused as to what it was all about.

> For Hans Meijer, a multihull sailor from Virginia Beach, Va., a tomato is anything but a piece of fruit. It has gotten him into trouble twice now in ocean racing, and both times, he has had to head for the beach. Not a good place for tomatoes.

The first sentence of the second paragraph, also composed entirely of words I recognize and understand, let me know that writer Barbara Lloyd was having a bit of fun with readers. "So what is this circuitous connection between a tomato and sailing?" Then she confirms my guess by naming the event, a 1,000 mile catamaran race called the Worrell 1000. In her third paragraph, I learn that Meijer's catamaran is named *Pomodoro,* the Italian word for tomato. While it was necessary for me to read ploddingly to the end of the article to "get the whole picture," a sailor, particularly a catamaran racer, reading the same article would have gotten the meaning in a fraction of the time.

Being able to identify words quickly and knowing their meaning is an important part of reading, but I used far more than my knowledge of words to understand the article. I have already mentioned two aspects of text that helped—the photograph and my familiarity with the format and style of newspaper reporting. I was also able to draw on the very little knowledge I have of sailboats and racing. As an experienced reader, I expect a piece of writing to be organized into paragraphs of several sentences and that each paragraph will provide more detail about the topic. I also expect the paragraphs to be arranged in a such a way so that ideas lead to a logical conclusion. I also know that newspaper writing must be concise and that each paragraph will begin with a topic sentence identifying its purpose to the reader. And, speaking of sentences, I, like all other language users, know how sentences in English are put together. This I know intuitively from hearing and speaking the language all of my life and from school studies in reading, writing, grammar, and foreign language study.

Words and Learning to Read

Readers who agree with my point that reading involves much more than word identification, however, may believe that new readers are different from experienced readers. In some respects they are, because beginning readers need to learn how to decode unfamiliar words, as well as develop an expanding core of words they can quickly and easily identify during reading. They are helped by learning how the alphabetic system works, the relationships between sounds and letters, and more sophisticated ways of analyzing print to solve "unknown" words. They also need to learn how to interpret the conventions of written language, as well as make sense of the syntax and organization of book language, which differs from the language of conversation. Children come to school knowing many words, and continue learning new words throughout their school years. According to one study, most six-year-olds have mastered a speaking vocabulary of 14,000 words (Carey 1978, cited in Smith 1994).

Pioneering research by Marie Clay (1968, 1982, 1991) and Ken Goodman (1965, 1996) provided a critical perspective for understanding the reading process by systematically observing children reading and making sense of their reading. By analyzing children's reading behaviors, each documented that when readers substituted one word for another, their errors, or miscues, often were meaningful and grammatically acceptable in the passage they were reading. Ken Goodman describes miscues as "windows on the reading process" (1996, 61). For example, suppose a reader comes to the sentence *I like to race in the yard* and misses the word *race.* It is more likely that this reader would substitute the word *run* than the word *rainbow,* because *I like to run* is a meaningful sentence in English, whereas *I like to rainbow* is not. The reader who substitutes *run* for *race* is using several sources of information to make sense of the text. First, he is reading for meaning, because the words can be used interchangeably; second, his substitution resulted in a grammatically correct sentence; and third, the two words are visually similar.

Moreover, both researchers observed that many readers spontaneously corrected, or attempted to correct, their errors. Each stressed that children have more opportunity to develop useful reading strategies when they read from texts that reflect the language they speak fluently. The children Marie Clay observed were five-year-olds learning how to read, and the self-correction behavior she observed suggested these readers had developed ways of learning from their errors. Based on these observations, she called for providing children with texts rich in cue sources.

> Words in sentence structures which mirror the syntactic and semantic forms of the language which the child speaks fluently will increase the child's opportunities to detect errors and develop error-correcting strategies (1982, 46).

A good example of a book that fits this profile is *The Ghost,* written by Joy Cowley and illustrated by Robyn Belton. On the cover is a picture of a child wrapped in a white sheet looking in the mirror, and on the floor is a paper bag with eyes and mouth cut out. Most young children have made costumes or played dress-up, and most have played peek-a-boo games with their parents, so readers of this book could draw on their own experiences to predict that this ghost is about to surprise someone. Below is the text, only twenty-six words.

> I see the door.
> I see the window.
> I see the table.
> I see the cat.
> I see the chairs.
> I see Mum and Dad.
> Boo!

There are many ways this book connects young readers with the new world of print. I mentioned the dressing-up image on the cover; if that is familiar, so is the image of the child sneaking up ever so slowly on her parents. The sentence structure, or syntax, is simple, but one that a young reader would probably use in conversation. The objects the "ghost" encounters on her travels are likely to be recognizable to young readers as well—*door, window, table, cat, chairs,* and *Mum and Dad.* The illustrations on each page clearly show the object "the ghost" sees, providing a way for the reader to confirm the identity of the word in print.

The print is centered at the bottom of each page and there is ample room between words for the young reader to see the space between them. This space between words is sometimes called a "finger space," because it is wide enough to accommodate a child-sized finger, and it helps new readers clearly see the boundaries between words. Although *The Ghost* is a simple book, it takes new readers into a world that is both imaginary and real, allowing them to re-member a similar personal experience and to read about another character doing the same thing.

Moving into Literary, or Book, Language

While students who have just learned to read *The Ghost* are engaged in the same reading process as more experienced readers, they still have much to learn about written language. As Frank Smith (1994) emphasizes, written lan-guage is not talk written down. While spoken and written language share the same grammar and vocabulary, there are different conventions for each. In part, this is because during conversations, the participants usually discuss a topic of common interest. They communicate not only through what they say, but also through gesture and intonation. Listeners can interrupt and ask the speaker to clarify a point. Speakers can respond to puzzled facial expressions by rephrasing a statement, then checking to see if their meaning was then un-derstood. Certain forms of writing, such as letters, have characteristics of spo-ken language. And, print that appears in the environment, such as the word *stop* on red octagonal signs, can be interpreted by seeing where it is placed.

In contrast, writers cannot stop their writing in order to determine whether or not readers understand their message. Nor can readers look up from the text and ask the writer what was meant by the statement on page twenty-four. Writers must use different techniques so that their intended ideas and the relationships between them are expressed entirely through their use of language. Written language is grammatically more complex than spo-ken language. Writers have time to carefully construct their thoughts and arrange them according to the conventions of the kind of document they are preparing, whether it is a report, a set of instructions, or a story. Of course, some forms of spoken language, such as a formal speech, have certain charac-teristics of written texts.

That was a very cursory discussion of a complex subject, but adequate for thinking about new readers who need to move on from books like *The Ghost* to those that are more in the style of written, literary language. To illus-trate, let's take a small leap to the book *The Carrot Seed,* written by Ruth Krauss and illustrated by Crockett Johnson. A little boy plants a carrot seed and those around him keep telling him it won't come up. First his mother, then his father, and finally his big brother tell him. Then, the three of them look him in the eye and point to the ground. The texts says:

> Everyone kept saying it
> wouldn't come up.

It does, of course, and the story closes with these words:

> And then, one day,
> a carrot came up
> just as the little boy
> had known it would.

It is not unusual for a speaker to use the phrase "everyone kept saying" in the context of a conversation. In fact, I have often heard children begin a sentence with this phrase. However, the syntax and phrasing of the closing sentence of the story are much more book-like. This is the kind of language readers meet in stories and not in casual talk.

A Sense of Story

In writing about *The Ghost* and *The Carrot Seed,* I focused on language at the sentence level. However, there are other ways in which knowing the language of books helps children learn how to read. Say the words *once upon a time* to a group of young children, and they know immediately that someone is about to tell or read them a story. Ask children about pigs or wolves or a young woman named Cinderella, and most can tell you who those characters are and how they act. In the words of Arthur Applebee, "Children gradually develop quite firm expectations about these story characters" (1978, 48).

Children also learn how stories unfold. Consider the story of "Little Red Riding Hood." Little Red Riding Hood's mother sends her to grandmother's house in the woods. On the way, she meets a wolf and tells him she is on her way to visit her sick grandmother. The wolf is a dangerous character who causes plenty of trouble, but with help from a woodsman, the story ends happily. The story of *Wiley and the Hairy Man,* retold and illustrated by Molly Bang, begins with a young boy getting ready to go into the swamp to cut some bamboo. His mother warns him to watch out for the Hairy Man. Like Little Red Riding Hood (Hyman 1983), Wiley meets a frightening creature on his journey, but unlike Little Red Riding Hood, Wiley outwits his adversary. These two stories are not identical, but they share similar plots and characters.

I use the phrase "literary partners" to describe stories that are similar in some way. There are many books for new readers that can help them develop a "sense of story," or understanding of the many different ways stories can be framed and plotted. *The Ghost* is a very simple story, one that I call a "sneaking up" story because readers do not see the "whole picture" until the very end. Similarly, Ruth Brown's *A Dark Dark Tale,* begins in a dark, dark moor, and takes readers on a slow journey through a wood, and into a house, where they meet a surprise on the last page. Books like *Titch* and *The Carrot Seed* can be thought of as literary partners because they each feature characters who, although they are the youngest and smallest, triumph in the end.

Learning from Students' Readings of Books

In the second phase of my dissertation research, I wondered if there were some places in texts that led to more errors than others. I selected twenty-two books used in Reading Recovery and compared running records of students' readings of those books taken during Reading Recovery lessons. Every day, Reading Recovery teachers select a new book for each of their students, choosing one that will support the individual student's current knowledge and strengths and provide a small amount of new challenge. The teacher carefully introduces the book, drawing the child's attention to the important ideas in the text and one or two new words. With support from the teacher, the student reads the book once or twice. The next day, the teacher takes a running record of the student's reading of the book introduced the day before.

Running records are valuable because they capture many observable reading behaviors, and teachers can study them to see how children are using meaning, the structure or syntax of the language, and print or graphophonemic clues in their reading (Clay 1993a 2000; Johnston 1997; Taberski 2000). There are two kinds of calculations from running records, error rate and self-correction rate, that serve as a quick shorthand for showing how well a student read a particular text. The error rate is usually converted into a percentage of words read accurately. Roughly, a text read with an accuracy of 95 to 100 percent (not more than one error for every twenty words read) is considered easy for the reader. A text read at between 90 and 94 percent (not more than two errors for every twenty words read) is considered to be at an instructional level for the reader. Peter Johnston uses the phrase "learning text" to describe a text read within the instructional range, "because children actually learn from it" (1997, 213). Michael Opitz uses the phrase "just-right" to describe books that children can read with good understanding (1998, 66). When a book is read with less than 90 percent accuracy, it is generally too difficult for the reader to manage without assistance. Opitz calls these "challenge books."

When children self-correct their errors during reading, it is an indication they are learning from their mistakes. The self-correction rate is calculated by adding together the number of errors and the number of self-corrections (self-corrections start out as errors, before they are corrected). This total is divided by the number of self-corrections. Self-correction rates are expressed as ratios. For example, a self-correction rate of 1:4 indicates that the reader corrected one out of every four errors. Clay notes that among *good* readers between the ages of five and eight, self-correction ratios of 1:2 to 1:5 are typical. "When children read texts of appropriate difficulty for their present skills (i.e., at or above 90 percent accuracy) this gives enough support from familiar features of text, enough time for reading work, without losing the meaning" (1991, 337).

Here are some examples of students reading texts rich in cue sounds, taken from my research. The first book I looked at was *The Ghost*, written by Joy Cowley and illustrated by Robyn Belton, one of the easiest books used in the program. Although this is a simple book, it nevertheless takes new readers into a world that is both imaginary and real, allowing them to remember a similar personal experience and to read about another character doing the same thing.

I had thirty-two running records of readings of *The Ghost* to compare. Twenty-seven of these readings were above 90 percent accuracy, indicating the text was in the instructional or easy range for those students. Five of the readings were below 90 percent, indicating the text was too difficult for those students. First, let us take a look at the errors and self-corrections on readings above 90 percent. There were two places in the text that resulted in the highest number of errors. One was the very first sentence, "I see the door." Two readers began, "I like," and then promptly self-corrected and changed "like" to "see." One began, "I is," and immediately self-corrected, while another read "I can," and corrected her response after reading the entire sentence as "I can the door." Note that two of those initial substitutions, *I like* and *I can*, are the beginnings of acceptable and common sentences. The first two readers were able immediately to correct their errors, probably by noticing visual information from the printed word *see*. The third reader needed to work through the whole sentence to make the self-correction. It seems likely that the child who began *I is* noticed right away that the phrase did not sound right, and used both her intuitive knowledge of the structure of English and the visual information of the print to self-correct. (Note: While running records of children's readings provide teachers with helpful information, they can only record observable behaviors, not everything a child knows or can do.)

Self-Corrections in the First Sentence of The Ghost

I see the door.

Student	First Reading	Self-correction
1	I like	I see
2	I like	I see
3	I can the door	I see the door
4	I is	I see

Now, let us take a look at the two readers who did not self-correct on the first sentence. Note that each of these substitutions results in an acceptable English sentence and one that is meaningful in the context of the entire book.

Student	First Reading	Self-correction
5	This is	no self-correction
6	I saw	no self-correction

Now, let's shift our perspective from the readers' actions to the book itself and consider how the features of the text supported them. Each sentence begins *I see,* which provides a predictable framework as the beginning of the sentence on each page. Once the first four readers corrected their initial error on *see,* they finished reading the book without further errors. Student number 5 substituted *this is* for *I see* on the first sentence, but read the remaining sentences accurately. Student number 6 read *I saw* on the first two sentences, but thereafter accurately read *I see* on the remaining four sentences. Each of the readers made these changes independently, without prompting from the teacher. The repetition of the pattern supported their problem solving by providing them opportunities to revisit and look more closely at the letters and words before them.

The errors in the running records of students who read the book with an accuracy below 90 percent reveal that the text was supporting the learning of those readers. For example, one student read *I saw* for four of the five sentences, resulting in an accuracy of 84 percent. Nevertheless, the repetition of the *I see* pattern allowed her to do some valuable sorting out. This is how she read the text.

> I saw the door.
> I saw the window.
> I saw [repeats this phrase] I saw the table.
> I saw the cat.
> I saw the [repeats this phrase] I saw the chairs.

Finally, on the last page, she read the entire sentence accurately.

> I see Mum and Dad.

Learning of any kind involves exploration, tentative behavior, and making errors. Experienced teachers know it is much easier to teach students who are risk takers than students who are afraid to try something new because they might not be right.

Increasing the Challenge

When someone is learning how to drive, they might begin by cruising a shopping center parking lot after hours when there is little traffic. In order to learn to be a good driver, a bit more challenge is needed—quiet neighborhood streets, for example. Similarly, most beginning readers quickly master books like *The Ghost* and are ready to try their developing strategies out on more difficult texts. The next book I discuss, *Look for Me*, written by June Melser and illustrated by Lynette Vondruska, can be thought as the move that puts the student driver on neighborhood streets during the morning rush hour.

Look for Me is the story of a simple hide-and-seek game in which Mum looks for her son David in several places. Like *The Ghost*, it is a story set in the familiar environment of a child's home, and the plot develops as the main character, the mother, moves through the house. And, like *The Ghost*, it ends with a surprise. The structure, or syntax, of the sentences and the vocabulary are well within the range of five- and six-year-olds, but there are several ways in which the book provides readers with more challenge than *The Ghost*. There are almost three times the number of words in *Look for Me* than in *The Ghost*, and each sentence is a few words longer. Also, there are three lines of print on all but one of the pages, so readers must be secure in their control over following the print from left to right and making the return sweep to the left. Instead of one sentence pattern being repeated throughout the book, there are two sentence patterns that alternate. The illustrations show where Mum is looking, allowing readers to check them to confirm the identity of words such as *chimney* and *clock*; however, readers must be able to read most of the words without supporting picture clues. Here is the text from the first two pages.

> Mum looked for David
> in the toy box.
> "No, he's not here," she said. (2)
> She looked for him
> up the chimney.
> "No, he's not here," she said. (3)

As you can see, the structure of the first sentence on each page is the same, but with small variations. Throughout the book the first sentence tells where Mum looked. Readers must be able to make the shift from the proper nouns—*Mum* and *David*—to the pronouns *she* and *him;* they must pay close attention to the print. They are supported, however, by their intuitive use of language they have used for many years, because in speaking we generally switch to pronouns once the subjects of conversation are clearly understood by the speakers. Readers must also pay close attention to the print in order to notice the change in the prepositions from *in the toy box* to **up** *the chimney.* Again, however, they receive support from their intuitive use of English phrasing. While it would not be wrong to say *in the chimney,* **up** *the chimney* is more likely to roll off the tongue of children whose first language is English. These are good examples of how students draw on their experience as speakers of the language to assist them in noticing the details of print, which in turn, supports their developing knowledge of how letters are combined to make words, and how words are used to make stories.

When I studied the running records of *Look for Me,* they were more interesting than those of *The Ghost* because there are many more examples that showed children engaged in productive reading work. The phrase "No, he's not here," is used four times. This is how one student sorted out some confusions on that phrase.

On page 2 she read:

"No, he's he's [repetition of the correct word] not here," she said.

On page 3 she read:

"No, he No he's [repetition from the beginning and self-correction on *he's*] not here," she said.

On page 4 she read:

"No, he he's [self-correction] ain't not [self-correction] here," she said.

On page 6 she read:

"No, he's not here," she said. [accurate reading, no self-corrections]

Not knowing this student, I can only speculate that in conversation she used the phrase "he ain't," and in the course of working on this book, she learned to check the print closely to read the exact words on the page. Another student's readings of this same phrase demonstrate how a mismatch between a child's oral language and printed book language prompted a close search of the text that led to self-correction.

On page 2 he read:

"No, he's not *in the* No, he's not here [as if starting to read *not in the toy box,* then returning to the beginning of the sentence and self-correcting his errors]," Mum she [self-correction] said.

On page 3 he read:

"No, he's not *in* here not here [return to *not* and self-correction]," she said.

On pages 4 and 6 he read the sentences accurately, without repetition or self-correction.

One miscue that I found very interesting focused on the word *mat*. The story concludes with Mum finding David. On page 7 there is a picture of David hiding under a small rug on the floor. His head and shoulders are peaking out. Mum has one foot on the rug, clearly positioned on top of David. She is looking up in the air, saying "Where is that boy?" Those words are not printed like those in the rest of the book; rather, they are encased in the kind of speech bubbles often used in comics. Next to David is a speech bubble that says, "Giggle giggle." The text on the last page follows the pattern of text on the previous pages, with the exception of the variation in the language, because David has been found.

> Mum looked for David
> under the mat.
> "**Here** he is," she said.

When I compared running records of *Look for Me*, I made an interesting discovery. The little word *mat* received the highest number of miscues, far more than the longer word *chimney*. I examined a total of seventy-five running records of students who read *Look for Me* with an accuracy of 90 percent or higher, and there were twenty-six miscues on the word *mat*. Of those twenty-six students who miscued on *mat*, only one miscued on *chimney*. In the whole group of seventy-five running records, there were only four miscues on the word *chimney*. How could that be? *Mat* is such a simple word; furthermore, it is very much like *cat, sat, hat,* and many other common words that are easy to spell.

Here are the words readers substituted for *mat: cover, covers, carpet, rug, quilt, mattress, sheet,* and *cushion.* Five readers used the word *rug,* the most frequently used substitution. Each of these words is a meaningful substitution for the word *mat,* although none visually resemble *mat.* Some readers made substitutions that were not meaningful, however the substitution resembled *mat* in some way: *snap, mit, mar, him, mom,* and *map.* Why should so many readers who read the rest of this book with such ease have trouble with such a small word? Not knowing those children I cannot say for sure; however, I think the key to understanding the problem is that the word *mat* is not a word commonly used in the United States to refer to a small rug. Consequently, I suspect that readers substituted words they knew to describe what they had seen in the illustration. *Look for Me* was written and published in New Zealand, where I assume the word *mat* is frequently used to describe a small rug.

A similar phenomenon occurred with the word *hose,* in a book called *Saturday Morning,* a Ready to Read book from New Zealand written by Leslie Moyes. In this story, a family of five and their dog spend their Saturday morning having breakfast, cleaning the car, and watering the garden. *Saturday Morning* is far more challenging for readers than *Look for Me* because there are several characters interacting with each other and the sentence patterns are varied, with little repetition. There are ten sentences using the words *hose* or *hosed*. *Hosed* is used four times and *hose* six times. It is used as a verb nine times, with three different meanings. In the first example, Mum is washing the car. In the second example, Mum is going to water the garden. In the third, the children ask to be sprayed with water.

> Mum *hosed* the car.
> I'm going to *hose* the garden now.
> "Please will you *hose* me," said Helen.

Only once, at the end of the story, is *hose* used as a noun.

> "Look, he's playing with the *hose*," said Mum.

While *hose* is probably a familiar word to most children in the United States, it is typically used as a noun and not as a verb. In a sample of thirty-two running records at 90 percent or higher accuracy, there were eighteen miscues on the first use of *hose*, "Mum *hosed* the car." The most common substitutions were *washed* or *cleaned*. In the second instance, however, when the garden was the object of *hosing*, the substitutions were words such as *spray* and *water*. As you can see, these miscues fit both the meaning of the story and the syntax of the sentence. Seven of the readers who miscued the first time *hosed* was used, read the word accurately throughout the rest of the book. At most, readers miscued three times on the word *hose* or *hosed*. Thus, the number of miscues on *hose* decreased as readers moved through the text, suggesting they engaged in problem solving as they progressed, visually analyzing the print to come up with the precise word in the text.

The Right Book for the Right Child at the Right Time

Throughout this book, I continue to write about books and children who have read them. By reading widely and closely observing how children read and interact with books, we can learn a great deal about how to support and encourage them in becoming better readers. The more we know and the more closely we observe, the more effective we become as their teachers. I cannot stress strongly enough, however, that there is no one book or set of books that will transform a new reader into a voracious reader. Librarians have often used the phrase "the right book for the right child at the right time" to describe the care with which an adult should place a book in a child's hands.

To help beginning readers find just-right books in the library, I put baskets of easy books in English and Spanish that I have grouped by levels of difficulty on shelves that are easy for them to reach. The baskets are close to tables, and I encourage the children take the baskets off the shelves and spread books on the tables to get a closer look at them. I separate the English and Spanish books and keep them in different colored baskets to help readers find the language they are looking for. Colored dots on the books and the baskets help students and teachers find books they can read "right now." Often called "little books" by many teachers, they are similar to books like *The Ghost, Look for Me,* and *Saturday Morning.* In each basket there are books from several publishers' series, both fiction and nonfiction. If I sort through the baskets, I can quickly tell which books are most popular. I call them "wrinkled books" because their worn appearance shows they have been read over and over again. If I place a few wrinkled books side by side, I notice how different one is from another, even though they are not too far apart with respect to difficulty. Selections include both fiction and nonfiction. Some, like *Animal Homes* by Peter Sloan and Sheryl Sloan, provide factual information about animals and are illustrated with photographs. Others, like *Fix It, Fox,* written by Patricia Ann Lynch and illustrated by Jane Caminos, are comical stories with cartoon-like pictures.

Books about cats are often wrinkled books. *I Am a Cat,* written by Teresa Chin and illustrated with photographs by Graham Meadows, is written in the first person, like a biography. *The Cat Who Loved Red,* written by Lynn Salem and Josie Stewart and illustrated by Holly Pendergast, is a short narrative that begins like an old, old story, "Once there was a cat who loved red." Each page after the introduction begins with the phrase, "She loved to . . ." Here are some of the things she loved to do:

> She loved to eat from a red dish. (3)
> She loved to play with a ball of red yarn. (4)
> She loved to sleep on a red pillow. (7)

Most of the time, I do not know which students connect with which books, but Melissa is an exception. In the spring of her first-grade year, she asked me to help her find a book she could read. As I had done with many students before her, I took her to the baskets of books, pulled out a few titles and asked her to give them a try. She ultimately selected *The Cat Who Loved Red* and read it with minimal help from me. The broad smile on her face revealed all—she had found *the* book! Several times during the next few weeks, she would bring the book to the library, wait patiently until she could have my full attention, and show off her newly discovered ability to read an entire book.

Many wrinkled books are not little books that fit in baskets, but popular children's literature books. When first grader Emanuel asked me to listen to him read *Bears in the Night* by Stan and Jan Berenstain, I could tell he had made the passage from seeing himself as a learner to being a reader. For Kathleen, the magical book was Dr. Seuss' inimitable *Green Eggs and Ham*, which she read to me a little bit at a time over the course of several weeks. Popularity, however, is not the only indicator of a book that has launched a child into reading. When Amy was in kindergarten, she found *Amy Goes to School*, written by Jenny Harris and illustrated by Phyllis Pollema-Cahill, and read it over and over with her mother until she could read it all by herself. Although she could have learned to read with many other books, finding one with her name in the title was magic for Amy.

Each of the books I just mentioned have several features in common, most notably a story or information that draws children inside and keeps them turning the pages. Some are serious in tone, and others are funny; some illustrated with photos, others with drawings or paintings. All have short sentences written with sentence structures, or syntax, used by most five- and six-year-olds. While there may be an occasional word or two that may be unfamiliar to a reader, most words used in these books are found in the spoken vocabulary of most five- and six-year-olds. Each of these books is rich in cue sources that assist children with reading the print and understanding the story or information in the book.

Only one of these books, *Fix It, Fox*, is composed of words that most people would call "decodable." The word study page on the back lists eight words: *box, fan, fix, fox, pen, pig, pot,* and *put*. These words, including repetitions of them, are used a total of thirty-one times in the text. There are ten other words used in the text: *said, it, the, in, mouse, pan, cat, dog, we'll,* and *help*. The author, Patricia Ann Lynch, has written a clever and engaging story with these words in which several characters bring in something for Fox to fix—a *pot*, a *pan*, a *pen*, and a *fan*. "'Fix it, Fox,'" each character says, putting the item needing repair on the counter in Fox's fix-it shop. Jane Caminos' humorous pictures are essential for readers to follow the story line, and young readers respond especially to the changes in Fox's facial expressions. He starts out with a smile as he puts each object in his collection box. As the box starts filling up, Fox looks worried, and by the time everyone has given him their items to repair, he looks completely overwhelmed. Fortunately, his friends understand his dilemma, and the story concludes with their offers of help.

Fix It, Fox is a well-loved book in our library, and I have no doubt that it has launched more than one young reading career. However, a reader's success with reading the text is not dependent on the almost exclusive use of short words that can easily be sounded out and decoded. Children who become good readers learn to draw on several sources of information to read and make sense of a book, and graphophonemics is one useful source of information. To become good readers, however, children also need texts that are meaningful and written in language familiar to them. *Fix It, Fox* fills all of these criteria, but so do many other more complicated books. Just as there is no one food that provides all the nutrients required by the human body, there is no single style of writing that will transform all learners into readers.

Decodable Texts

There is nothing inherently wrong with a book filled with words having some alphabetic or phonetic features in common. Such texts may be useful in helping some children sort out some of the letter-sound relationships and spelling patterns they will encounter in their reading. However, as Regie Routman points out, decoding is not useful for finding out the meaning of words students have never heard of or do not know the meaning of (1996, 94). Teachers strive to find books that support their students, and sometimes the best choices are decodable texts, as Heidi Anne Messmer (1999) determined when tutoring a second-grade student who had not learned how to read in first grade.

Teachers and librarians should be wary of sweeping generalizations, asserting that decodable texts are necessary or advantageous for all beginning reading instruction. This simply is not true. To demonstrate, I will return to *The Ghost*. As "the ghost" moves through the house, she sees several things: *the door, the window, the table, the cat,* and *the chairs.* With the possible exception of *cat,* these are not easy words for a beginning reader to decode. However, in the twenty-seven running records I examined, all readings above 90 percent accuracy, there were very few miscues on these words. They are summarized below.

Word	Miscues Self-corrected (sc)	Miscues Not Self-corrected
door	window/sc	
window		windows
table	cat /sc	kitchen
cat	no miscues	no miscues
chairs	couch /sc	furniture
		white furniture
		door
		couch

In twenty-seven readings of *The Ghost*, there were very few miscues on the words *door, window, table, cat,* and *chairs.* Furthermore, each of those substitutions was meaningful in the context of the story. Undoubtedly, readers were assisted by the illustrations, and had they been asked to read the same words from a word list or flash cards, it is probable that their accuracy rate would have been much lower. This brings me back to the point I have made several times, and will continue to make throughout this book: Reading is much more than word identification. Well-written books given to the right child at the right time contribute to the learning of new words. When new readers know they can check illustrations to confirm the identity of a word or two, they can use that information to learn how letters are arranged to make those words. The examples I gave were running records from each student's second reading of the book. In subsequent lessons, it is likely they read it several more times, thus having more opportunities to learn from the text.

In some respects, the notion of *decodable texts* is as vague a term as *predictable texts.* Two researchers, Richard Allington and Haley Woodside-Jiron (1998), attempted to clarify the definition of decodable texts by analyzing many of the various policy and advocacy documents that call for the use of decodable texts in beginning reading. In all of the documents they reviewed, they found two features that seemed to distinguish decodable texts from other kinds of texts. First, decodable texts are composed of phonetically regular words, and second, those texts are composed of words constructed from phonic elements previously taught to students. More ambiguous, however, was whether or not a decodable text was defined as one composed exclusively of decodable words, or a text with a few sight words was also considered decodable. Compounding the problem of defining decodable texts is the matter that, in English, a sequence of letters may have different pronunciations in different words, so decoding is not always a simple matter. For example, consider the following word pairs: *how* and *show; read* and *read; love* and *move; put* and *shut.*

Children Need Books

Far more important than trying to characterize the best books for beginning readers by using ambiguous phrases such as *decodable texts* or *predictable books* is the necessity of making sure that all classrooms and school libraries are filled with an abundance of books that meet the diverse needs and interests of all students. There is no single book or series of books that will be perfect for all children, and children are best served when teachers have a wide selection of books to choose from for reading instruction. Jeff McQuillan, in the last chapter of his book *The Literacy Crisis: False Claims, Real Solutions* (1998), reviews and synthesizes many research studies on children's reading achievement. While each of these studies focuses on a different group of students, a key ingredient for high reading achievement in each situation was access to a wide range of books. Stephen Krashen (1995) analyzed data from forty-one states on the fourth grade reading test of the National Assessment of Educational Progress (NAEP), and found that one of the best predictors of scores was the number of books per student in school libraries.

Access to books, however, is not equal among school children. As Krashen (1997/98) points out, there are vast differences in the numbers of public, school, and classroom library books available to students from affluent communities in contrast to students from high-poverty areas. In another study designed to investigate literacy instruction in high-poverty schools, Sherry Guice and her colleagues "were especially disturbed by the lack of books provided to these children" (1996, 197). Furthermore, they discovered that 40 percent of the teachers in their study used personal funds to purchase the majority of the books in their classroom collections. Imagine going to work for Microsoft® and finding out you needed to purchase a computer for your office so that you could do the job you were hired for. You might argue that Microsoft® is more flush with cash than most school districts, but I would counter that if making readers of *all* of our children were truly a priority in this country, policy makers would rush to see that all classrooms and school libraries were well stocked with large collections of books.

The Books Children Need

Currently, there are thousands of wonderful "little books" created especially for children who are learning to read, and there are thousands of children's literature trade books for readers of all ages. Children who are learning to read need access to a great many books. They need picture books with exquisite illustrations in a variety of artistic styles. They need poetry and stories written in rich, imaginative language. They need poetry and stories that will make them laugh. They need poetry and stories that feature characters of many races and cultures. They need nonfiction books about a wide assortment of subjects. Children need books that are too difficult for them to read on their own, and they need books they can read independently. Most of all, they need books they love so much that they want to keep reading more and more and more.

Good books are an important component of a successful classroom literacy program, but good teachers also provide their students with a whole range of reading and writing lessons that support their growth as readers (Morrow, Tracey, Woo & Pressley 1999). From the beginning, children need texts that foster the development of a range of strategies simultaneously. They learn best from texts that reflect the grammar of the language they speak and the vocabulary they use in conversation. Good teachers provide their students with books that will teach them something new. That something new might be language that is more book-like than talking, a less predictable text where the identity of an unfamiliar word cannot be found by checking the illustration, or a text about a subject new to the reader.

One concern of mine has been the lack of a large core of books for new readers featuring characters from the diverse cultural and ethnic groups in this country. Slowly, this is changing for the better. The "Piñata Books" published by Celebration Press have long been popular with the students at my school because the stories in many of the books reflect events from their personal family stories. The "Visions™" series of emergent reading books from The Wright Group features African American families, and a brand new series from Lee & Low publishers called "Bebop Books" features books about children from Latin American, African American, Asian American, Native American, and other diverse backgrounds. Multicultural libraries are important for all of our students. Violet Harris' book *Using Multiethnic Literature in the K-8 Classroom* (1997) is an excellent resource for teachers and librarians.

Literary Pathways is a book about selecting and evaluating books for independent reading. The pages of this book are filled with descriptions of many, many books, but please keep in mind that for every book I write about, there are scores of wonderful books I have no room to mention. Many of the books I discuss are not the most recently published, because the examples come from several years of my own teaching. In general, the date a book was originally published should not be of concern to teachers if it is a story of enduring quality that appeals to contemporary readers. My goal in writing *Literary Pathways* is to provide a foundation and starting point for continued exploration and discovery of books that will turn new readers into eager readers.

Summary

Understanding text complexity is an important consideration for teachers and librarians who select books for new readers. While readability formulas can be effective for organizing books along a gradient of difficulty, they are not finely tuned for analyzing books for beginning readers. The concept of predictability is useful because it guides teachers and librarians into thinking about texts in relationship to their readers. However, it is important to keep in mind that texts can be predictable on several levels. At the word or sentence level, predictability may mean a repetition of words or phrases, with a change of a word or two. At the story level, predictability may indicate a story such as a cumulative tale that follows a particular pattern. Predictable texts may be those constructed around a pattern of days of the week or number sequences. Thus, a predictable text is not necessarily an easy text, and the notion of predictability is not adequate for explaining why a particular text is easy or difficult for readers.

Research in emergent literacy has been very helpful in understanding readability in texts for beginning readers because this research is rooted in extensive observations of how children learn language and how they learn to read and write. Research in miscue analysis has provided powerful insights into the reading process, and has provided an important foundation for research into how texts support beginning readers. There is no research evidence showing that any one kind of text is superior to another for teaching children to read. Most important is having large and varied classroom and school library book collections so that teachers and librarians can always choose *the right book for the right child at the right time.*

Closing Points

- Any book can be assigned a level.
- A book with a level is no guarantee of its quality or appeal to children.
- Levels do not provide sufficient information for purchasing books for a meaningful reading and literature program.
- Texts can be predictable in several ways, including repetition of a sentence pattern; repetition of a cycle of events; use of familiar sequences, such as numbers or days of the week; or characters who act in unique ways.
- A predictable text is not necessarily an easy-to-read text.
- Children's early experiences with stories, language, and writing influence the types of texts that support their learning to read.
- Children need books they love so much they want to keep reading.
- Classrooms and school libraries should be filled with great quantities of books to meet the reading needs and interests of all students.

Bibliography

Children' s Books

1. *Frog and Toad Are Friends* by Arnold Lobel. HarperCollins, 1970.
2. *Brown Bear, Brown Bear, What Do You See?* by Bill Martin. Illus. by Eric Carle. Holt, 1992.
3. *Titch* by Pat Hutchins. Simon & Schuster, 1971.

4. *The Three Billy Goats Gruff* retold and illus. by Paul Galdone. Houghton Mifflin. 1979.

5. *The Three Billy Goats Gruff* retold and illus. by Janet Stevens. Harcourt, 1990.

6. *You'll Soon Grown Into Them, Titch* by Pat Hutchins. Greenwillow, 1983.

7. *Tidy Titch* by Pat Hutchins. Greenwillow, 1991.

8. *Whose Mouse Are You?* by Robert Kraus. Illus. by Jose Aruego. Simon & Schuster, 1986.

9. *Mary Wore Her Red Dress, Henry Wore His Green Sneakers* by Merle Peek. Clarion, 1985.

10. *Amelia Bedelia* by Peggy Parish. Illus. by Fritz Siebel. HarperCollins, 1963.

11. *The Duchess Bakes a Cake* by Virginia Kahl. Scribner, 1955 (out of print).

12. *Nate the Great and the Sticky Case* by Marjorie Weinman Sharmat. Illus. by Marc Simont. Dell Yearling, 1981.

13. *There's a Nightmare in My Closet* by Mercer Mayer. Dial, 1984.

14. *Have You Seen My Cat?* by Eric Carle. Simon & Schuster, 1997.

15. *Frog and Toad* books by Arnold Lobel. HarperCollins.

16. *Magic School Bus* books by Joanna Cole. Illus. by Bruce Degen. Scholastic.

17. *The Ghost* by Joy Cowley. Illus. by Robyn Belton. Wright Group, 1983.

18. *The Carrot Seed* by Ruth Krauss. Illus. by Crockett Johnson. Harper-Collins, 1945.

19. *Little Red Riding Hood* retold and illustrated by Trina Schart Hyman. Holiday House, 1983.

20. *Wiley and the Hairy Man* by Molly Bang. Simon & Schuster, 1996.

21. *A Dark Dark Tale* by Ruth Brown. Dutton, 1992.

22. *Look for Me* by June Melser. Illus. by Lynette Vondruska. Wright Group, 1982.

23. *Saturday Morning* by Leslie Moyes. Learning Media, 1983.

24. *Fix It, Fox* by Patricia Ann Lynch. Illus. by Jane Caminos. Silver Burdett Ginn, 1996.

25. *I Am a Cat* by Teresa Chin. Photos by Graham Meadows. Rigby, 1997.

26. *The Cat Who Loved Red* by Lynn Salem and Josie Stewart. Illus. by Holly Pendergast. Seedling Publications, 1992.

27. *Bears in the Night* by Stan and Jan Berenstain. Random House, 1971.

28. *Green Eggs and Ham* by Dr. Seuss. Random House, 1960.

29. *Amy Goes to School* by Jenny Harris. Illus. by Phyllis Pollema-Cahill. Rigby, 1997.

30. *Piñata* (Spanish) and *Mas Piñata* (Spanish and English). Celebration Press.

31. *Visions*™ Books. Wright Group.

32. *Bebop Books.* Lee & Low Books.

3

Sorting Books Along a Gradient of Difficulty
Starting the Conversational Dance

In the previous chapter, I demonstrated ways of thinking about texts and illustrations in books for beginning readers, and showed how observing readers is an essential part of the process of understanding what makes books easy or difficult for them to read. I used the metaphor of mapping an elephant to illustrate the immensity of figuring out where to begin. In this chapter, we will take a tour of a broader range of books, keeping in mind the perspective of the seventh mouse who did not mistake the parts of the elephant for the whole. I have found that the most effective way to describe these differences is to select books on a particular topic or theme from a range of several levels, and discuss them in relation to each other. Previously, I have written about books with an "all fall down" theme (Peterson 1991). For this book, I have chosen fictional books with surprise endings and nonfiction books about frogs, and I will present them in order of difficulty, from easier to more complex.

Many factors influence the choice of a level for a particular book, including content in relation to children's personal experiences, language patterns, vocabulary, illustration support for the meaning of the text, and narrative style. Making a decision about an appropriate level for a book is a process of examining the relationship of such features within the context of an entire book. Furthermore, assigning a level to a book is also a process of estimating its placement in relation to other books, so it is important for teachers and librarians to know many books. Aside from the book itself, the child who reads the book is the most important consideration.

Consequently, assigning a level to a book is always a "best guess," until that book has been read by a large number of students. For a leveling system to be effective, it is important to make provisions to review the levels assigned to new books once they have been read by several students. In my experience, some books are easy to level immediately, while others must be tried at two or even three levels. Ultimately, however, as Marie Clay cautions, "A difficult text is a text which is difficult for a particular child. An easy text is easy because a particular child can read it" (1991, 201).

Beginning the Conversational Dance

Some of the books I write about in this chapter have been used in Reading Recovery for several years, and consequently have been assigned Reading Recovery book levels. Reading Recovery levels are a useful frame of reference, but like any leveling or readability system, they are useful only if teachers and librarians know their children and the literature they provide for them. I do not refer to those levels in this chapter, because I want to focus on the books themselves. Instead, I will carry on a "conversational dance" around many books in order to describe how I estimate how easy or difficult a book is in relation to others by looking at different aspects of texts and illustrations.

It is rare that I can read through a book once and be sure where it fits along a gradient or in a series of levels. Instead, I think things to myself like: "This book reminds me of . . . [another book]. Most readers would know these words, but the syntax of the sentences is a little more complex than most books at this level; on the other hand, this sentence pattern is repeated several times and that will help readers; this book about dinosaurs has some very hard words, but dinosaur fans probably know them already; and, this book about the solar system has many features in common with the dinosaur book I just leveled, but it is about a subject that is new to most of my students, so I think I had better place it at a higher level." When I finish talking to myself about a book, I usually have a much better idea about where to level a book in relation to other books, but I will not know for sure until I have observed children reading it.

Almost every book I write about in *Literary Pathways* is one I know through the eyes of children, by way of teaching, book discussions, and informal conversations. There are many styles of writing in children's books, and different features can influence how easy or hard a book is likely to be for most readers. Sometimes vocabulary can make one book more challenging than another; sometimes, the challenge lies in the syntax and sentence length. A reader's prior knowledge is a strong factor influencing the readability of a text, and children bring different interests to their reading. As Paula Moore points out in her article about selecting nonfiction literature for emergent readers, ". . . when reading nonfiction texts, prior knowledge or interest about the topic is the factor most likely to determine how 'readable' the text is" (1998, 78).

Practice Texts

To demonstrate a few of the challenges present in trying to level books into a sequence of difficulty, I have created three practice texts. Picture in your mind an easy book with illustrations showing the actions in the following sentences. We will call this hypothetical text *Animals Move.*

> Dogs run.
> Bears climb.
> Birds fly.
> Fish swim.

If you wanted to level this book, that is, find its place in relation to other books, you might start by thinking that children are probably familiar with each of those animals and would be able to check the picture to confirm the identity of the word. You might also reason that the verbs are all words that children use in conversation. Furthermore, the meaning of each phrase would be easy for a young reader to grasp.

Now, let's alter the text a bit by changing the names of the animals, but leaving their actions the same. We will call this one *Unusual Animals.*

> Coyotes run.
> Koalas climb.
> Condors fly.
> Barracudas swim.

You probably would not consider this text easier than the first, but do you think it would be about the same or more difficult? You could reason that most children might not be familiar with some of these animals, so the second text would be harder. Of course, you might know one particular student with a wide knowledge of animals, and for that student, the two books might be about equal in challenge. Now, one more variation, which we will call *I Like Animals.*

> I can run like a dog.
> I can climb like a bear.
> I can fly like a bird.
> I can swim like a fish.

Where do you think this text falls in relation to the other two? Perhaps you have already decided that the book *Unusual Animals* would provide the greatest challenge for most readers, and that a child who could easily read the words *coyote, barracuda, condor,* and *koala* was ready for more challenge than a series of two word sentences. If you were to consult Thomas Gunning's

(1996) Primary High Frequency Word List to see which words are most frequently used in books for first graders, you would find the words in all three texts, with the exception of *coyote, barracuda, condor,* and *koala,* a good indicator that the text with those words might be too hard for most early readers.

Now, you have to decide if *Animals Move* is easier or harder than *I Like Animals.* On the surface, it looks as though a two-word sentence should be easier than a six-word sentence, particularly for a child who is learning how to match spoken words with written words and read the spaces between words. However, each word in the two-word sentence is a high content word that carries half the meaning of the sentence. Although very young children who are learning how to speak go through a period of time using short phrases comprised of high content words, most children start school having well-developed semantic and syntactic systems (Lindfors 1987). Five- and six-year-olds, like adults, do not typically speak in two-word sentences. Two-word sentences can be hard to understand because their meaning passes quickly. Longer sentences can actually help listeners and readers by giving them time to process the speaker's or writer's thoughts.

The six-word sentence *I can* _____ *like a* _____ gives readers time to understand its meaning, and the repetition in each sentence of *I can* and *like a* gives readers a predictable framework that frees them to attend more closely to the high content pairs in each sentence: *dog, run; bears, climb; birds, fly;* and *fish, swim.* The repetition of the sentence pattern also gives readers time to sort out confusions and correct errors, in the same way many real readers did with *The Ghost,* which I wrote about in the previous chapter. This text might be a little bit easier for most readers than the *Animals Move* text, but you would not know for sure until you had tried the books with several readers.

The concept of *word density ratios* (Hiebert 1999) provides another useful way of thinking about this puzzle. The texts with two-word sentences have no words that are used more than once. Thus, each word is a unique word and the word density ratio for each is 1:1. The third text has a total of twenty-four words, but only twelve unique words because several words are repeated. Thus, its word density is 1:2, suggesting this text would be slightly easier than the other two texts. Ultimately, you would need to put both texts in the hands of many young readers to know for sure.

Reading Explorers

Now it is time to turn our attention away from practice texts and hypothetical readers to real books and real readers. When I started writing *Literary Pathways,* I knew I would need some help in knowing how to write about books for children moving into the short, illustrated chapter books, sometimes called "easy readers" or "transitional books." I knew how to write about books for beginning readers because I have taught several children how to read, and my dissertation research was on selecting and evaluating books for beginners. However, I wanted to see books like *Henry and Mudge* through the eyes of the children for whom they were written. As Susan Hepler and Janet Hickman learned from their classroom research, some children's response to literature is social. I was inspired by their idea of "a community of readers," and I hoped that by bringing students together to talk about books, they would create their own learning communities.

> We have proposed the idea of a "community of readers" to let us talk about how children, in alliance with friends and teacher, work together to help each other learn to read. Our observations have been made in classrooms where school reading does not differ from reading which the rest of the world does—where children read for pleasure and learn to read by reading books (1982, 279).

I asked Lynda Brady, a second-grade teacher at Tully, if she and her class would help me out. When we first talked, I was not sure of what I was looking for or how they could help, but Lynda thought it would be a good idea for me to meet regularly with groups of students reading at similar levels. My goal was to find out what they liked to read by listening to what they had to say about books—not by giving them reading instruction. They became the Reading Explorers, and the voices of two years of Reading Explorers fill this book. While I let them know that their mission was to help me learn more about books and readers, they once told a new student that the purpose of Reading Explorers was to help them become better readers!

Like most classes, there was a wide range of reading levels in Lynda's classes. At the beginning of the first year of Reading Explorers, the lowest level reader was able to point to and accurately read the phrase "I went walking" in the picture book *I Went Walking* by Sue Williams and illustrated by Julie Vivas, while the most proficient reader read and discussed in great detail *The Chocolate Touch* by Patrick Catling, a short chapter book with a well-developed plot inspired by the ancient story of King Midas and his golden touch. From this range, Lynda and I created four groups that I met with weekly. They read from the regular library collection, their own books, from sets of trade books I have in the library for teachers to borrow for their classrooms, and from books I purchased for them that stayed in their classroom. My conversations with the Reading Explorers kept me in touch with real readers as I read from a wide range of books.

Fiction / Nonfiction

Before I launch into book discussions, I would like to say a few words about the terms *fiction* and *nonfiction*. Many of us who teach are prone to use these terms as though they were completely separate categories, as though all works of fiction tell lies and all works of nonfiction present truths. In reality, there are many styles of writing in fiction and many writers of fiction conduct exhaustive research to ground their stories in authentic places or periods of history. As Gordon Wells has pointed out, "... all fiction is firmly based in fact ..." (1986, 204). Readers of fiction know the powerful pull of the worlds their favorite writers create, which seem every bit as real to them as their everyday lives. Novelist, poet, and essayist Barbara Kingsolver writes of the reality of fiction in her essay "Jabberwocky," included in her book *High Tide in Tucson.*

> A novel works its magic by putting a reader inside another person's life. The pace is as slow as life. It's as detailed as life, so that the story feels more personal than the sets designed by someone else and handed over via TV or movies. Literature duplicates the experience of living in a way that nothing else can, drawing you so fully into another life that you temporarily forget you have one of your own (1995, 230).

There are also many styles of writing in nonfiction, and few are mere recitations of "just the facts," like almanacs and field guides. Russell Freedman, author of many biographies for children, including the Newbery Award winner *Lincoln: A Photobiography,* emphasizes the importance of a strong story line, or narrative, in nonfiction.

> Certainly the basic purpose of nonfiction is to inform, to instruct, hopefully to enlighten. But that's not enough. An effective nonfiction book must animate its subject, infuse it with life. It must create a vivid and believable world that the reader will enter willingly and leave only with reluctance. A good nonfiction book should be a pleasure to read. It should be just as compelling as a good story. After all, there's a story to everything. The task of the nonfiction writer is to find the story—the narrative line—that exists in nearly every subject (Freedman 1992, 3).

Most of us readily talk about different genres of fiction. We expect science fiction to be different from historical fiction and poetry to be different from prose. On the other hand, we sometimes overlook the variety of styles of writing in nonfiction. For example, let's take a look two pieces of writing about jackrabbits and their afternoon resting places. One appears in a field guide, a genre of nonfiction writing designed to provide concisely written facts about plants and animals. The other is a two-page article from *Arizona Highways,* a popular publication with informative articles written in a conversational style.

The Audubon Society Nature Guide *Deserts* tells readers that "By day, it generally rests in dense vegetation or in a shallow depression, or form, becoming active in late afternoon" (MacMahon 1985, 566). On the same topic, naturalist Tom Dollar writes in his article "Focus on Nature":

> Day after day, throughout the hottest desert months, I've watched black-tails and other rabbits and hares return to the same shady bush to siesta. They remain in these small basins for hours on end, rising occasionally to stretch or to nibble on nearby forage but never abandoning their cool refuges unless startled (July 1999, 33).

Both pieces of writing are nonfiction, but each serves a different purpose. Each provides accurate information, but Dollar takes readers into the jack-rabbits' world, making them feel as though they, too, are a part of the scene. Readers of this kind of writing are usually looking for both information and style, or, in Rosenblatt's terms, they approach reading both efferently and aesthetically. These same sentences could also be woven into a novel to describe what a fictional character observed during an extended camping trip in the desert.

I do not mean to gloss over differences between fiction and nonfiction, however. There are features of nonfiction writing, sometimes referred to as expository texts, that are important for teachers to keep in mind when guiding new readers. Foremost, we expect the information to be accurate, and we look for photographs, maps, and other illustrations to complement the written text. Rick Kerper emphasizes that nonfiction is more than information conveyed through words, calling it "a *literature of* fact that combines both verbal and visual texts" (1998, 55). Clarity of presentation is essential so readers can understand the subject every step of the way, unlike the plots of many stories that are designed to keep readers in suspense until the end. And, while there are many exceptions, the nonfiction that children encounter is usually written in the present tense, while many fictional stories are written in the past tense.

When I tried to assign levels to nonfiction books for Reading Recovery, I found it difficult to do because so much depends on the knowledge a child brings to reading. A child with an interest in the solar system would have little or no trouble reading the names of planets, whereas a dinosaur fan could quickly identify words like *triceratops* and *Tyrannosaurus rex.* A dinosaur aficionado with no interest in the solar system, however, would have a difficult time with a book about planets, even though a text about dinosaurs with a similar structure would be an easy one to read. While there are some characteristics of texts that indicate they are nonfiction, and there are some ways of reading that are more typical for nonfiction than fiction—paying attention to the captions on photos and diagrams, interpreting data in charts, using indices and tables of contents, for example—nonfiction is not so different from fiction that it should be considered a completely separate literary form. While I explore fiction (books with surprise endings) and nonfiction separately (books about frogs), it is with the purpose of demonstrating differences *and* similarities. After all, much of what is classified as nonfiction is real-life experience told in story form such as history or biography.

Looking at Books with Surprise Endings

Most readers enjoy a surprise. They do not want to read something that is so predictable it makes them drowsy. No young readers have ever told me they like books with surprises, but when they ask for something funny, scary, or with a puzzle, I know they want to be surprised in some way. It is a mistake to think that only advanced readers can encounter such surprises in their independent reading. Page-turners can be found among the simplest books for the newest readers. My intention in this section is to discuss books from a range of levels (easier to more difficult) to show some options a writer has in creating a story with a surprise, and to demonstrate how teachers can put together a group of books with similar themes at many levels.

Focus Books

1. *Too Many Balloons* by Catherine Matthias. Illus. by Gene Sharp. Rookie Reader. Children's Press, 1982.
2. *Just Like Daddy* by Frank Asch. Simon & Schuster, 1981.
3. *Hattie and the Fox* by Mem Fox. Illus. by Patricia Mullins. Simon & Schuster, 1987.
4. *And I Mean It, Stanley* by Crosby Bonsall. An I Can Read Book. HarperCollins, 1974.
5. *The Napping House* by Audrey Wood. Illus. by Don Wood. Harcourt, 1984.
6. *Little Chick's Friend Duckling* by Mary DeBall Kwitz. Illus. by Bruce Degen. An I Can Read Book. HarperCollins, 1992.
7. *Poppleton and His Friends* by Cynthia Rylant. Illus. by Mark Teague. Scholastic, 1997.
8. *Bear's Hiccups* by Marion Dane Bauer. Illus. by Diane Dawson Hearn. Holiday House, 1998.

Too Many Balloons

One of the easiest books with a surprise ending is *The Ghost,* which I discussed in Chapter 2, in which the reader is taken through a house and each sentence begins with "I see" and ends with a familiar household object such as a couch or chairs. The surprise occurs at the end when a child covered with a sheet shouts "Boo!" A book that is longer and more challenging than *The Ghost* is *Too Many Balloons.* The plot is simple and cumulative. A little girl goes to the zoo and buys a red balloon to show to the lion. Next, she buys two yellow balloons and shows them to the giraffes. She makes eight more stops at the balloon man's stand, buying three balloons, then four balloons, and on up to ten balloons for her last purchase. Observant readers will notice that she never puts any balloons down, so by the end of the story, she is holding fifty-five balloons. The surprise ending, of course, is that she is carried into the air by the balloons.

The entire text of *Too Many Balloons* is long—182 words—much longer than other books that present similar challenges for readers. However, there are many aspects of the text that make it highly predictable for readers and support their learning of new words. First of all, each episode consists of three small events that provide a predictable framework throughout the book. There are ten episodes in the story. Once readers have read one or two episodes, they understand how the story continues and can make useful predictions that give them a head start with each new event.

1. Buying a balloon
2. Showing the balloon to an animal or animals
3. Acknowledgment that the animal(s) liked the balloon

The sentences describing each of these events are written in syntax used by children in conversation, and also follow predictable patterns. Readers must closely attend to the print because there are slight changes in wording, as each new color of balloon and new animal is introduced. If readers are not certain of the color words in print, they can check the colors in the illustrations. The colors in the illustrations provide readers with support for learning to read the words in print. The colors of the balloons would be familiar to most readers: red, yellow, blue, green, orange, white, pink, and purple. The last two sets of balloons are striped and polka-dotted, and while they are not colors, students who have read this book to me have not had any trouble making the switch.

Just Like Daddy

Just Like Daddy has long been a favorite of Tully students because the twist at the end is truly a surprise to them. A young bear begins his day doing everything "Just like Daddy," and that phrase is the refrain in the text that follows bear's descriptions of his actions five times in the story. He gets up, has breakfast, and goes fishing with his mother and father. The big surprise at the end is that the young bear catches a fish "Just like *Mommy!*"

Like *The Ghost* and *Too Many Balloons*, readers of *Just Like Daddy* receive support from repetition of sentence patterns and phrases. *Just Like Daddy* is more challenging, however, because the action is more varied, and consequently, there is a greater variety of words that are used only once in the story. While most readers are likely to understand the meanings of words like *yawn, breakfast, worm,* and *hook,* and the meaning of the events in which they are used, it is still challenging for them to continually confront different words. Also, there is a greater variety of sentence patterns in *Just Like Daddy,* and many sentences begin with adverbial clauses. Being able to read individual words may not be sufficient if readers do not grasp how they fit together and serve as an introduction to the rest of the sentence. From a teaching perspective, *Just Like Daddy* is a perfect book for providing readers with many opportunities to read and understand syntactically complex sentences.

Hattie and the Fox

Hattie and the Fox ends with a big surprise for some of its characters, but not for readers who quickly see the story unfolding through Patricia Mullins' collage illustrations. Hattie is a hen who worriedly reports to her barnyard friends that she sees a nose in the bushes. Their responses show they are not at all concerned. "'Who cares?' said the sheep. 'So what?' said the horse." Hattie persists in reporting her observations, but each time she mentions something else she sees—eyes, ears, legs, and a body—the animals respond with the same chorus of boredom. The exchange continues until Hattie sees the tail and shouts. "It's a fox? It's a fox!" All of a sudden, their chorus becomes one of alarm, but the cow's loud "MOO!" frightens the fox away.

Hattie and the Fox is a book that has delighted countless children, young listeners and older, newly independent readers alike. In comparing it with *Just Like Daddy,* it is easy to see at a glance that *Hattie and the Fox* is likely to be more challenging because it has a greater number and variety of words and expressions that may be unfamiliar to readers. Furthermore, many of the actions of the unnamed young bear in *Just Like Daddy* are similar to children's every day lives, making it a bit more accessible to some readers than the world of Hattie and her friends.

These two books, however, have a similar structure that provides readers with a grounding in how some stories "work." First, there is an event (a young bear waking up; Hattie noticing a nose in the bushes) followed by a response in the form of a refrain ("Just like Daddy"; "'Who cares?' said the sheep."). As the events of the plot progress, the refrains give readers a chance to "rest" with anchor-like passages that become easier to read as they continue through the text. Think of learning to drive in an unfamiliar city, and how reassuring it is to find distinctive landmarks to help you find your way. Being certain of those landmarks allows you to direct your attention to new features in the environment.

And I Mean It, Stanley

And I Mean It, Stanley is a book with a surprise ending that is more challenging for readers than *Hattie and the Fox,* even though the text is shorter and the words look like they should be easier for readers to identify. The primary reason for this difference lies in the structure of the story and the style of writing. In each of the four books I have just discussed, there is an element of mystery and a surprise ending, but the reader is told immediately about the nature of the journey. In *The Ghost* it is a walk through a familiar home setting; in *Too Many Balloons,* it is the common experience of visiting a zoo; in *Just Like Daddy* it is a cozy family day; in *Hattie and the Fox* it is the recognizable danger a fox presents for a hen.

The direction of *And I Mean It, Stanley* is less clear from the beginning. The illustrations show a pile of trash—coat hangers, cracked pails, bits of wood—and a small girl, wearing her baseball cap backwards, scrunched up on the ground peeking through a fence. The entire text of the story is a first person monologue in which the girl tells Stanley she doesn't care if he plays and that she's having a lot of fun and making a "really, truly great thing" (Bonsall 1974, 15). When this story is introduced to new readers and read aloud to them in an expressive voice, they quickly recognize the tone of voice as one they have either used or heard between friends annoyed with each other.

What makes this text challenging for readers is that taken sentence by sentence, it is difficult for some to figure out precisely what is happening. Experienced adult readers are accustomed to styles of writing in which the author intentionally leaves out information and ties loose ends together at the close of the story. Young readers, however, may be confused by a book in which Stanley's identity is not revealed until the end. This style is, of course, why *And I Mean It, Stanley* is a terrific book for readers when they are ready, because they must work through a very small bit of confusion before they finally understand what the story is about. Stanley appears, finally, on page 30, and he is a big, fuzzy, friendly dog! He bursts through the fence, and knocks down the "truly great thing." On the last page, Stanley is licking a smiling face, and the closing words are "Aw, Stanley."

The words and phrases of the text are easy for readers to understand, but there are no convenient refrains to serve as anchors of support. Instead, there are many repetitions of phrases within sentences and restatements of the same ideas in slightly different ways. For example, the text on three pages uses different approaches for the girl to tell Stanley she doesn't care if he stays away.

> But I don't care, Stanley.
> I don't want to play with you.
> I don't want to talk to you. (8)
> You stay there, Stanley.
> Stay in back of the fence.
> I don't care. (9)
> I can play by myself, Stanley.
> I don't need you, Stanley.
> And I mean it, Stanley. (11)

Quite often, figuring out whether one book is easier or more difficult than another is a hard call when the two books seem similar to each other. I asked second grader Daniela to read *Hattie and the Fox* and *I Mean It, Stanley* on two different occasions while I took a running record of each reading. She read *Hattie and the Fox* fluently and expressively, with an accuracy rate of 96 percent and a self-correction rate of 1:3. *And I Mean It, Stanley* was more challenging for her. She read more hesitantly, missing words such as *talk, made,* and *making* that are quite easy for her in other texts. Nevertheless, her accuracy rate of 91 percent was within an appropriate instructional range, and several comments she made about the story ("it's probably the cat" and, referring to the girl's finished creation, "it looks like a person") showed she was following the action.

Louise Rosenblatt emphasizes that ". . . reading is a matter of inferring, creating meaning" (Karolides 1999, 168). In reflecting on Daniela's reading of *And I Mean It, Stanley*, it seems to me that because so much of her attention was focused on creating meaning from the words and pictures that she miscued on words she read easily in other contexts. Consequently, she was learning to read like a more advanced reader, without having all of the facts placed immediately before her, continuing reading without quite knowing everything she needed to know to fully understand the meaning of the story.

The Napping House

Next, I will discuss two texts that are similar in the level of challenge they provide readers, but that are very different in structure and vocabulary. *The Napping House* has a cumulative text with a rich, literary vocabulary. *Little Chick's Friend Duckling* develops in episodes and has a varied vocabulary, but words that are likely to be known by young school children. Both are engaging stories that present different kinds of challenges and consequently, important literary experiences for children.

There is a surprise ending for *The Napping House,* and it can also be seen as an "all fall down" story. It begins on a rainy day in a napping house where everyone is sleeping. Granny is stretched out on the bed, and one by one, a child, a dog, a cat, a mouse, and a flea pile on top. When the flea bites the mouse, a chain reaction begins, and one by one, each goes flying off. That description makes it all seem "ho-hum," but Don Wood's lush, expressive double-page spreads create a visual feast as worthy of attention as Audrey Wood's lively text.

The structure of the story will be familiar to any child who has heard other cumulative tales. Below are the first three sets of text.

There is a house,
a napping house,
where everyone is sleeping.

And in that house
there is a bed, a cozy bed
in a napping house,
where everyone is sleeping.

And on that bed
there is a granny,
a snoring granny
on a cozy bed
in a napping house,
where everyone is sleeping.

The granny is joined by a *dreaming child, a dozing dog, a snoozing cat, a slumbering mouse,* and a *wakeful flea.* Once joined by the flea, the quiet fades because the flea bites the mouse, which starts a chain reaction that sends all the characters flying.

I think it is apparent that this would be a very challenging text for a new reader, in spite of the repetitive, cumulative structure. From a teaching perspective, I think of this clearly laid out, predictable structure as one that allows readers to focus their attention on literary language and extend their knowledge of those delicious descriptions, much in the same way the repetitive structures of books like *Just Like Daddy* and *Hattie and the Fox* help readers make new discoveries about language. When I first asked Alex and Frederick to read *The Napping House,* they took one look at words like *slumbering, snoozing,* and *dozing* and emphatically declared it too hard for them. However, before they started reading we took a close look at all those wonderful words for sleeping, and talked about their meanings and how to analyze the letters and groups of letters to pronounce the words. Once they learned how to solve those new words, they were on their way. Frederick asked if he could borrow the library's big book version of *The Napping House,* and the next day I saw him in the hall carrying the book, and with a broad smile, he told me he was taking it to read to some younger children. I could tell from the huge grin on his face that he had found the book that transformed his perception of himself from struggling reader to "real" reader.

Little Chick's Friend Duckling

Frank Smith writes, "One of the beautiful things about written language that makes sense (to the child) is that it increasingly provides learning assistance to the child" (1994, 202). This is true of books with refrains and cumulative language, as well as stories that develop as a series of events or episodes. *Little Chick's Friend Duckling* tells a story of the value of friendship and gives readers experience in reading a quiet story that unfolds slowly. The surprises are subtle—several shared small discoveries, and an important one for Little Chick that her mother, Broody Hen, will always have room for her, even after her six eggs hatch. The story opens with Little Chick running out of the hen-house after declaring, "There is no room for me!" Next, she meets her friend Duckling and together they reveal to each other their secret fears of places each one finds scary.

Readers of this story not only meet characters whose behavior is influenced by their feelings; they gain experience with descriptive language and some of the ways authors tell about their characters. The following description shows how writers can create an image in simple but engaging language, and while the sentences are short, reading them aloud reveals a graceful, gentle rhythm that is consistent with the tone of the story.

> Little Chick and Duckling
> ran to the barn and looked in.
> A big, scary thing
> stood in the stall.
> It stamped its hooves
> and swished its tail.
> It put its head
> over the stall door. (16)
> "Oh, Duckling," said Little Chick.
> "That is not a scary thing.
> That is a horse." (18)

Thus, while newer readers may focus on reading to understand what is happening in a story, their encounters with various styles of writing provide far more powerful learning opportunities than merely identifying and learning new words. I am reminded of Katie, who easily read the sentence "'There is no room for me!' cried Little Chick." (8). She stopped, and with a puzzled look on her face, told me she didn't know what that meant. I started explaining that Little Chick was cold, but when she tried crawling under Broody Hen's wing the space was filled with six eggs, Katie jumped in, saying, "Oh— I thought that was a *real* room!" She returned to the first page, and re-read fluently, with understanding.

Dialogue, or conversation, is another aspect of text that can influence text difficulty. Many easy books show characters talking, and encase their words in quotation marks, which gives readers experience with the conventions of dialogue. For example, in the book *Look for Me,* which I wrote about in Chapter 2, whenever Mum looks for David but does not find him, her response is in the form of a quotation.

> "No, he's not here," she said.

Thus, readers have the opportunity to become familiar with the print conventions of talk, but they do not follow a dialogue in which one or more people are contributing a variety of thoughts. In contrast to *Look for Me,* a large portion of the text of *Little Chick's Friend Duckling* is a conversation between Little Chick and Duckling. Genuine dialogue often helps a plot to advance and one challenge for readers of dialogue is figuring out who is talking. Katie, for example, was initially confused at the identity of "she" in the following interaction.

> "Hello, Ducking," said Little Chick.
> "Why are you here
> and not swimming in the pond?"
> "The pond is covered with ice,"
> said Duckling.
> "Oh," said Little Chick.
> She hopped up and down.
> "I am cold," she said.
> "Me, too," said Duckling. (10)

Note that Katie's confusion had nothing to do with word knowledge. In her previous reading experience, she read stories in which one character talks, the other replies, and so on. *Little Chick's Friend Duckling* provides more challenge, however, because after Little Chick says "Oh," readers encounter a brief description of her actions ("She hopped up and down."), followed by another bit of talking by Little Chick ("I am cold"). Once I demonstrated how to pinpoint the identity of "she," Katie was on her way. She also politely told me that

I did not have to sit so close to her while she was reading because she didn't need any more help!

Bear's Hiccups and Poppleton and His Friends

Paying attention to dialogue is one way to examine text complexity; considering how a story begins and the amount and style of descriptive language are other telling features. About two months into her second-grade year, Nancy came to me with two library books she had borrowed the week before. "I'm returning this one," she said, handing me *Bear's Hiccups*. "It has too many hard words," she said emphatically. Then she opened *Poppleton and His Friends* to the story called "Dry Skin" and continued by telling the story, vibrantly recounting every detail. *Bear's Hiccups* and "Dry Skin" have surprise endings, so they fit in with this discussion, as well as provide the opportunity to discuss how they are more challenging for readers than books such as *Little Chick's Friend Duckling*.

Descriptive Language. First, let's take a look at the text Nancy told me had too many hard words. The first chapter is called "Looking for Trouble."

> It was the hottest day
> of the entire summer in the forest.
> Every leaf on every tree hung limp.
> Flowers wilted.
> Bees bumbled home for a nap. (6)
> The pond lay flat and still,
> like a scarf dropped in the grass.
> Otter was so hot he quit playing.
> Frog was so hot he quit croaking. (8)

Nancy is a strong, confident reader, always ready to try something new. I could see a few words that might be unknown to her—*limp* and *wilted,* for example, and possibly *scarf* and *croaking,* but I suspected there were reasons other than vocabulary that caused her to put the book down. (I decided not to push the issue, however; putting myself in the position of interrogator certainly would not have encouraged her to talk to me about her reading.)

The challenges Nancy encountered in *Bear's Hiccups* can be made visible by looking at the beginning of "Dry Skin."

> Poppleton looked in the mirror
> one morning.
> "Yikes!" he cried. "Dry skin!"
> He looked closer.

"I am flaking away." (20)
Poppleton called Cherry Sue.
"Cherry Sue," said Poppleton,
"I am dry as an old apple.
What should I do?" (20)
"Put on some oil," said Cherry Sue.
"All right," said Poppleton.
He put on some oil. (23)

I have quoted approximately the same amount of text so we can look beyond individual words to gain a better understanding of why *Bear's Hiccups* is a more challenging story for independent reading than "Dry Skin." Readers of "Dry Skin" find out the direction of the story in the second sentence and immediately are drawn to the absurdity of a pig announcing he is "flaking away." The images are very concrete—any seven-year-old I know could draw a picture of a pig with flaking skin, probably laughing the whole time. In contrast, readers of *Bear's Hiccups* encounter descriptive language that sets a quiet tone and creates images that are poetic and subtle. Experienced readers can recognize the purpose of such an introduction and revel in Bauer's exquisite language, knowing they will soon come to the action in the story. Newer readers, on the other hand, even those like Nancy who have large reading vocabularies and an eagerness to discover new stories, may have trouble when they first encounter an unfamiliar style of writing because they cannot figure out exactly what they are supposed to find.

Story Structure. Had Nancy continued to the third page of text, she would have found out that Bear was hotter than anyone in the forest. She might also have felt very hot herself when she finished reading about bear's discomfort. She would not, however, begin to understand the direction of the story until page 13 when Bear first speaks.

"This is a very small pond,"
Bear said.
"And I am a very large bear.
So the rest of you can go away.
This pond is mine. All mine."

Frog disputes the ownership of the pond, which leads to an argument and the disappearance of Frog. All the animals of the forest are worried about him, but Bear's attack of incurable hiccups distracts their attention. The big surprise comes when Bear sneezes and something pops out of her mouth—Frog.

The structure or shape of a story can also influence how challenging it is for readers. When some elements of a story are repeated with some variations, they provide a framework that helps readers anticipate the direction of the story, which in turn can free up some attention to figuring out unfamiliar words. A quick look at "Dry Skin" shows some repetition of events.

1. Poppleton discovers dry skin.
2. He asks Cherry Sue for advice.
3. She makes a suggestion.
4. He follows her advice.
5. Dry skin is back.
6. He calls her again.
7. She makes another suggestion.
8. He tries again.
9. Dry skin is back.
10. Cherry Sue visits Poppleton.
11. She looks at his dry skin.
12. She announces he doesn't have dry skin; he has *lint*! (the surprise)
13. The story continues for five more pages, while Poppleton cleans up.

"Dry Skin" (as well as the stories in all the *Poppleton* books) is more accessible to newly independent readers than *Bear's Hiccups,* but there are some important similarities to note. I wrote about the elegant descriptive language in *Bear's Hiccups,* but there are also splendid descriptions in "Dry Skin" that delight readers and immerse them in memorable language. When Poppleton calls Cherry Sue about his problem, he first says he is "as dry as an old apple" (22); then, he is "as dry as a dandelion" (24); and finally, he is "as dry as a desert" (27). When Cherry Sue suggested he try oil, Poppleton replied, "It just made me want french fries." When she asked him to try honey, it made him "want biscuits." When readers experience colorful language like Rylant's, they not only learn new words, they learn that putting words together in unexpected ways opens up new worlds for the imagination.

Characterization. Both books have characters with distinctive personalities. We can laugh at Poppleton's dilemma, but we can also feel a twinge of sympathy for him when Cherry Sue chides him for wearing his sweater for three days ("'I can be such a pig,' he said."). We laugh, too, at Bear and Frog when they each declare emphatically that the pond is "mine," and might even see the irony in their very human-like proclamations. Young readers do not need to be able to talk about characterization in stories, but they can begin to develop an awareness for the different types of characters who populate the landscape of their stories. Having experience with all sorts of characters provides a good foundation for understanding characters in the more complex stories they will read later.

By the way, I did ask Nancy if she would read *Bear's Hiccups* to me, but I waited until the end of the school year. There were some words that were new to her—*limp, wilted, quivered, chattered,* and *stoutest,* for example—but she read fluently, engrossed in the story. When she finished the book, she said, "I liked it. It makes me feel hot. I just get into the story and pop right into the pond."

Looking at Books About Frogs

For a closer look at the landscape of nonfiction, I selected the topic of frogs because there are many books about them for young readers, and it is a popular topic of study at my school. I began by making a chart to compare features of each book. My categories were: author, title, scope, vocabulary, and level of detail. When I finished, I had some ideas about which books might be easier or more difficult, but I never know for sure until I observe students reading them. I asked third graders Javier and Marina, to help me out. They remembered a little bit about their second grade frog studies, each is a capable reader, and each was willing to read several books to me and answer my incessant questions about the texts. I met with Marina twice and with Javier three times. I want to emphasize that my asking these students to read frog book after frog book while I took running records did not create authentic teaching or learning sessions. While our time together was relaxed and each was interested in what they were reading, my purpose was to gather information from them, not to encourage them to extend their learning. They did not read the first two books on the list because I did not own them at the time.

Focus Books

1. *Tadpoles and Frogs* by Jenny Feely. Photos by Michael Curtain. Alphakids. Sundance, 1999.

2. *Frogs* by Laura Driscoll. Illus. by Judith Moffatt. All Aboard Reading. Grosset & Dunlap, 1998.

3. *Frog (See How They Grow)* by Kim Taylor and Jane Burton. Dutton, 1997.

4. *The Frog* by Sabrina Crewe. Life Cycles. Raintree Steck-Vaughn, 1997.

5. *Frogs and Toads and Tadpoles, Too* by Allan Fowler. Rookie Read-About Science. Children's Press, 1992.

6. *From Tadpole to Frog* by Wendy Pfeffer. Illus. by Holly Keller. Let's-Read-and-Find-Out-Science. HarperCollins, 1994.

7. *Frogs* by Michael Tyler. MONDO, 1997.

8. *Frogs* by Gail Gibbons. Holiday House, 1993.

Tadpoles and Frogs (Jenny Feely)

Tadpoles and Frogs is one of a series of books created especially for emergent readers, and a fine example of how a text can contribute to learning more about reading and confirm or add to a child's knowledge about a subject. In a mere forty-one words, using simple sentence structures and vocabulary familiar to young readers, Feely describes a frog's developmental cycle, Curtain's close-up photographs clearly illustrate the points in the text, and on the last page, a simple chart of words and photographs summarizes the life cycle. While some of the words like *hatch, tadpole,* and *shrinks* might be new for readers, most are likely to be familiar. This is an attractive book, and while there are repetitions of phrases, the text is not boring or monotonous. It is a simple text, without being simplistic. Each page states one fact, allowing readers to gradually build an understanding of the phases of the cycle from egg to frog.

> The frog lays eggs
> on the water. (2)
> Tadpoles hatch
> from the eggs. (4)

Frogs (Laura Driscoll)

If you were to place *Tadpoles and Frogs* (Feely) alongside *Frogs* (Driscoll) you would immediately see one difference. *Frogs* has many more pages and words (twice the number of pages, and 325 more words). Quickly scan the pages and you will notice many words not used in *Tadpoles and Frogs,* such as *webbed, amphibians,* and *croak.* Right away, you would decide that *Frogs* is the more challenging of the two books for readers. And, while both books tell about the change from eggs to tadpoles to frogs, the scope of the book *Frogs* is broader than *Tadpoles and Frogs.* About half the text is devoted to information about several kinds of frogs and their predators. Now, let's refine our observations and take a close look at a portion of the text of *Frogs,* the portion that tells what happens after the eggs hatch.

> The eggs hatch.
> Frog babies swim out.
> They look like fish.
> They swim like fish.
> They even breathe
> underwater like fish. (8)
> But they are not fish.
> They are tadpoles. (9)

This is the more challenging of the two texts, yet note how carefully the author layers in bits of information to help readers gradually expand their understanding of tadpoles. Many children have never seen tadpoles, but most have seen fish swimming. By comparing tadpoles to fish, readers can visualize how a tadpole acts. Then, to avoid misunderstandings, the author states emphatically that they are not the same.

Using Running Records to Establish a Gradient of Text Difficulty

Sorting books into a gradient of difficulty does not require magical powers. Teachers and librarians possess a wealth of knowledge about texts and how students learn, and this experience is the most important factor in leveling books. Simply, read the books and think about the texts in relation to other books you have used with students. Then, arrange them in the order of challenge you think they present to readers. Sorting texts in this way will ususaly serve the needs of most teachers and librarians, especially if they observe how children read those books, and re-level them if necessary.

Sometimes, however, it is interesting and instructive to take running records of children reading those books. Before asking Javier to read the following four books, I predicted the order of difficulty they would present to him, but my predictions were not confirmed until I compared the running records of his readings. Of course, data from one student is not adequate for generalizing how a large number of students will respond to a group of books. Most of the time however, comparing one or two students' running records of a particular book provides sufficient information for figuring out where that book falls in relation to others.

> *Frog (See How They Grow)* by Kim Taylor and Jane Burton: 96 percent accuracy
>
> *The Frog* by Sabrina Crewe: 92 percent accuracy
>
> *Frogs and Toads and Tadpoles, Too* by Allan Fowler: 90 percent accuracy
>
> *From Tadpole to Frog* by Wendy Pfeffer and Holly Keller: 89 percent accuracy

Frog (See How They Grow) (Kim Taylor and Jane Burton)

Frog (See How They Grow) is approximately one hundred words shorter than *Frogs* (Driscoll) and about the same level of difficulty. Javier read this with 96 percent accuracy, and several of his miscues were the kind often made by proficient readers because they were appropriate for the meaning and syntax of the sentence and were visually similar to the word in print: *feather* for *feathery, the* for *this, twenty* for *twelve.* He asked for help with only three words— *spawn, surrounded,* and *spend.*

The style of writing is in the form of a personal narrative, with a frog telling the story of its development from an egg to the age of one year. I usually dislike books in which an animal narrator uses human language to provide information because they have a tendency to sound coy or cute, but in this case, the first-person style of narration is a useful way of taking readers inside the process of transformation. Each double-page spread of the book addresses a different topic, which is highlighted in bold print in the upper left corner.

This book is designed so that the printed texts serve as captions to photographs, which dominate the pages. These captions range from one to three sentences, and visually resemble small paragraphs. Understanding the concept of a paragraph is not important to young readers, but having the experience of reading a group of sentences that elaborate on one aspect of a subject supports their growth as readers. Like *Tadpoles and Frogs* (Feely) this book provides a visual and textual summary at the end of some of the stages from egg to frog.

Sentence structure and length are more varied than in *Tadpoles and Frogs* (Feely) and *Frogs* (Driscoll), yet the concepts are presented in small chunks to help readers slowly build their knowledge. Note that the specialized word *spawn* is introduced in the context of words the reader is likely to know already, thus supporting the reader's learning of a new word and concept. Additional details about the eggs are included, and while readers may need assistance identifying a word or two, they are likely to already know the meaning of those words.

> The eggs
> are called
> frog spawn. (6)
> Each black egg is
> surrounded by clear
> jelly, and
> they all stick
> together. (7)

The Frog (Sabrina Crewe)

The next book I asked Javier to read was *The Frog* by Sabrina Crewe. The text is quite long, more than 700 words, and each topic is covered in more detail than in the other texts. In addition to describing the change from tadpole to frog, other topics are addressed, such as food, molting, camouflage, predators, hibernation, and habitat. Some of the artwork is photographs and some is drawings. Each shows detail that enhances the written text (or vice versa). At the end of the narrative, there is an illustration labeling parts of the frog, a map showing the location of leopard frogs in North America, a glossary, and an index. The layout of the pages makes it a useful book for children reading at different levels. Illustrations are generally centered on each page. Above the illustration is a short sentence in bold print that lower level readers could read as the main text, or that higher level readers could read as captions or introductions to the two- and three-sentence descriptions on each page that form the main body of the text.

This book was more challenging for Javier than *Frog (See How They Grow)*, but his fluent reading and 92 percent accuracy rate showed that the book is one he could understand and learn from. Some of his miscues were those typically made by fluent readers—*tadpole* for *tadpoles,* for example, understandable because most of the text uses the plural form. In contrast to *Frog (See How They Grow),* there were many more words that stumped him: *suckers, lungs, camouflage, predators, amphibians, vocal sacs, fertilize,* and *polluted,* for example. Most of these are words he knew the meaning of, such as *lungs, camouflage,* and *predators,* so that the explanation in the surrounding text helped him to recognize them if they appeared again in the text. However, concepts like *fertilize* and *amphibian,* were new to him, so he missed them in other books about frogs, as well as this one.

In spite of the considerable difference in the overall length and the range of topics covered, there are strong similarities in how language is used to present information in these two books. Each topic or main idea is presented entirely on one page in two or three sentences, and each block of text is framed by considerable white space, clearly signaling what the reader should attend to. Additionally, the photographs and sentences in bold print at the top of the page help readers to confirm the meaning of what they find in the longer text. They expand their knowledge of frogs, while reading text that broadens their experience with new vocabulary and a variety of sentence structures that will support their reading of more complex texts that do not have immediately recognizable patterns or structures. Two pages about frog predators provide good examples of how this book supports and stretches readers. Note how the author has provided readers with many ways to build up the concept of predation.

The snake is dangerous.
(color drawing of snake)

Frogs have many **predators.** Turtles and fish catch frogs in the water. Snakes, birds, and bigger animals try to catch frogs when they are on land. (18)

The frog leaps out of danger!
(color photograph of frog leaping out of water)

The frog's legs are very strong. The frog can leap far on land or jump high out of water. This is how it escapes from predators. (19)

Frogs and Toads and Tadpoles, Too (Allan Fowler)

Sometimes, it is easy to look at a book and make a reasonable guess as to the support and challenges it will provide readers. The books I have just discussed have clearly defined structures that alert readers to what they should pay attention to. Other times, it is necessary to observe readers to learn more about a book. Two books that puzzled me with respect to how challenging they would be for readers were *Frogs and Toads and Tadpoles, Too* by Allan Fowler, and *From Tadpole to Frog* by Wendy Pfeffer and illustrated by Holly Keller. Both books were designed with younger students in mind, but their formats are very different from one another. Fowler's book, illustrated with photographs, makes comparisons between frogs and toads. While some of the sentences in the book are short and grammatically simple, others challenge readers to read and comprehend syntactically complex sentences.

Note that the vocabulary and information in the following sentence is similar to that in the quotations from *Tadpoles and Frogs* (Feely) and *Frogs* (Driscoll). However, the information is more densely packed into one sentence in the Fowler text, and readers must see the relationship between the facts in each clause in order to comprehend the message of the text. As Marilyn Adams (1990) pointed out, younger readers' "syntactic senstivities" are not well developed. One way to help students develop an eye and ear for syntactically complex sentences is to provide them with books such as *Frogs and Toads and Tadpoles, Too.*

> Most toads and frogs lay
> their eggs in water, where
> the eggs hatch into tadpoles. (24)

I asked both Javier and Marina to read *Frogs and Toads and Tadpoles, Too.* Javier read it with an accuracy rate of 90 percent, and Marina's accuracy rate was 96 percent. A 90 percent accuracy rate suggests the text is at the low end of the reader's instructional level. An accuracy rate of 95 percent or higher suggests the book is an easy one for the reader. At first glance, *The Frog* (Crewe) looks like a much more challenging book for readers than *Frogs and Toads and Tadpoles, Too* (Fowler) because the Crewe text has three times the number of words as the Fowler text. However, if you examine the texts more closely, you will see that the sentence lengths in each are similar. The shortest sentence in Fowler's book has five words and the longest has sixteen words. The shortest sentence in Crewe's book has three words, and the longest, eighteen words. Both books have words that would challenge many readers.

The organizational structure of each book is quite different from the other. In contrast to the logical progression of information given in Crewe's book, the information in Fowler's book does not follow a clearly defined pattern. The first five pages tell about the sounds various frogs make, and the next page mentions that frogs and toads are amphibians. The next few pages compare frogs and toads. While two pages tell about frogs' feet, no information is given about toads' feet. The book closes with a discussion about eggs and tadpoles. *Frogs and Toads and Tadpoles, Too* was Javier's favorite book. The small differences in the percentages of his running records suggest that there are not wide variations in difficulty from one book to another.

From Tadpole to Frog (Wendy Pfeffer)

From Tadpole to Frog has some characteristics of an informational storybook because the information about frogs is presented in the framework of a story (Leal, 1993). Take a look at the opening two pages—the language sounds very different from that in the other frog books, which focus on telling facts.

> This is Frog Pond.
> But where are the frogs? (5)
> When winter winds whistle, the frogs hide. They
> sleep at the bottom of the pond in the soft mud.
> Frogs hibernate in their hideaway all winter long. (6)

The words, syntax, and sentence lengths in *From Tadpole to Frog* are no more challenging than passages from books I have previously quoted. Yet, in these first thirty-six words, Javier made five miscues, and on the next page he miscued eight times in forty-one words. A few miscues were meaningful and did not disrupt the flow of his reading (*safe mud* instead of *soft mud,* for example), but most, even though they had some visual similarities to the words in the text, did not make sense in the sentence as he read them. His accuracy rate for the first two pages was 84 percent, and, not wanting to force him to read a book that was too hard, I asked him if he wanted to stop. He chose to continue reading.

What made this book more challenging for Javier? I think it is the story-like beginning and poetic imagery, which do not signal clearly to readers looking for information, how to find the facts. The information about frogs is embedded within the story, and phrases like "when winter winds whistle" are not the style of writing found in most information books. At the end of his reading, Javier said, "I didn't know they hibernate—I thought only bears hibernated—that they can go in the mud and under the mud and sleep." Interestingly, although he had a difficult time reading several passages of this book, it was the only time during his reading of any of the frog books that he spontaneously told me about something he learned. This small example is consistent with Leal's (1993) observations that informational storybooks are more engaging to children than those that provide just the facts.

Frogs (Michael Tyler) and *Frogs* (Gail Gibbons)

Marina read *From Tadpole to Frog* (Pfeffer), with an accuracy of 95 percent. Most of her errors were the kinds of substitutions made by proficient readers: *there* for *here*, and *don't* for *do not*. I also asked her to read selections from two books that I thought would be too difficult for Javier. Interestingly, her accuracy rate for the 150-200 word passages she read was 95 percent, the same as for the easier books she read. When she came to unfamiliar words—*species*, *oxygen*, and *embryo*, for example—she asked what they meant and read them accurately if they appeared again. I did not ask her to finish the books because I wanted to maintain an informal, conversational exchange, and she liked to stop reading and reflect on what she was learning. When she shifted from the book to conversation, she wove in anecdotes about the frogs she had seen the previous summer while visiting family in rural Arizona.

The two books I asked Marina to read are both titled *Frogs*. One was written by Michael Tyler, and the other was written and illustrated by Gail Gibbons. In many respects, Tyler's book resembles *The Frog* (Crewe), because it is organized by topic, information is presented in concise paragraphs, and it is copiously illustrated with photographs and diagrams. In contrast, the text of Gibbons' book is a continuous narrative, making it similar in style to *From Tadpole to Frog* (Pfeffer and Keller). Both books are much longer than other books I have discussed—more than 900 words for Gibbons', and more than 1,400 words for Tyler's. The extra length allows for more detailed descriptions, as well a closer look at differences in some species of frogs.

The best way to show how these books challenge young readers is to select passages about the same topic. I consider Tyler's book to be the more difficult of the two, because, while he describes the most common behaviors, he often lets the reader know there are variations from one species to another, and his descriptions are more condensed than Gibbons' descriptions. However, like Marina, readers who are interested in the topic would find both books valuable because each author highlights and extends information in different ways. Gibbons begins her discussion by showing spawn floating on water. Her use of short sentences allows readers to process one fact at a time. Slowly, she leads readers to relate one bit of information to the next, allowing them ample time to think and make connections.

> Frogs lay their eggs in water or wet places. Otherwise, the eggs could dry up and die. These eggs do not have shells. They are inside jellylike coverings. As they float, the jelly lets the sun's warmth come through to the eggs inside.

While Tyler describes the breeding process as it takes place in the water, he also tells readers about exceptions to this practice. In contrast to Gibbons, he often presents information in compound and complex sentences, making readers sort out the relationships in the space of a single sentence. To understand these passages, readers must be able to recognize words and also understand the meaning created in each separate sentence. Like the seventh mouse in *Seven Blind Mice,* they must learn how the smaller parts fit together to create a meaningful whole.

> Some frogs do not lay their eggs in water. They lay them in little nests on moist ground so that the eggs do not dry out and there is enough water for the tadpoles to begin to grow in their jelly capsules. When heavy rain falls the tadpoles are washed into a pond where they complete their growth (Tyler, 24).

I loved my time with Marina and Javier, both of whom I have known since they were in kindergarten. I secretly hoped each would want to continue helping me out with my research; however, they let me know politely they had indulged my probing long enough. Of course, they continued using the library for recreational reading and research, so I continued working with them all year long.

Working with Javier confirmed my belief that the best way to sort books along a continuum of easier to more difficult is to put them in the hands of readers, and pay attention not only to the percentage of words they read accurately, but also to the nature of their reading errors and self-corrections. Although I had predicted accurately the gradient of difficulty of the four books he read, I did not begin to develop a sense of the supports and limitations each book provided for readers until I observed Javier reading them. Each book contributed a slice of new information that helped him with understanding the information and learning some of the specialized vocabulary used to describe tadpoles and frogs.

Ironically, I learned less from Marina about individual books because she read everything I asked her to read at an accuracy of 95 percent or better. Most of her errors were typical of the errors we all make when we are reading; the kind that, if someone were to ask us to reread a passage, we would read accurately. When she came to a word she already knew the meaning of, but did not recognize in print, she would either figure it out herself or ask. If it appeared again in the text, she would read it accurately without hesitation. More telling, is when she came to words representing concepts new to her—*embryo* and *species* are two examples—she asked me the meaning of the words, indicated she understood, and kept right on reading. Clearly, she was capable of reading and understanding most any book in our elementary school library, independently or with the assistance of a more experienced reader.

The most important lesson I learned from Marina and Javier is how essential it is to provide children with a wide variety of texts about the subjects that interest them, and to give them plenty of time to explore those subjects.

Marina and Javier may have grown tired of serving as my research subjects, but they always approached each new book I gave them with enthusiasm. They looked through them, studied the illustrations, noticed captions, and talked about how each new book was alike or different from the others.

Throughout their readings, which took place over several days, I was fascinated by the way Marina and Javier kept making these "new connections," and how each text helped broaden their knowledge. I could also see that Marina's recent first-hand experience with observing frogs in their natural settings strongly contributed to her understanding of her reading. Merely providing students with a book or two they can read is not adequate for them to develop an understanding of a subject. We should be careful not to confuse fact gathering with developing knowledge. Writers approach their subjects from different perspectives, which, in turn, supports readers in learning about the many ways language can be used to communicate ideas.

Summary

We have taken a long journey in this chapter to demonstrate the many ways of exploring and talking about books. I have used words such as *style, vocabulary, syntax, illustrations, structure, fiction,* and *nonfiction.* I have talked about similarities and differences in books, and brought in children as guest readers. I have suggested ways of determining if one book is easier than another, but always with the caveat that reader interest and prior knowledge play a very important role in making that assessment.

Another way of thinking about this journey is to imagine yourself visiting a large city for the first time. You have taken a taxi or shuttle from the airport to your downtown hotel, so you are only vaguely familiar with the maze of freeways and city streets the driver has followed. When you first venture out of your hotel to explore the surrounding area, you are reluctant to travel out of sight of the hotel, for fear you may get lost. You pay close attention to street signs and distinctive landmarks to help you in finding your way back to the hotel, should you go a little further than you intended.

Think of yourself in the same city and hotel a few days later. You have gotten more acclimated to your surroundings, and you do not need to consciously focus on signs and landmarks. You know the major streets and how they intersect, so you are not alarmed if you wander off a main thoroughfare and forget to notice exactly where you are. You are confident that you can find your way back to a street that will take you to your hotel.

Now, as comfortable as you have become navigating the downtown area of the city, you know little about the city at large—its residential, business, and industrial areas. In order to truly find your way around a city, you must know all of its neighborhoods and their geographical relationship to each other. You must be able to find your way from any one section of the city to another, regardless of your starting point. If you encounter an unexpected street closure, you should be able to easily select another route.

Each of these three scenarios can be related to the following three chapters of this book. The books I write about in Chapter 4 are for those readers who are just starting to know the surrounding terrain; they need distinctive landmarks to help guide their journey through a book. For example, a reading landmark could be an illustration, a repeated sentence pattern, or a memorable refrain. The books I write about in Chapter 5 are for those readers who are comfortable leaving the immediate vicinity of their hotel because they know how to reach the main routes back; they are ready for stories with more detail and plots that take them on small journeys, out of sight of the opening scene of the book. The books I write about in Chapter 6 are for those readers who know a city well enough to confidently explore its many neighborhoods beyond the downtown area. They understand the general layout of the city, so if they get confused about their location, they can do a bit of quick thinking and regain their bearings. They are ready to explore some neighborhoods in depth, the way a reader might read many books of historical fiction or about dinosaurs. As always, keep in mind that readers, like travelers, have different interests and learn by taking different pathways.

Closing Points

- Knowing many books and the children who read them is the most important factor in leveling books.

- A reader's prior knowledge is a strong factor influencing the readability of a text.

- Text features influencing readability include vocabulary, syntax or sentence structure, dialogue, descriptive language, and story structure.

- Most readers enjoy a surprise—they do not want to read something so predictable it makes them drowsy .

- Page-turners can be found among the simplest books for new readers.

- Children need a wide variety of books and plenty of time to read and explore subjects that interest them.

- Providing students with many styles of writing to read gives them a good foundation for beginning to read more complex texts.

Bibliography

Children's Books

1. *The Ghost* by Joy Cowley. Illus. by Robyn Belton. Story Box. The Wright Group, 1983.

2. *Henry and Mudge* books by Cynthia Rylant. Illus. by Suçie Stevenson. Simon & Schuster.

3. *I Went Walking* by Sue Williams. Illus. by Julie Vivas. Harcourt, 1989.

4. *The Chocolate Touch* by Patrick Catling. Morrow, 1979.

5. *Lincoln: A Photobiography* by Russell Freedman. Clarion, 1978.

6. *Too Many Balloons* by Catherine Matthias. Illus. by Gene Sharp. Rookie Reader. Children's Press, 1982.

7. *Just Like Daddy* by Frank Asch. Simon & Schuster, 1981.

8. *Hattie and the Fox* by Mem Fox. Illus. by Patricia Mullins. Simon & Schuster, 1987.

9. *And I Mean It, Stanley* by Crosby Bonsall. An I Can Read Book. HarperCollins, 1974.

10. *The Napping House* by Audrey Wood. Illus. by Don Wood. Harcourt, 1984.

11. *Little Chick's Friend Duckling* by Mary DeBall Kwitz. Illus. by Bruce Degen. An I Can Read Book. HarperCollins, 1992.

12. *Poppleton and His Friends* by Cynthia Rylant. Illus. by Mark Teague. Scholastic, 1997.

13. *Bear's Hiccups* by Marion Dane Bauer. Illus. by Diane Dawson Hearn. Holiday House, 1998.

14. *Tadpoles and Frogs* by Jenny Feely. Photos by Michael Curtain. Alphakids. Sundance, 1999.

15. *Frogs* by Laura Driscoll. Illus. by Judith Moffatt. All Aboard Reading. Grosset & Dunlap, 1998.

16. *Frog (See How They Grow)* by Kim Taylor and Jane Burton. Dutton, 1997.

17. *The Frog* by Sabrina Crewe. Life Cycles. Raintree Steck-Vaughn, 1997.

18. *Frogs and Toads and Tadpoles, Too* by Allan Fowler. Rookie Read-About Science. Children's Press, 1992.

19. *From Tadpole to Frog* by Wendy Pfeffer. Illus. by Holly Keller. Let's-Read-and-Find-Out-Science. HarperCollins, 1994.

20. *Frogs* by Michael Tyler. MONDO, 1997.

21. *Frogs* by Gail Gibbons. Holiday House, 1993.

4

Little Books for Emergent Readers

In Chapter 3, I wrote about a broad sweep of literature for beginning readers, and likened the process of figuring out how easy or difficult a book might be for a reader to a conversational dance with the text. I concluded Chapter 3 by comparing new readers with someone visiting a city for the first time. A brand new reader is like the person who stays near his hotel while he gets his bearings, and pays close attention to distinctive landmarks and street signs to keep from getting lost. The books that support new readers have memorable signposts to assist them on their journey. Familiar oral language patterns, repeated phrases, patterned stories, and simple illustrations are a few of the features of these books. The subjects of the books, whether fiction or nonfiction, should be of interest to readers and make connections to their prior knowledge.

These readers are often called "emergent readers" because they are learning how to look closely at print. They are learning the directionality of print and how to match spoken and written words. They probably know a few words in print, and are learning how to identify unfamiliar words. They are learning how to check pictures to help with their overall understanding of what they are reading and, when necessary, to help identify unknown words. Readers, like travelers, however, learn and expand the boundaries of their explorations. Gradually, readers learn to navigate longer stretches of text because they develop a larger core of known words, as well as strategies for solving new words. They become more fluent in their phrasing, and read longer sections of text without stopping. The illustrations of a book provide a frame of reference for following the story, but readers rarely consult them to identify an unknown word.

In Chapter 3, I wrote about a handful of books for this range of readers. In this chapter, I use a close-up lens to examine more than twenty books, and describe how each one provides readers with valuable experience in reading different kinds of texts. It is important to keep in mind that these very easy books comprise only one slender thread of an effective reading program; care should be taken to carefully select books that will send children along exciting literary pathways. As Charlotte Huck wrote, "We don't achieve literacy and then give children literature; we achieve literacy through literature" (1989, 258). The books I write about in this chapter are simple texts, but when carefully selected and introduced to young readers, they can set the pattern for building foundations to lead them to more complex literature.

The simplest of texts can use language within reach of a reader and tell a story so compelling readers will return to it again and again. There is a huge qualitative difference between a *simplified text* and a *simplistic text*. A dictionary definition of *simplify* is "to reduce in complexity or extent." In contrast, *simplistic* refers to "the tendency to oversimplify an issue or a problem by ignoring complexities or complications." (*The American Heritage Dictionary of the English Language,* 3rd ed. 1996, 1683).

Ken Goodman uses the phrases "authentic texts" and "artificial texts" to describe the differences between texts that support readers and those that can interfere with learning how to read.

> Artificial texts that control word frequency and disrupt sentence structures don't provide readers with cues for predicting and expecting. Authentic texts, on the other hand, not only control their own vocabulary but also have predictable, authentic grammar and thus provide natural grammatical cues for readers (1996, 77).

Fortunately, today, there are a great many simplified, but authentic texts that both support and appeal to beginning readers. *The Ghost,* which I discussed in Chapters 2 and 3, is an example of an authentic text that tells an inviting story about a familiar childhood experience in language commonly used by young readers. The best way to get to know an easy book is to read it out loud. If a story or informational narrative sounds good to your ear, and if the topic appeals to you, there is a good chance that it will appeal to your students. If the narrative sounds forced, contrived, or artificial to you, there is a good possibility it will be a poor choice for young readers.

To help take the mystery out of finding appropriate books for the earliest of readers, I suggest you think of some things you have learned to do throughout your life — ride a bike, swim, play basketball, or use a computer, for example. For most of these activities you may have had formal or informal instruction, or perhaps you learned by carefully observing others and teaching yourself. No matter how you learned something, however, you probably learned by engaging in the entire process at once, starting clumsily, but gradually refining and improving your work. You did not spend hours learning to pedal before your parents would allow you get on your new bicycle, nor were you required to pass pedaling before you were allowed to practice steering, although you probably had special support from training wheels and a watchful parent. Riding a bicycle requires coordinating several actions simultaneously, as well as being alert to traffic and road conditions.

Lest you think learning to read and learning to ride a bicycle are vastly different activities that should not be compared, consider how young children learn to speak. They are not given sounding out lessons before they are permitted to utter a complete word or sentence, nor are they given a new list of words to memorize every week. Indeed, linguist Michael Halliday's (1975) extensive observations of his infant son Nigel demonstrated that babies' first sounds are meaningful verbal communications, and that, through continued interaction with adults, they gradually expand and refine their use of language.

Readers, like cyclists, must learn to coordinate several actions at once— left-to-right directionality, one-to-one matching, word recognition, and solving unknown words, for example. They learn to make connections between what they know and what they are reading, and expect the entire process to be meaningful. When Margaret Meek (1988) writes about the "untaught lessons" embedded in the reading process, I am reminded of my grandson Dominic at the age of two and half. His parents read aloud to him frequently, but made no attempt to teach him how to read by drawing his attention to the printed texts. One afternoon, I read several versions of *Goldilocks and the Three Bears* (Galdone 1972; Barton 1991) to him, and then showed him Brinton Turkle's *Deep in the Forest,* a wordless "reverse" story in which a baby bear intrudes on a human family, causing the same kind of destruction Goldilocks caused in the bear family home. I introduced the book to him by saying it was a little bit like the Goldilocks stories, but it didn't have words and we would have to use our own words to tell the story from the pictures. He looked at me quizzically, pointed to the words on the title page, and emphatically said, "Those are words!"

By carefully selecting books for emergent readers, teachers can support the obvious lessons of how to decode print, but they can also guide a much broader range of learning that makes reading both a source of pleasure and a source of information. Untaught lessons for new readers include learning to look at the illustrations for clues to the meaning of the text (more than just a source for identifying unknown words), recognizing that characters behave in different ways, understanding that events follow each other in a logical sequence, and expecting most stories to have a surprise or something unusual happen at the end. They expect informational books to tell them something they already know and help them learn something new. While it is important to keep in mind that children, as well as adults, often hold widely differing opinions about the value of any given book, all texts are not equal. Some are much richer in providing readers with opportunities to learn the pleasures of reading and prepare them for entering wider realms of literature.

To Level or Not to Level . . .

In Chapter 2, I described my dissertation research, in which I evaluated books used in Reading Recovery during its first two years in the United States and compared students' readings of many of those texts. Originally, I intended to identify the key characteristics of each of the twenty levels used in the program, but I found that to be an impossible task because there are so many variations in books at one level, and books at several levels may have many features in common. I discovered that it was more meaningful to discuss characteristics of texts in groups of levels, and explain how texts in one group might be more or less challenging than another group.

The books I discuss in this chapter roughly span the first fifteen used in Reading Recovery. Rather than describe them by separate levels, I have organized them by the categories that emerged from my research. There are two reasons for this. First, Reading Recovery is a short-term, temporary intervention for first-grade students having difficulty learning how to read, and Reading Recovery teachers must finely tune their book selections in a way that is not necessary for regular classroom instruction. The twenty-level system was constructed to serve the unique needs of Reading Recovery, but there is nothing magical about it. It is a sorting system that facilitates choosing an appropriate text for a lesson. Through specialized and intensely focused training, Reading Recovery teachers learn how to evaluate and select texts for their students, and they quickly discover that levels are just a starting point.

Second, I have always been fearful that any system in which levels are too closely defined has the potential of blinding us to the needs and interests of the diverse students we work with every day. Kathy Short clearly expresses the trap we can unwittingly ensnare our young readers in if we depend on levels to guide our selection of literature for them.

> Learning to handle a range of difficulty enables readers to develop strategies for reading all kinds of books. We handicap children and prevent them from developing the strategies they need when we insist that they read only at their "instructional" level (1997, 15).

Shelley Harwayne describes the pros and cons of leveled books in her discussion of the Manhattan New School's process used to establish a short list of benchmark books at different levels for teachers to use to assess readers' progress as they moved to the next grade. She takes care to emphasize that brief assessments using benchmark books do not reveal or express all there is to know about who a child is as a reader, and cautions parents to avoid placing undue value on these assessments. While acknowledging the value of having a uniform process developed by the school for *their* students, she also worries that an emphasis on benchmark books "will lead to an overreliance on and a glaring presence of leveled books" (2000, 348).

Kathryn Mitchell Pierce addresses the limitations of a system of levels in her provocative article, "'I Am a Level 3 Reader': Children's Perceptions of Themselves as Readers." She was surprised to discover that some of the students in her multi-age primary class were defining themselves as readers solely by the level of books they could read independently, even though her classroom is filled with a rich variety of children's literature and the reading of leveled books comprises a very small portion of their reading. She continues by explaining how she led her students to broaden their views of themselves as readers and reflects on the experience in her classroom.

> I am concerned that in an effort to provide children with books "at their level," teachers are moving away from involving children with books grouped according to the other ways that literate individuals organize books. In our classroom the children often formed groups according to friendship patterns or grouped books according to what their friends were reading (1999, 373).

I urge all readers of this book to keep in mind that children not only need books they can read by themselves; they also need more complex literature to explore on their own or with a friend, and they need to hear many, many stories read aloud. They need to hear stories like *Chrysanthemum* by Kevin Henkes and *Swimmy* by Leo Lionni long before they are able to read them independently. Good instructional programs provide students with a wide range of books, only some of which are closely tied to their current instructional levels. Even when the focus is on texts for reading instruction, it is important to provide children with books from a range of levels and subjects. Mary Jo Fresch found that when students in one first-grade class self-selected books for reading, they moved back and forth between easy and difficult texts.

> The pattern suggests that the children were taking risks while building confidence. They would select something that challenged their new strategies and then return to something familiar or well within their consolidated word knowledge. Self-selection allowed the children to make the decision about the kind of text they were willing to attempt at the time (1995, 223).

Lucy Calkins and her colleagues at the Teachers College Reading and Writing Project grappled mightily with how to achieve the right balance between leveled and non-leveled books, and worked out effective ways to incorporate libraries of leveled books into classrooms, keeping in mind that "there is a thin line between leveling books and leveling children . . ." (2001, 120). Project classrooms are filled with rich collections of books, and leveled books comprise only about one-third of the books in any classroom, and children receive a lot of support in learning how to find books that make them feel strong as readers.

Tim Rasinski emphasizes the importance of choosing the right texts so that children develop speed and fluency in their reading, which will lead to improved comprehension.

> One key to nurturing fluent reading is finding the appropriate text for the reader to read. Texts that are too difficult, overly dense with unfamiliar vocabulary and concepts, can make any otherwise fluent reader disfluent (2000, 148).

One of the greatest joys I have had as a teacher is watching a child finish a book, and smile broadly because he has read it all by himself. As a librarian, I have observed that stronger readers find pleasure in books that are easy, as well as those that challenge them; unfortunately, I have also observed that weaker readers, if unguided, will fill their arms with books too difficult for them, but not select *any* they can read fluently. I often lead younger readers to the baskets of leveled books I have in English and Spanish, pick out a few and ask them to read to me. I can quickly find which basket is just right for them, and encourage them to borrow one book from that basket, along with their other selections from the entire library. (The books in each basket comprise three Reading Recovery levels and are coded with colored dots that match the dots we put on sets of leveled books teachers use for instruction. Books in English and Spanish are kept on different shelves so children are clear which language they are looking at. It is not uncommon for a second or third grader to ask me if a book is in English or Spanish, so I think it is important to keep them separate.)

If teachers have read from a wide range of children's literature and know some guidelines for evaluating text complexity, they can put wonderful books in the hands of all readers. Some children enter first grade having read independently books like *Charlotte's Web,* while other students may need very simple texts with repeated phrases in third and fourth grade. Most children fall somewhere between these extremes. It is important to keep in mind that most children do not need to read books from every point on a continuum. Some will benefit from a gradual introduction of slightly more challenging texts, while others will make gigantic leaps once they grasp what it means to be a reader. In particular, I am thinking of Eric, currently a kindergartner at Tully, who started the school year reading books like *The Ghost* and three months later began devouring *Nate the Great* mysteries. During this same time, a group of fourth-grade students at Tully found those same mysteries a good match for their current reading interests and abilities.

A Few Words About Picture Books

Picture books are an important part of any literature program. There are so many wonderfully exciting books to read aloud to children, and there is no sight more splendid than watching children explore the pages of a picture book. However, teachers and librarians need to be very conservative in leveling picture books for a reading instruction program. Book leveling is a process for sorting books along a gradient of difficulty that focuses primarily on written text. Illustrations are considered during the leveling process, but only to the extent they depict the meaning of the written text. Picture books are filled with art and meant to be looked at slowly and carefully. Stories in picture books are told through both the art and the written text (if there is text). Barbara Kiefer explains it this way.

> . . . the picturebook is a unique art object, a combination of image and idea that allows the reader to come away with more than the sum of the parts. We can no more look at a single illustration in the book or examine the words without the pictures than we can view 5 minutes of a 2-hour film or see an opera without hearing the singers' voices and say we have experienced the whole (1995, 6).

I have spent many happy hours with preschool, kindergarten, and first-grade children poring over the picture books of Donald Crews. *Freight Train* seems to be everyone's favorite. The children respond enthusiastically to the colorful freight cars on each page, but their favorite pictures are always those that show the freight train moving very fast. They have so much to talk about when they look at any Donald Crews book. There are very few words in *Freight Train,* and some of those would be hard for a new reader ("crossing trestles," for example). If *Freight Train* were leveled for beginning reading instruction, its intended audience might never see it. Furthermore, if *Freight Train* were used in reading instruction, the focus would likely be on the words, and readers might not be given time to enjoy the illustrations. While there are many picture books, such as *Brown Bear, Brown Bear, What Do You See?* that are quite suitable for early reading instruction, many others are best reserved for reading aloud, reading together, or reading alone.

Focus Books

In this chapter, we will look at books that range in difficulty from *The Ghost* and *Tadpoles and Frogs* to books like *Hattie and the Fox*, *The Napping House*, and *Frog (See How They Grow)*, which I discussed in Chapter 3. The easiest books are composed of repeated sentences with a few word changes, while the most difficult typically have several sentence patterns, a greater variety of words, and some descriptive language. I have selected approximately five or six books to use as examples of texts at each group of levels. Some books are children's literature picture books, while others represent some of the many series of "little books" created especially for beginning reading instruction. I chose books with different subjects and styles of writing to show how teachers and librarians can develop meaningful and interesting sets of books for the newest of readers. I have used many of the books I write about in my own teaching, so I know they are books with "kid appeal." Please remember, however, that the books I feature are only a very small portion of the high quality texts being published today.

Getting Started (Reading Recovery Levels 1–4)

Summary of Levels 1–4

- consistent placement of print
- repetition of one or two sentence patterns
- oral language structures commonly used by young children
- vocabulary commonly used by young children
- unusual words, if used, are carefully framed in the context of supportive language structures
- familiar objects and actions
- illustrations provide high support for the printed message
- a story may have an opening and closing event, but the sequence of most events could be changed without changing the meaning of the whole book

---

Focus Books

1. *What I See* by Holly Keller. Green Light Reader. Harcourt Brace, 1999.
2. *Ouch!* by Lucy Lawrence. Illus. by Graham Porter. Literacy Tree. Rigby, 1989.

3. *The Sausage* by Jillian Cutting. Illus. by Peter Stevenson. Sunshine Extensions. Wright Group, 1992.

4. *The Chase (Hey, Tabby Cat)* by Phyllis Root. Illus. by Katharine McEwen. Brand New Readers. Candlewick, 2000.

5. *All Fall Down* by Brian Wildsmith. Cat on the Mat Books. Oxford University Press, 1983.

6. *Butterfly* by Jenny Feely. Photos by Michael Curtain. Alphakids. Sundance, 1999.

Readers who are just starting to look at print need books with familiar ideas or concepts and memorable, repeated language structures that reflect their speech. These books should also have attractive, uncluttered illustrations that clearly show the objects or action in the text. Readers are learning to observe the directionality of print and match each spoken word with a printed word. They learn how to check the pictures to confirm the identity of a word in print. As they gain experience, readers learn how to locate and use a beginning letter to confirm the identity of a word. They also begin to self-correct some of their errors. While the following books are simple texts that support early learning, they are very diverse in topic and style. Easy books do not have to be boring books.

What I See

I began with *The Ghost* in Chapter 2, showing how a simple surprise story was created by using four- and five-word sentences, each beginning with the child-familiar phrase "I see the . . ." Another book that explores the child's world from the perspective of "I see . . ." is *What I See*. A school-age boy walks around his house and yard noticing various objects and animals. Two-thirds of each page is filled with Holly Keller's delicate watercolor illustrations, while the four-word sentences are clearly visible centered in the white space below the illustration. The objects and animals are ones most children could easily identify from their prior knowledge and from the illustrations. Furthermore, words on the facing pages rhyme, and all but one of those pairs follows the same spelling pattern.

> I see a fly.   I see a pie.
>
> I see a cat.   I see a mat.

As simple as it appears on the surface, this book is much more than a verbal and visual catalog of recognizable objects. Rather, it is a personal narrative describing a small journey around a child's familiar landscape, ending with the boy looking at his reflection in a pond, saying, "I see me." Readers can read the words and check the illustrations to confirm the identity of words, but if they look more carefully, they will also see action taking place in those still pictures. For example, on one page, the boy is looking at some toys on a shelf and the text says, "I see a top." On the next page, the top lies on the floor, and on the foreground of the picture are a pail, a puddle of water, and a mop. The text says, "I see a mop." Readers who are observant or encouraged by noticing teachers will pick up on the unwritten story—that the boy's actions with the top lead to the appearance of the mop.

Ouch!

Other stories for beginners appeal to their delight in slapstick. One "wrinkled," well-used book in my library is *Ouch!* A comical boy has Band-Aids® scattered on various parts of his body. Phrases, not full sentences, comprise the text on each page.

> Band-aids on my fingers.
> Band-aids on my nose.
> Band-aids on my shoulder.
> Band-aids on my toes.

At school, whenever I read a story that has rhymes to children in preschool through second grade, they delight in letting me know every time they hear a rhyme. One reason I think *Ouch!* is so popular is that the second and fourth lines rhyme, as do the sixth and eighth lines, giving the text a sing-song feel of a chant children would say out loud if they were covered in Band-Aids®.

For books to be slightly more challenging to readers, they must present more variation from these books, but only slightly. This might occur because sentences are longer, requiring more attention to print, as well as to the greater amount of ideas or action that longer texts permit. There may be more variation in sentence patterns and vocabulary, while still providing strong support for the knowledge readers bring and ideas that can be easily communicated through pictures as well as print.

The Sausage

The Sausage, another well-worn book in our library collection, is a good example of a text that provides more challenge, but not too much. Readers of these stories must follow two lines of print and speech marked by quotation marks. The first story, "The Sausage" is the most dramatic. It begins with a giant happily eyeing a large sausage he is about to cut into. Observant readers will spy the head, paws, and tail of a mouse watching from the edge of the table.

> "My sausage,"
> said the giant.

The picture on the next page shows a mouse pushing the sausage off the table and a grinning cat peeking out from behind the table cloth.

> "My sausage,"
> said the mouse.

A most important aspect of developing readers is providing them with attention grabbing texts. "My Sausage" certainly does that, because, though simple, it hooks readers in an adventure that keeps them anticipating and predicting what will happen next. And, like many good stories, there is a surprise ending. After the cat grabs the sausage, it is picked up by a dog, a pig, a sea gull, and finally . . .

> "**My** sausage,"
> said the shark.

The other two stories in the book are not as dramatic as the first, but nevertheless engaging for readers. "The Tree House" shows the homes of various animals, and "Dinner" features foods for zoo animals. Each employs a repetitive sentence pattern in language easily controlled by most beginning readers, and only one word is changed on each new page. The animals are those likely to be known by readers, and the illustrations clearly show those animals.

> "The Tree House"
> "Here is my house,"
> said the owl.

> "Dinner"
> "Look at my dinner!
> said the elephant.

The Chase (Hey, Tabby Cat!)

Many experienced readers are drawn to stories with memorable characters. *Frog and Toad* and *Henry and Mudge* are familiar personalities on the literary landscape, but characters with distinctive personalities are less common in very easy books. Two who come to mind immediately are *Huggles* and the inimitable *Mrs. Wishy-Washy,* and the much-loved stories written about them by Joy Cowley and illustrated by Elizabeth Fuller. Now, there is a new character, *Tabby Cat,* who is certain to capture the attention of beginning readers. There are eight little books of approximately forty words each that feature this mildly mischievous, but thoroughly lovable cat. *Tabby Cat* is one of several characters in the Brand New Readers series published by Candlewick Press.

One of these books, *The Chase,* is a good example of a text that provides slightly more variation in sentence structure and vocabulary than the books I previously discussed, but which keeps readers within the framework of familiar language and an easily followed story line. The narrative follows a simple pattern of chase and escape, or action and reaction. First, the cat chases a mouse, but the mouse runs away. Next, he chases a butterfly, and then a frog. Those animals also escape. Lastly, Tabby Cat chases a flower, which, of course, he catches. Readers follow two alternating sentence patterns. The design of the book helps to create dramatic tension, because readers must turn the page to find out what happens each time there is a chase. For example, the first page of the story is on the right-hand side of the book. The illustration shows an orange cat with red stripes and a smile on his face running after a white mouse. The text says:

> Tabby Cat chases a mouse.

When readers turn the page, they see a picture with only the mouse, in an enlarged, close-up view. Standing on two legs, head turned to the left, this object of the chase has a facial expression that clearly shows who the winner is. The text says:

> The mouse runs away.

The pictures of *The Chase,* like all very easy books for beginners, provide very important support for readers. Obviously, they can help readers confirm the identity of some of the written words, and teachers can guide students to making connections between the illustration, the printed word, and the arrangement of letters that makes up the word. More importantly, however, the illustrations can set the tone and flesh out the story by communicating small details that readers are not ready to manage in the printed text. Think about a time when you have tried to describe an event such as a concert or a ball game to a friend, but you just could not seem to find all the right words. Instead, you throw your hands up in the air, and say, "Well, you just had to *be* there." Similarly, the illustrations in a book allow readers to *be there,* freeing them to focus their mental energy on reading the printed text.

Tabby Cat does not catch the mouse, but a colorful butterfly goes by. Following the same pattern of the opening sentence, but with the change of one word, the text says:

> Tabby Cat chases a butterfly.

The follow up sentence follows the same pattern or syntax as the one in which the mouse escapes, but readers have a two-word change. The text says:

> The butterfly flies away.

There is a plot, or flow, to the events in *The Chase;* however, like most easy books, it makes no difference to the outcome of the story whether or not Tabby Cat chases the mouse, the butterfly, and the frog in that particular sequence. He could have chased the frog, the mouse, and then the butterfly without dramatically altering the nature of the story. Admittedly, there would be a subtle shift in the story by making such a change because Tabby Cat becomes more rambunctious as he pursues animals that fly and hop, so there are sound reasons why the book's creators used the mouse, butterfly, and frog sequence. From the beginning reader's perspective, it is often easier to follow a narrative without too many things happening at once. In this case, readers can read about the mouse chase, but then leave that behind to focus on the butterfly chase. When reading about the frog chase, it is not necessary for readers to keep in mind what happened with the mouse and the butterfly in order to understand what is happening with the frog. This attention to the interchangeability of events might seem trivial or unimportant, but remember that beginning readers are learning to coordinate a whole range of behaviors, only one of which is understanding a line of thought.

Notice that I have used a great many words to describe what is happening in the first three events of a thirty-six word text. Still, I have more to say. *The Chase* is a satisfying read because it is a page-turner that leads readers to an unexpected outcome. When Tabby Cat chases the flower, he not only catches it; he crash lands on top of it, breaking the flowerpot, and ending up with the flower, torn apart from the plant, grasped in his paw. Readers get a good laugh at the outcome of Tabby Cat's antics. Thus, the plot of *The Chase* is simplified for readers because they do not have to remember a complicated series of events. However, the narrative leads to a conclusion that is credible based on Tabby Cat's actions; even though it is simple, it has the shape of an authentic story. And, readers who love Tabby Cat will be ready to meet his literary cousin Cookie, star of *Cookie's Week,* discussed later in this chapter.

More on Words...

You may have noticed that in this discussion of four books for very beginning readers, I have written about story events, characters, and sentence patterns, but nothing specifically about words or vocabulary. That was an intentional move because it is much too tempting for adults to focus only on words and ignore all the other aspects of books that lead young children into reading. It is important to consider how an *entire* book helps readers coordinate all of the actions needed to become a reader, in the same way the seventh mouse grasped the identity of the elephant by understanding the relationship between the parts and the whole. Good teachers try to keep their students' knowledge and interests in mind when they select books for them; further-more, they usually introduce a new book by moving through the pages and talking about the action, and any words that might be challenging, before ask-ing them to read it.

Most of the words in the books I just discussed will be known to most readers. The word *sausage* might be new to some, who might want to call it a *hot dog.* That, however, could lead to an impromptu lesson on sounds in words and word-by-word matching. Think, too, about the word *away* in *The Chase.* By itself, the word does not have a meaning that is easily grasped by young readers. However, the chance to encounter it three times (*runs away, flies away,* and *hops away*) in natural, authentic language can provide a solid ref-erence point for readers who see the word in other books.

All Fall Down

One word that I have often found to be troublesome to new readers is *and,* be-cause, like *away,* it is not a word that signals a clear meaning or image for young children. That is the reason why *All Fall Down* is a bit more difficult than the other books I have discussed, but very useful in helping readers grasp the con-cept of *and* and recognize it in print. I usually introduce *All Fall Down* by ask-ing if the student has ever stacked one block upon another, and so on. Before I can finish describing the scenario, the student inevitably jumps in with "all fall down," thus taking ownership of the book she is about to read. Next, we look through the book to see that this tower is made up of a bee, a butterfly, a bird, a rabbit, a seal, and a ball. Wildsmith slowly builds up this image in words and pictures by adding something new on each double-page spread.

> I see a bee.
> I see a bee and a butterfly.

Finally,

> I see a bee and a butterfly and
> a bird and a rabbit and a seal
> and a ball.

Then, the inevitable conclusion,

> All fall down.

Before leaving this discussion of *All Fall Down,* it is important to stress that I have never selected this book for readers solely because I have found it helpful for teaching the concept and print identity of the word *and.* I do some-times select a book for a child to support her learning a specific word or two, but I would not chose a book solely for this purpose. I have selected this book primarily because it is one children love reading! Brian Wildsmith is an acclaimed artist and illustrator of many picture books too difficult for beginning readers to read independently. Here, however, is a delightful story, illustrated with his signature splashes of bright color, that new readers can read independently. Borrowing Ken Goodman's phrase, it is an "authentic text."

Butterfly

The quantity and quality of nonfiction books designed to support the developing and changing needs of beginning readers is starting to catch up with an impressive range of fiction currently available. Thoughtfully written texts, coupled with clearly drawn or photographed illustrations, create books that children can read and learn from. A perfect example is *Butterfly*, written and illustrated by the same author and photographer who created *Tadpoles and Frogs*, a book I discussed in Chapter 3.

Comparable in difficulty to *All Fall Down*, the text of *Butterfly* carefully frames the life cycle of a butterfly in repeated sentence patterns using simple syntax. The left-hand pages hold only the text, while the right-hand pages are filled with dazzling photos that show exactly what is described in print. Each page describes one new step in the cycle from egg to butterfly. The first pair of pages shows a butterfly on a leaf. The second pair (pages 4 and 5) shows the egg left by the butterfly. The photograph shows an enlarged, close-up view of a leaf, which takes up about one-third of the page, and the egg is about the size of a pencil eraser. While there are other leaves in the photo, they are not in focus, so the reader's attention is drawn clearly to the leaf and the egg. The text says:

> Then there was
> an egg
> on a leaf. (4)

The next set of pages refers to the caterpillar, and again, the photograph focuses on the caterpillar and stem.

> Then there was
> a caterpillar
> on a stem. (6)

Note that readers must follow three lines of print, and that the sentence patterns are similar, but they also must read many words that may be unfamiliar, as well as grasp relationships that may be new to them. Teachers should also recognize that there are different ways of thinking about new words. There are words like *butterfly* and *caterpillar* that most of their students know and use in their spoken vocabularies. When new readers first see these words in print, they may need help in analyzing the letters or groups of letters that make up the word, but they generally learn to recognize the printed word in the future. More challenging are words like *chrysalis*, which is used on the next set of pages.

> Then there was
> a chrysalis
> on a leaf (8).

If *chrysalis* is a completely new word and concept to a child, these two pages of text and the photograph will be much more difficult than the others in the book. However, notice that there is only one small bit of information that is likely to be completely new to most readers. With a supportive introduction and conversation about the subject, most readers will easily incorporate this new information and vocabulary into what they already know about butterflies and caterpillars.

Little Adventures (Reading Recovery Levels 5–8)

Summary of Levels 5–8

- repetition of two to three sentence patterns (phrases may change)
- opening, closing sentences may vary from the interior text
- oral language structures predominate, with a gradual introduction of literary, or written language structures ("book language")
- many familiar objects and actions
- illustrations provide high to moderate support for the printed message
- most stories have an opening and closing event, but the sequence of the events between the opening and closing could be changed without affecting the meaning of the whole book

---

Focus Books

1. *I'm Bigger Than You!* by Joy Cowley. Illus. by Jan van der Voo. Sunshine Books. Wright Group, 1987.
2. *Cat Tails* by Kittie Boss. Illus. by Erin Marie Mauterer. Books for Young Learners. Richard Owen, 1999.
3. *It's Game Day* by Lynn Salem and Josie Stewart. Illus. by Tim Collins. Seedling, 1992.

4. *Green Footprints* by Connie Kehoe. Illus. by Terry Denton. Literacy 2000. Rigby, 1989.

5. *Where's Spot?* by Eric Hill. Putnam, 1980.

6. *The Turnip* retold by Harriet Ziefert. Illus. by Laura Rader. Puffin Easy-To-Read. Puffin, 1996.

7. Tolstoy, Aleksei. *The Gigantic Turnip.* Illus. by Niamh Sharkey. Barefoot Books, 1998.

To progress to more complex text, readers must develop a range of strategies for solving the identities of unfamiliar words, and learn to more keenly analyze print. Books like those I have discussed in the previous section present readers with interesting stories or information using repeated sentence patterns, syntax, and vocabulary familiar to most young children. Such texts not only allow them to engage in the same range of actions as more proficient readers; they also provide an important framework that allows readers to explore and make new discoveries. The next group of books I write about are some that require more flexibility from readers. Most of the ideas, concepts, and vocabulary presented in this next set of books will be familiar to readers. Repetition continues to be an important feature in these texts, but readers may encounter two or three sentence patterns, or they may encounter slight variation in phrases that requires them to more closely monitor print than was necessary with easier texts.

I'm Bigger Than You!

I am reminded of Veronica, a second-grade student I tutored a few years ago. She could read books like *The Ghost*, easily matching word by word and checking the illustrations to confirm the identity of each object. However, there were many upper- and lower-case letters she could not identify by letter name, sound, or by naming a word beginning with the letter. When I began working with her, she scored twenty-three out of a possible fifty-four on the Letter Identification task on Clay's Observation Survey (Clay 1993a). I bring her up at this point because there is a widespread belief that children cannot learn to read until they know all letters of the alphabet. While it is certainly a good thing for children to know all letters, it has been my experience that many children will continue learning letters and sounds *while* they are learning to read from interesting, meaningful texts.

During the first few weeks of daily reading lessons, Veronica read several patterned texts in which she needed to notice one change of word in the same place in subsequent sentences. When I thought it time for her to move on, I introduced *I'm Bigger Than You!* In this story, two characters, Rooster and

Goose, are arguing over which one of them is bigger. *Bigger* and *biggest* are frequently used words in this text. I knew that Veronica used those comparative forms naturally in her oral language, so the sentence structures would not be difficult for her. Thus, I thought this book provided a good opportunity to focus on letters, or visual features of print.

The pages of the book are laid out in double-page spreads. The illustrations begin on the left-hand page and continue on to the right. The printed text is placed on white space of the left-hand page. The illustrations show Rooster and Goose each stretching to be taller than the other. Then, as the competition escalates, these silly characters climb up on old barrels and other bits of trash. At last, the entire heap tumbles down, and Rooster and Goose land on the ground smiling, each announcing, "We're the same." The slight changes in the sentences on pages 2 and 4, and on pages 8 and 10, gave Veronica opportunities to pay close attention to letters and words.

> "I'm bigger than you,"
> said Rooster. (2–3)
> "No, I'm bigger than you,"
> said Goose. (4–5)

She read the first page accurately, but then began the next page just as she had the first. She started, "I'm bigger . . . ," then stopped and looked to me for help. My reply, "You read," sent her back to the beginning, and she looked carefully at the word "no" and self-corrected her miscues, finishing the sentence accurately. Pages 6 and 8 repeat the exchange of "No, I'm bigger than you," but on page 10, Rooster changes the pattern.

> "I'm the biggest," said Rooster. (10–11)

On this page, Veronica read, "No, I'm bigger than you said . . ." When she said "said," she realized she had run out of words in the sentence because there was no printed word where she put said. Next, she returned to the beginning of the sentence and reread it accurately. She was learning to pay closer attention to print by reading a text that provided an anchoring support for her using her strengths (reading for meaning and natural use of the forms of written English syntax) to free her to explore and make discoveries in her areas of weakness (knowledge of letters and attention to print).

Cat Tails

Sometimes a text can be challenging, even though the same sentence pattern or patterns are repeated throughout a book. One example is *Cat Tails*. Each page describes a different style of cat tail using a very simple sentence structure. The adjectives used to describe the tails are ones most children know and understand—*fluffy, striped, straight,* and *crooked.* They are, however, more challenging to read than adjectives like *red, blue, big,* or *little,* which are used frequently in casual conversation. If the descriptive words were common colors, for example, and the cats' tails were clearly painted those colors, the text would be easier for readers. Readers of *Cat Tails* are supported by a framework of repeated sentence patterns and illustrations that provide clues to the identity of some words. These kinds of support allow readers to devote most of their reading work to solving new words by checking beginning and ending letters and searching for meaningful chunks or groups of letters.

> There are cats
> with fluffy tails. (2)
> There are cats with striped tails. (3)

An additional challenge is added on the last two pages with humorous language play that gives readers something to ponder and also leads them to closely attend to the words in print.

> There are cats
> with no tails. (6)
> And there are cattails—
> tails with no cats at all! (8)

Texts with slight variations in word arrangement can also be used to effectively help readers gain familiarity with prepositions and adjectives that are essential to most written texts, but which are difficult to recognize as strings of letters because they do not refer to familiar objects.

It's Game Day

It's Game Day tells about a day in the life of a young soccer player. Because it is a subject with a vocabulary many young readers know well, most will be able to manage the shifts and variations in the sentence patterns. The opening sentence is reminiscent of the cumulative sentences of *All Fall Down.*

> I put on my soccer shirt,
> my soccer shorts,
> and my soccer shoes. (2)

The text on four pages tells about kicking the ball. Note how the consistent introduction on each page serves as an anchor to focus the reader's attention on where the ball goes.

> I can kick the ball up the field.
> I can kick the ball to my friend.
> I can kick the ball down the field.
> I can kick the ball in the goal. (4–7)

It's Game Day also provides readers with an early introduction to a personal narrative style of writing, one students in my school are expected to learn in the first and second grades. While there are many fine examples of personal narrative to read aloud to young children, most are too complex for them to use as models for their own writing. Books like *It's Game Day* can be read independently by beginning readers, and allow them to internalize the style of personal narrative writing in their own language.

Green Footprints

I like to look for easy books that have something in common with longer books that new readers can understand and enjoy, but that are too hard for them to read on their own. I call these pairings "literary partners." One picture book my younger students love to hear me read aloud is Pat Hutchins' *Where's the Baby?* It is one of five entertaining stories about Billy and Hazel and the rest of their monster family. In this story, baby Billy travels through the house leaving a trail of messy handprints and footprints as he gets into everything. Hazel follows the prints and finds him asleep in bed covered with splotches of paint, but looking quite angelic. A fine, easy literary partner for *Where's the Baby?* is *Green Footprints*. In this book, an unknown narrator follows a path of green-paint footprints from the bedroom, through the kitchen, out of the house, and up in the tree. Like *It's Game Day*, repetition of the beginning sentence pattern helps anchor readers so attention can be focused on the rest of the sentence.

> Green footprints
> across the floor. (6)
> Green footprints
> out the door. (7)

The culprit here is the cat, who has walked through a wet painting that has been left on the floor. The pictures in the book illustrate all the places where footprints were left, thus giving readers a source of information to support their reading of the written text. However, checking the pictures will only reveal the identity of key nouns in the sentence, such as *floor* and *door*. To read the book successfully, readers must also identify several prepositions, such as *under, across* and *out*. Books like *Green Footprints* and *It's Game Day* are excellent examples of texts that support word recognition and analysis by drawing on the phrasing and syntax young readers have been using orally for several years.

For example, a reader looking at the illustration on page 6 for the words "Green footprints across the floor," would see a line of footprints that stretch from the left edge to the right edge of the picture. While it would sound right and make sense to say, "Green footprints *on* the floor," most readers would notice that the word they are looking at—*across*—is much longer than *on* and that it does not contain the letter *n*. Depending on the student and teaching moment, a teacher might say the word or encourage the reader to engage in some problem solving. For example, in response to a student's substituting *on* for *across,* the teacher might say. "You read *Green footprints **on** the floor.* That certainly makes sense and sounds right, but let's take a closer look at that word." In the ensuing conversation, the teacher and student could discuss the word *across,* perhaps noting the initial letter *a* that is pronounced like the word *a*. They could also refer to the illustration and point out how the footprints can be seen traveling *across* the floor.

Where's Spot?

The puppy Spot is the star of a series of lift-the-flap books by Eric Hill, and a favorite character of preschoolers, kindergartners, and first graders at Tully. *Where's Spot?,* the first book in this series and the easiest to read, provides a perfect example of a text that supports readers through repetition, but which also prepares them for the varying styles that are found more often in written language than oral conversation. This story opens with Spot's mother looking for him because he has not eaten his dinner. She looks for him in many places—*behind the door, inside the clock,* and *in the piano,* for example. The text on most of the pages is a question followed by the response *no.*

> Is he behind the door?   No.
> Is he inside the clock?   No.
> Is he in the piano?   No. No.

Thus, readers soon find out that each left-hand page has a question that begins, "Is he . . ." and upon lifting the flap, an animal inside the object will respond with the word *no.* Although readers may read *in* for *inside* and not notice they have not read the entire word, most who can read books at the level of *It's Game Day* and *Green Footprints* will be able to easily read the question-and-answer portions of *Where's Spot?* What makes this a more challenging text, however, are the opening and closing pages of the book.

> That Spot!
> He hasn't eaten
> his supper. Where can
> he be?

Readers beginning this page are not given many clues to its meaning. Most notice the pictures of two dog dishes—one that is empty has *Sally* printed on the front; the other says *Spot* and it is filled with food. They can see Spot's mother Sally walking in the direction of the next page, so they know she is going to start looking for him. Most readers have spent a lot of time with this book and heard it read to them long before they begin an independent reading, so they are well aware of the sequence of events, and most easily find and read the name *Spot*. What they are not prepared for, however, is a very writerly text composed of words they must identify almost exclusively from the letters that form the words. Readers who successfully read *Where's Spot?* are those who can flexibly draw on several sources of information to read, and who are learning word strategies for analyzing and solving words new to them.

The Turnip

Folktales are one kind of story loved by all children. Currently, we are fortunate to have an abundance of beautifully illustrated versions of familiar and less well-known stories from many cultures. Most of these, however, are beyond the reach of beginners for independent reading because the texts are written in descriptive, literary language. For example, consider *The Turnip*, the old Russian story told by Aleksei Tolstoy, about a man who plants a turnip that grows so big that it takes a string of people, animals, and finally the tiny mouse to pull it up. One picture book version of this story is *The Gigantic Turnip*, retold and illustrated by Niamh Sharkey. The illustrations are comical and quirky and the language, vivid and dramatic. Her cast of characters includes the old man and his wife, plus canaries, geese, hens, pot-bellied pigs, and a cow. They do not simply pull to get the turnip—they heave, tug, and yank.

> The old woman wrapped
> her arms round the old
> man's waist. Both of
> them pulled and heaved
> and tugged and yanked,
> but still the turnip would
> not move.

Some kindergarten, and most first- and second-grade classrooms have children who can read Sharkey's text independently or with a little help, but for many children in those classrooms, it would be too difficult. While it is important for beginning readers to hear books like *The Gigantic Turnip* read aloud and to explore them on their own or with friends, it is also valuable for them to have versions they can read themselves. Harriet Ziefert's retellings of familiar tales, including *The Turnip*, *The Gingerbread Man*, and *The Little Red Hen*, are superb because they retain all of the zest and liveliness of longer, more complex versions, but they can be read independently by children much sooner than most picture books. The easiest of Ziefert's retellings is *The Turnip*. The language is simple, but rolls off the tongue. Now, look at the language in the scene with the man and woman pulling on the turnip, and compare it with Sharkey's version.

The old woman pulled the old man.
The old man pulled the turnip.
They pulled and pulled.
But they could not pull it up.

At first glance, *The Turnip* looks more challenging than *Where's Spot?*, because sentences are longer, and the entire text contains approximately four times the number of words as the Spot book. However, much of the extra length occurs because of the repetition in action, giving readers a chance to sort out and correct confusions along the way. Furthermore, the repetitive chain of events is quickly grasped by children, even those who have not heard it before, and it is an easy story to retell. Thus, most children come to the reading with a vivid picture of the action in their minds.

Cassandra's readings of both books helped me better understand why each is about the same level of difficulty, and also what each contributed to her growth as a reader. She was a second-grade student with whom I worked two or three times a week from March through May. I had been noticing that whenever she borrowed books from the library, she usually took books that were well beyond the interest and reading ability of other second graders. I have never told children not to borrow books that were too hard for them because I encourage them to explore the entire library. However, I was worried that Cassandra had no notion of how to find books she could read independently. One day, I asked her if she would like to read *Where's Spot?* to me. She consented, and I took a running record of her reading. She made eleven miscues, and self-corrected one of them, for an accuracy rate of 85 percent and a self-correction rate of 1:11. All but two other students in her class were currently reading much harder books, ranging in difficulty from *Little Bear* to *Bunnicula,* and I was concerned because our school year ends mid-May and she would not be ready to read third-grade material the following year.

One observation is not enough to understand everything about how a reader reads, but in looking over her running record, I noted that most of her reading was accurate and fluent. Furthermore, the comments she made during the reading showed me that she was familiar with the book and liked reading it. However, I also noted that she made no attempts to read five words in the text, and consequently, I was concerned that she had not developed strategies for analyzing unfamiliar words. I asked permission from her teacher to give her some reading lessons, and within two months she was capably reading books like *Little Bear* and Arnold Lobel's *Mouse Tales.* Within the context of reading fiction and nonfiction of interest to her, she learned to pay closer attention to features of words and to use this information to help her solve the identity of words she did not immediately recognize.

During her first reading lesson, I asked her to read *Where's Spot?* This time, she read it with a 92 percent accuracy. Two sessions later, I gave her a copy of *The Turnip*, and before opening the book, she told me most of the story, saying it was one she had learned in kindergarten. Then she read the whole book easily and fluently. Her accuracy rate was 94 percent and her self-correction rate was 1:3, which means that she corrected one out of every three miscues she made. As Cassandra's teacher, I was delighted with her progress (as was she) and as the writer of this book, I could see that *Where's Spot?* and *The Turnip* are similar in the level of challenge they provide for readers. Of course, observing one student in one instructional context is not sufficient for knowing how most children will respond to a particular book and where it is best placed along a continuum, but it does give a teacher a starting point.

Let me now show how the shape of the narrative and repetition of sentence patterns in *The Turnip* helped Cassandra do some reading work and sort out a confusion she was having. The story is probably one you know—an old man plants a turnip, which grows so big, he cannot pull it up. He proceeds to call first the old woman, next the little girl, next the big dog, followed by the cat. Each time, the string of characters pulls and pulls, but the turnip does not budge. First, the old man tries, and the text says:

> He pulled and pulled.
> But he could not pull it up.

Then, with the shift from *he* to *they,* the following two sentences are repeated four times:

> They pulled and pulled.
> But they could not pull it up.

Like many young readers, Cassandra's everyday oral language influenced her reading, and in this story, *couldn't* rolled off her tongue more readily than *could not.* From the perspective of meaning and comprehension, *couldn't* is a perfectly acceptable substitution for *could not.* However, the first two times she read the sentence, she read *couldn't not,* showing that she noticed each printed word. The third time, she read *couldn't not,* repeated the word *not,* then self-corrected her miscue and read *could not.* The fourth time, she read *could not* accurately, but the fifth time, reverted to *couldn't not.* Thus, in the context of a story she already knew and could read above 90 percent accuracy, the repetition of phrases gave her several opportunities to work independently to learn more about words. Although her miscue on the fifth *could not* indicates she had not completely sorted out the differences in the words, she gained valuable experience in managing her own learning. After she finished the book, I gave her a mini-lesson on contractions, asking her to write both the two-word form and the contracted form on the blackboard, and describe the differences.

As you can see from the examples I have given, there are not enormous differences between the first group of texts and the second. If you compare the easiest book in the first group—*What I See*—with the most challenging in the second group—*Where's Spot?*—it is easy to describe the differences. It is much more difficult to decide if a book like *All Fall Down* is easier, more difficult, or similar in challenge to *Cat Tails*. There are broad features that are more characteristic of one group of texts than another, but it is difficult to know where to place some books without first putting them in the hands of readers. I can estimate an initial level for a book by examining the story, sentence patterns, and vocabulary, and by comparing it to books I know well; however, it is not until I place the book in the hands of readers that I can make a more accurate determination of level.

Expanded Narratives (Reading Recovery Levels 9–12)

Summary of Levels 9–12

- repetition of three or more sentence patterns
- varied sentence patterns (repeated phrases or refrains)
- blend of oral and written language structures
- subjects include familiar experiences and imaginative events
- illustrations provide moderate support for the printed message
- events in many stories follow a sequence in which one event leads to another; order of events could not be changed without affecting meaning
- greater vocabulary, more descriptive language, more details

Focus Books

1. *Sharing Danny's Dad* by Angela Shelf Medearis. Illus. by Jan Spivey Gilchrist. Little Celebrations. Celebration Press, 1993.
2. *Cookie's Week* by Cindy Ward. Illus. by Tomie dePaola. Putnam, 1988.
3. *Tiny's Bath* by Cari Meister. Illus. by Rich Davis. Puffin Easy-to-Read. Puffin, 1998.
4. *The Changing Caterpillar* by Sherry Shahan. Books for Young Learners. Richard Owen, 1997.

5. *I'm a Caterpillar* by Jean Marzollo. Illus. by Judith Moffatt. Hello Science Reader! Scholastic, 1997.

6. *More Spaghetti, I Say!* by Rita Golden Gelman. Illus. by Mort Gerberg. Hello Reader. Scholastic, 1993.

When readers can read books like *Where's Spot?* fluently and with expression, they are ready for less patterned stretches of text with more events and greater detail. To manage these increased demands, however, readers still need texts developed around a familiar structure or framework along with the repetition of some sentences or phrases. Sentence patterns are more varied, and literary language more evident. Some books have repeated sentence patterns, but often this repetition exists in the form of a refrain or a repeated phrase that leads into sentences with varied endings.

Sharing Danny's Dad

Sharing Danny's Dad is a good example of how a writer can give shape to a story with a definite opening and closing, but at the same time support readers with a repeated sentence framework in the middle of the narrative. I think of *Sharing Danny's Dad* as a "slice of life" story, because the characters and events resemble those we all have known, in one way or another. Even though they are fictional characters, they seem like real people with emotional lives, and were this a longer book with many chapters, it would be called "realistic fiction." The story line is simple—a young boy is sad because his father must go to work, so he goes to his friend Danny's house to play. His friend Danny greets him, saying, "Don't feel sad. Today we can share my dad!" The interior of the story tells about everything that the three of them do together, and at the close of the narrative they share a hug.

Like the interior events of *Where's Spot?*, those in *Sharing Danny's Dad* follow a sentence structure that is repeated several times. However, those in *Sharing Danny's Dad* are more challenging for readers because they are longer, compound sentences formed of two clauses joined by the word *and*. Note how the following three sentences provide readers with a predictable framework, but also demand they have enough word knowledge to flexibly manage the slight variations in wording. Readers must also hold the meaning of the first phrase in mind while reading the second clause. In order to understand the meaning of the entire sentence, readers must understand the relationship between the two clauses in each sentence.

> Danny's dad threw a ball to him, and then he threw it to me.
> Danny's dad chased him, and then he chased me.
> Danny's dad pushed him on the swing, and then he pushed me. (8–13)

In order to read these sentences, as well as the others in the text that do not follow these patterns, readers must be able to identify words quickly and read them fluently so the meaning of the whole text comes through clearly. If they must focus too carefully on recognizing each and every word, they will have difficulty comprehending the story. Think of the difference between someone just learning to play the piano who plays note by note, giving equal emphasis to every sound, and an experienced pianist who plays the same set of notes accurately, but smoothly and fluidly so that the piece comes through as a cohesive whole and not as a series of separate notes. *Sharing Danny's Dad* challenges readers to develop fluency and phrasing, but the repetition in the text also supports their growing ability to read longer stretches of text in a meaningful way.

Cookie's Week

Cookie's Week has long been a favorite of Tully students—both as a read aloud they can chime in on and as a text for independent reading. Cookie is a lively house cat who has an adventure every day, and as a consequence of his actions, leaves some kind of mess. The text has several repeated, predictable elements. Each event begins with a day of the week in sequence, followed by a description of Cookie's action, and then by the consequence. Each day, Monday through Saturday, Cookie gets in trouble. On Sunday, there is a hint that Cookie might rest, and the picture shows Cookie curled up on a blanket. Alert readers notice, however, that one of Cookie's eyes is open and looking at a bee. I have never known any child to believe that Cookie will rest on Sunday!

Like the book *Where's Spot?*, *Cookie's Week* has a structure and repeated cycles of action that readers quickly grasp, and which support them while they tackle unfamiliar words. *Cookie's Week* presents more challenge, however, because each action is described using a different verb. The first page is easy because the verb is *fell*, one most children use in their oral speech, and thus, a word they can read easily in print. The verbs on subsequent pages, however, are not those children spontaneously use when looking at the pictures—*knocked* and *upset*, for example. There are also many nouns children know in their daily lives that are part of their speaking vocabulary, but which may be new to them in print—*kitchen drawer, clothes,* and *curtains,* for example.

Readers of *Where's Spot?* quickly learn that if they are unsure of where they are looking for Spot on a particular page, all they have to do is check the picture and they will immediately have the identity of the hiding place—*door, piano,* or *clock,* for example. There are not many words or many details in the pictures to confuse the reader. Readers may already know those words in print, but if they do not, they can use the pictures for help. In contrast, children who can read *Cookie's Week* independently, or with minimal assistance, are those who are able to pay close attention to the print features of a great many words.

Tiny's Bath

Many readers I know have laughed their way through *Tiny's Bath*. Tiny is a very large dog in need of a bath; he is owned by a very small boy who must use his ingenuity to make it happen. Like another well-loved "cleaning-up" story—*Mrs. Wishy-Washy* by Joy Cowley—this one ends, as readers will expect, with the cleaned-up animal rushing back to the mud. I especially like the way Tiny's size is compared to familiar objects.

> He is bigger than a bike.
> He is bigger than a chair.
> He is bigger than I am!

The sentences are short and some phrases are repeated, but there is more variation in sentence structure than is found in books at lower levels. The words, concepts, and actions in this story are likely to be familiar to readers and easy for them to grasp. The major challenge for them in this book, as well as others in this group, is being able to flexibly manage shifts in sentence structure and a plot that develops sequentially.

> Tiny likes to dig.
> He is dirty.
> He needs a bath.

Finally, when I think about features of texts that appear in small ways in this group of books, I look for a *few* examples of language that are more common in books than in casual, spoken conversation. This kind of language is sometimes referred to as *literary language*. For example, the use of *bigger* and *biggest* in *I'm Bigger Than You!* is in the context of an argument not unlike those we have observed in young children. In contrast, the use of the word *bigger* in *Tiny's Bath* is slightly different and more literary because it is used to compare his size with familiar objects. While the pictures show Tiny truly to be enormous in size, experienced readers recognize this use of language as exaggeration, or hyperbole, which is characteristic of tall tales.

Cassandra read *Tiny's Bath* the same day she read *The Turnip*. She read it with 90 percent accuracy, well within her instructional range, but her self-correction rate was only 1:6, leading me to think *Tiny's Bath* would probably be a more challenging book for most readers. She also read *Cookie's Week* in our previous session together with an accuracy rate of 92 percent and a self-correction rate of 1:3. *Cookie's Week* is a good frame of reference for me in leveling because it is a book I have observed many children reading. Both books require readers to read many different words. Many of those in *Cookie's Week,* like *knocked, upset,* and *kitchen drawer,* are more likely to be more unfamiliar to children than those in *Tiny's Bath.* On the other hand, readers of *Tiny's Bath* receive support from the repetition of phrases, but the overall language structure of alternating, repeated sentence patterns is not as immediately recognizable and thus predictable to readers.

The Changing Caterpillar and I'm a Caterpillar

During our time together, Cassandra also read nonfiction books about elephants, tarantulas, polar bears, caterpillars, and frogs. I quickly discovered that she was a font of knowledge about various animals and their life cycles, and prior to working on a new book, I would ask her to tell me what she knew already. Nonfiction books proved to be the turning point in Cassandra's reading. Watching how she became animated whenever I gave her a book about animals, I knew she had finally embarked on the literary pathway that would transform her into an eager reader.

During our conversations, I introduced specialized or unusual vocabulary she would encounter. Two books she read that fall within this group of levels are *The Changing Caterpillar* by Sherry Shahan and *I'm a Caterpillar* written by Jean Marzollo and illustrated by Judith Moffatt. Each presents the metamorphosis of a caterpillar into a butterfly, but through different writing and illustration styles, and along with the more simply written *Butterfly,* which I discussed earlier in this chapter, they make a fine text set for new readers.

Shahan's written text is illustrated with colorful, close-up photographs to show readers quite clearly what the written text describes. In fact, I would recommend that teachers encourage students to spend a lot of time scrutinizing and talking about the photos before they begin to read. That way, they can draw on their observations to support their reading. The text is brief (fifty-one words) and *chrysalis* is the only specialized word used. Some phrases are repeated, but the narrative is not patterned; it unfolds in a linear fashion, from caterpillar to chrysalis to butterfly.

> One day the caterpillar stops eating.
> It hangs upside down
> and changes. (4)
> The caterpillar changes into
> a little green pod.
> Now it is a chrysalis. (6)

I'm a Caterpillar is slightly more than three times the length of *The Changing Caterpillar,* and includes the whole cycle of change—caterpillar to chrysalis to butterfly to eggs to caterpillars. The illustrations are colorful collages, which support and illuminate the text, but which are not as instructive as the photographs in *The Changing Caterpillar*. The narrative clearly presents the facts of change, but they are told in a humorous way from the "first person" perspective of a caterpillar. Like *Butterfly*, there is an illustration on the last page that summarizes the cycle.

> I shiver.
> I twist.
> I split my skin! (eighth page)
> My old skin falls away.
> I am soft inside.
> I am a pupa (PEW-pah). (ninth page)
> I grow a shell
> to protect the pupa.
> I am now a chrysalis (KRIS-ah-lis). (tenth page)

I introduced both of these books to Cassandra on one day, and took running records of her readings on the next day. By the time I introduced these books to her, she had become much more proficient at word analysis, so both were easy enough for her to read fluently, but challenging enough for her to engage in productive reading work. She read *The Changing Caterpillar* at 94 percent accuracy with a self-correction rate of 1:3, and *I'm a Caterpillar* at 92 percent accuracy with a self-correction rate of 1:4. Both texts made important contributions to her growth as a reader because she gained experience from the different ways that writers present information. I was also encouraged by her high self-correction rate because it showed she was paying closer attention to print and using her awareness to notice details in words. As her word-solving skills increased, she became more confident in her ability to read new books.

More Spaghetti, I Say!

Children benefit from reading books from a range of subjects, writing styles, and vocabulary. To become more proficient readers, they also need to read longer and longer stretches of text quickly and fluently. *More Spaghetti, I Say!* is a rollicking tale in rhyme about a monkey named Minnie who refuses to play with her friend Freddy because she only wants to eat spaghetti. The text is 340 words (twice the length of *I'm a Caterpillar*), and filled with ways to eat and play with spaghetti. This brief selection from the book demonstrates how a text can support readers with repetition of phrases, but also can cause them to read many different words.

> I can run in spaghetti.
> And ride in spaghetti. (16)
> I can jump.

I can slide.
I can hide in spaghetti.
I can skate on spaghetti. (17)
and ski on spaghetti. (18)

Books like *More Spaghetti, I Say!* and the others in this group are like a bridge between lower level books composed of repeated phrases and higher level books with variations in sentence patterns. When readers are less dependent on repeated patterns, they can read stories or nonfiction that develop across a sequence of events. In some stories, like *Cookie's Week* and *Sharing Danny's Dad,* only the opening and closing are marked by time. It makes no difference to the story whether Danny's dad starts by throwing a ball to the boys or by pushing them on the swing. In contrast, the sequence of the events in *Tiny's Bath* is fixed because the humor of the story comes from Tiny being dirty, Tiny getting a bath, and Tiny jumping into the mud. Now, readers are ready for small stories, narratives with more details and more descriptive language.

Small Stories (Reading Recovery Levels 13–15)

Summary of Levels 13–15

- varied sentence patterns
- text may have repeated phrases or refrains
- greater variety of words
- specialized vocabulary for some topics (especially nonfiction)
- written language structures and literary language
- oral language typically appears as dialogue
- conventional story with simple episodes
- sequence of events usually occurs within an organizational framework readers can easily recognize and use as an anchor of support while working with more complex vocabulary, sentence structures, and variations in sentence patterns
- in fiction, illustrations provide low to moderate support for the printed message; the flow of events is often illustrated, but not specific words
- in nonfiction, meaning of ideas and concepts are enhanced by illustrations, diagrams, and photographs

Focus Books

1. *Building a House* by Byron Barton. Greenwillow, 1981.
2. *Tarantula* by Jenny Feely. Photographs by Michael Curtain. Alphakids. Sundance, 1999.
3. *Polar Bears* by Marcia Freeman. Pebble Books. Capstone Press, 1999.
4. *Old Grizzly* by Joy Cowley. Illus. by Jan van der Voo. Sunshine Books. Wright Group, 1987.
5. *Meet My Mouse* by Fay Robinson. Photos by Dwight Kuhn. Little Celebrations. Celebration Press, 1993.
6. *Who Took the Farmer's Hat?* by Joan Nodset. Illus. by Fritz Siebel. HarperCollins, 1963.

Readers who are ready to move into this group of books are like Cassandra. They have read and enjoyed various fiction and nonfiction books with differing narrative styles. They talk knowledgeably about stories and characters they like, and make connections between those that are similar. They read to find out about favorite subjects, and discover that it is useful to look at more than one book about the same topic. During reading, they look at the illustrations occasionally to help identify words, but they have also become very capable word detectives, using letters or syllables from known words to solve unfamiliar words. Particularly with nonfiction, they learn to study the pictures before and during reading, not so much to solve particular words, but to help them better understand the meaning of the concepts and ideas they encounter in print.

Books in this section challenge readers through the presence of more descriptive language, some words and concepts that may be unfamiliar to them, more complex language structures, and illustrations that support and enhance the text, but which do not provide ready clues to the identity of particular words. The overall text lengths are similar to those in easier books; however, these books are more demanding because readers must attend to more detailed information or story lines.

Building a House

Consider, for example, Byron Barton's marvelous book *Building a House*, which takes readers on a clearly written and illustrated tour of home construction. The entire text has eighty-three words; sentences range in length from three to ten words, and the colorful, full-page illustrations clearly show every step. Readers, however, encounter words like *bricklayers, carpenters, electrician,* and *plumber.* The following sentence, one of the most challenging in the book, is packed with information. "An electrician wires for electric lights." Unless the reader is someone who comes from a family of builders or is an avid fan of the television show "This Old House," *Building a House* would be a very challenging book to read for the first time, even though it looks like an easier book at first glance.

Tarantula and *Polar Bears*

Cassandra did not read *Building a House*, but she did read *Tarantula* and *Polar Bears*. Tarantulas are a familiar sight around Tucson neighborhoods, particularly during the summer rains when the males wander the desert in search of mates, and polar bears are especially fascinating to many Tucson students because they inhabit a world vastly different from our Sonoran Desert. Each of these books is one of a series designed for new readers. In addition to providing clearly presented information along with color photographs, the books include features typically found in more advanced nonfiction books, such as indexes (both books), maps and picture labels (*Tarantula*), tables of content (*Polar Bears*), and glossaries (*Polar Bears*). *Polar Bears* is one of a series of four books on bears published by Capstone Press, and *Tarantula* is one of the Alphakids Guided Readers.

Each is an example of the type of nonfiction book that makes a wonderful addition to a library or classroom collection because they are packed with useful information about their subjects, but at the same time are very accessible to lower level readers and to more proficient readers looking for introductory material about a subject new to them. Like *Building a House, Tarantula* and *Polar Bears* look much easier at first glance than they actually are for readers. According to the publishers of *Tarantula*, its Reading Recovery level is 11; and the publishers of *Polar Bears* have designated it a Reading Recovery level 9. From my work with Cassandra, I think those levels are little low so I decided to include them with this group.

Tarantula was the first of these two books I introduced to Cassandra. I decided to spend our first session just browsing through the book, talking about the information, and asking her to look for words she was not sure she knew. During the course of our conversation, she read the whole book, but it was a reading I supported considerably. More than any other book she had read for me, this one led to the most spontaneous and interesting responses. She moved back and forth between the printed text on the left-hand pages and the pictures on the right, enthusiastically interjecting her own questions, comments, and observations. She also spent a lot of time poring over the map of the United States that highlights the states where tarantulas are found, and learned how to use the index on the last page. One bit of information she found fascinating was that tarantulas shed their skin. In the chart below, note how the author of this text first states a fact about tarantulas, and then provides more detail in short, descriptive sentences. On the right, note how Cassandra's comments help her turn the printed information into understanding (Meek 1996).

Book Text	Cassandra's Comments
The skin of a tarantula does not grow.	"Ours does."
When a tarantula gets bigger, it crawls out of its old skin.	"It crawls out of its skin? It's like a snake."
Its new skin is very soft for a few days. (8)	"So when they molt out of their old skin, they stay soft!"

The day after this conversation and reading, I asked her to read while I took a running record. She read with an accuracy of 87 percent and a self-correction rate of 1:8. Two words she missed were *poison* (substituting *pointy*) and *paralyzes* (omitted, then I told her the word; during our conversation the previous day, she told me the meaning of *paralyze*, so I knew she understood the concept behind the word). The following day, I took another running record of her reading, and her accuracy rate improved to 91 percent and her self-correction rate to 1:6. This time, she read the words *paralyzes* and *poison* accurately. Most of her other miscues were on "easier" words, but her substitutions were meaningful—"grows big" instead of "gets bigger," for example. Interestingly, she substituted *mammals* for *mice* on both readings of the following sentence: "Some very big tarantulas feed on small mice and small birds" (10).

Three days later I introduced *Polar Bears* to her, and on the following day she read it with 90 percent accuracy and a self-correction rate of 1:8, numbers that are very close to her second reading of *Tarantula*. *Polar Bears* contains about half of the number of words as *Tarantula*, and on the surface, *Polar Bears* looks like the easier text because it has shorter sentences and fewer sentences on each page. The readings of one student do not provide enough information to predict how easy or difficult these books might be for a large number of students, but they do provide music for a conversational dance. It could be that *Tarantula* is indeed the harder of the two books, but Cassandra's prior knowledge and familiarity with tarantulas made it equivalent to *Polar Bears* for her. On the other hand, I think the text of *Tarantula* is better designed for helping readers build layers of understanding of the subject. Like the page on skin I previously quoted, each page features one topic and one or two additional sentences that provide additional detail. This framework supports readers' attempts at predicting the content in the second and third sentences.

The text of *Polar Bears*, on the other hand, is arranged so that most pages have only one sentence per page (two pages contain two sentences each). The narrative is well-written and flows well, but it does make demands on readers that may not be readily apparent to teachers. For example, consider the following double-page spreads. In each, there is a full-page color photograph on the left-hand page and written text on the right-hand page.

> Pages 10–11:
> Photograph on the left: close-up of a polar bear's foot
> Text on the right: Polar bears have
>   webbed toes.
>
> Pages 12–13:
> Photograph on the left: close-up of a bear swimming
> Text on the right: Webbed toes help
>   polar bears swim.

A glossary at the end of the book defines *webbed*, but its meaning cannot be inferred from the narrative or from the photographs. Most children I know who have read *Polar Bears* (it is very popular in our library) already understand the meaning and function of *webbed*, so additional explanation is not necessary. Keep in mind, however, that these short, simple sentences hold densely packed information, and thus may be more challenging for readers than they seem on the surface. There is a difference between a reader who knows the meaning of *webbed* and needs help identifying it in written form, and one who does not know the concept of the word even when told what word all of those letters make.

Generally speaking, books that are filled with descriptive language, such as *Tarantula* and *Polar Bears*, require readers who are able to quickly identify many words, solve for most unknown words, and remember words someone has told them (Cassandra's remembering of *poison* and *paralyze* once I had given her the words, for example). Readers who have developed this facility for knowing and understanding a great variety of words within a text are ready for books that require digging beyond the surface level to truly understand the ideas and concepts presented. Both of these books are good examples of texts that support students in expanding their reading vocabulary and in learning how to acquire new knowledge. Jerome Bruner's (1973) memorable phrase "going beyond the information given" is an apt description of what readers must be able to do in order to read books in the 13–15 level group.

Old Grizzly

In addition to Cassandra, there were two other Reading Explorers with whom I met for some extra reading lessons, Alex and Frederick, whom I introduced in Chapter 3. They progressed from reading *The Napping House*, to reading several books I write about in Chapter 5, such as the *Little Bear* books and Arnold Lobel's *Owl at Home*. In the beginning, however, each of the boys seemed very unsure of himself as a reader, although both were interested in books, read fluently, and were good at solving unfamiliar words by using letters, groups of letters, and links to words they already knew. I suspect, that like Cassandra, they were keenly aware that most of the other students in their class were reading much harder books than they were, and that their progress was limited by their perceptions of themselves as weak readers. Their teacher and I, on the other hand, were baffled, because we knew their potential. Ultimately, however, I began calling them the skyrocket readers, much to their delight, because of how fast they soared once each found their "just-right book."

Frederick's just-right book was the big book version of *Ratty-tatty*, which he picked up on his own at our first Reading Explorer's meeting. *Ratty-tatty* is the story of a clever rat who steals everyone's food without getting caught. Sprawled out on the floor with the book open, Frederick struggled to work his way through the text. When he finished, he was so excited that he pulled in several other students to listen to him read. Alex's just-right book was *Old Grizzly*. Both are part of the Sunshine Books series published by Wright Group, and both have been given a Reading Recovery level of 13.

In contrast to Frederick's persistence with *Ratty-tatty*, Alex took one look at *Old Grizzly* and told me it would be too hard for him. I did not ask why, but suspected that the seven lines of print on each page were the source of his doubt. I, on the other hand, knew from having observed him read easier books that *Old Grizzly* was just the book to launch him into longer texts with illustrations that set the scene, but which help only minimally with word identification. Grizzly Bear is a self-pitying character who sits in a chair watching a parade go by. First, the drummers invite him to "Come and play!", followed by the clowns and then the jugglers. Each time, his response is "No! Go away!" He complains that no one cares, but finally two dogs stop by and convince him to join them at the circus.

The structure of the story is well designed for leading readers into narratives with problems to solve and characters with personality. Grizzly Bear is the central character, so readers need only to pay attention to one character, and each scene takes place entirely on one double-page spread (text on the left, illustration on the right) so readers do not have to keep a thread of action in mind across several pages. Furthermore, the repetition of some phrases supports readers while they work with simple dialogue and with words that may be new to them. For example, the words on the first three pages are almost identical, except for the name of the circus people who go by. First go the drummers, then the clowns, and then the jugglers. In these three sentences, readers encounter complex sentences, dialogue, and a tone that helps them predict how Grizzly Bear will continue behaving.

> Grizzly Bear
> sits on a chair,
> watching the band go by.
> "Come and play!"
> the drummers say.
> But Grizzly Bear says,
> "No! Go away!" (2)

After these three pages, the narrative on each page begins with "Grizzly Bear," but then the sentences that follow are varied. Furthermore, in *Old Grizzly* they have a character with whom they can empathize, for who has not at one time lamented, "I'm all alone and it's just not fair"? The story takes a happy turn at the end, when two little dogs go by and invite him to join in on the fun. Notice how the text format on the last two pages of the book is similar in style to that on page 2, supporting readers' predictions about how sentences will be organized. At the same time, within that structure, there is quite a bit of variation in phrasing and vocabulary.

> Grizzly Bear
> jumps out of his chair,
> and gives a loud shout,
> "HOORAY!"
> And there are no more grumbles,
> or grizzles or mumbles . . . (14)
> . . . for the rest of the day. (16)

Meet My Mouse

Like *Old Grizzly*, *Meet My Mouse* has a clearly recognizable structure that provides readers with a strong framework for supporting their predictions about the organization of each page of text. The text is laid out in double-page spreads, with the words printed on the left page under a photo of "my mouse," and a full-page photo of other mice on the right-hand page. Each page tells something about the narrator's mouse from the first-person perspective, and then makes a comparison to all other mice.

> My mouse has brown and white spots.
> Like all mice, she has very soft fur. (4)

Each of the next six pages of text have two sentences, the first beginning with "my mouse," and the second beginning with "like all mice." These phrases give readers a running start, enabling them to focus their attention on the rest of the sentences, which describe mice in many different ways. Other topics are whiskers, teeth, tails, and activities. The page about teeth has three sentences, giving readers more detail about the subject.

> My mouse has long teeth.
> Like all mice, her teeth keep
> growing. She chews things to keep
> her teeth from growing too long. (8)

Not only is *Meet My Mouse* an attractive and compelling book for readers; it provides them with untaught lessons about how writers use comparisons to tell about their subject. Children are often asked to compare objects or events, and this book clearly and invitingly shows one way for them to proceed. *Meet My Mouse* is also a perfect literary partner for Bruce McMillan's splendid picture book *Mouse Views: What the Class Pet Saw,* a photographic journey of a wandering pet mouse's travels through a school.

Who Took the Farmer's Hat?

I want to close with one of my favorite books, *Who Took the Farmer's Hat?* It is the story of a farmer and his old brown hat. One day, the wind whisks it away. He looks everywhere, but no hat. One by one, he asks Squirrel, Mouse, Fly, Goat, Duck, and Bird if they have seen his old brown hat, but they each say they have not. Children find this delightfully funny, because the hat shows up in every scene, but each animal reports seeing it as something else—a bird, a mousehole, a hill, a flowerpot, a boat, and finally, a nest. Like the other books I have discussed in this section, *Who Took the Farmer's Hat?* has an organizational framework of repeated episodes that supports readers while they develop flexibility in working with varied sentence patterns and many different words. Each cycle of the story follows a similar pattern.

> He saw Squirrel. "Squirrel, did you see
> my old brown hat?" said the farmer.
> "No," said Squirrel.
> "I saw a fat round brown bird
> in the sky.
> A bird with no wings."

Children who like *Who Took the Farmer's Hat?* also enjoy Mem Fox's book *Hattie and the Fox,* which I discussed in Chapter 3. With their repeated and predictable cycles of events and relatively long texts, they tell exciting stories in memorable language and prepare readers for the more complex narratives of the books I write about in Chapter 5.

Summary

By the time new readers have read books like those I wrote about in this chapter, they have truly emerged as readers. They have read a variety of books for information and pleasure. Each of these books has a clearly laid out structure, which firmly grounds readers' expectations of how each narrative will unfold. Secure in understanding the framework of a story or narrative, readers are free to attend to learning more about words. Newer readers, like more experienced readers, have interests that influence how they will respond to different books. Frederick and Alex were transformed as readers when they each found stories they liked, but nonfiction marked Cassandra's turning point as a reader. Had I chosen books for them solely based on text level, they might not have soared so quickly. Too help all emergent readers soar, it is important for teachers and librarians to have large collections of books to capture every student's curiosity.

Closing Points

KEEP IN MIND . . . Very easy "little books" are only one component of an effective reading program.

Reading aloud from the rich treasures of children's literature is very important for the making of a reader; however, by carefully selecting little books, teachers and librarians can provide children with delightful and interesting stories for reading instruction.

KEEP IN MIND . . . There is a widespread belief that children cannot learn to read until they know all the letters of the alphabet. It has been my experience that many children will continue learning letters and sounds *while* they are learning to read from interesting, meaningful texts.

Emergent readers are new readers who are learning how to coordinate several behaviors at the same time.

- how to look closely at print
- the directionality of print
- how to match oral speech with printed words
- how to use their developing knowledge of print to check the identity of a word
- using illustrations for enjoyment and as a source of information about the meaning of a story

- developing a core of known words
- becoming fluent in phrasing

Teachers and librarians can support emergent readers by:
- giving them many different kinds of stories and nonfiction narratives
- putting books in their hands that will introduce them to the pleasure of reading
- carefully introducing books to readers, giving them a frame for understanding the text

Characteristics of little books for emergent readers include:
- familiar oral language patterns
- repeated phrases
- patterned stories
- illustrations depicting the message in the written text
- links to readers' prior knowledge

Book levels or readability levels are useful for:
- quick identification of several texts suitable for readers
- benchmarks for marking a reader's progress

Book levels are being used inappropriately:
- if children are confined to reading "at their level"
- if children are forced to read at every level on a continuum or a specified number of books at each level
- if they are used as a substitute for thoughtful consideration of the literary qualities of books
- if they are perceived as an inflexible sequencing of books

Bibliography

Children's Books

Getting Started

1. *What I See* by Holly Keller. Green Light Reader. Harcourt Brace, 1999.
2. *Ouch!* by Lucy Lawrence. Illus. by Graham Porter. Literacy Tree (Rigby). Mimosa Publications, 1989.

3. *The Sausage* by Jillian Cutting. Illus. by Peter Stevenson. Sunshine Extensions. Wright Group, 1992.

4. *The Chase (Hey, Tabby Cat)* by Phyllis Root. Illus. by Katharine McEwen. Brand New Readers. Candlewick, 2000.

5. *All Fall Down* by Brian Wildsmith. Cat on the Mat Books. Oxford University Press, 1983.

6. *Butterfly* by Jenny Feely. Photos by Michael Curtain. Alphakids. Sundance, 1999.

Little Adventures

1. *I'm Bigger Than You!* by Joy Cowley. Illus. by Jan van der Voo. Sunshine Books. Wright Group, 1987.

2. *Cat Tails* by Kittie Boss. Illus. by Erin Marie Mauterer. Books for Young Learners. Richard Owen, 1999.

3. *It's Game Day* by Lynn Salem and Josie Stewart. Illus. by Tim Collins. Seedling, 1992.

4. *Green Footprints* by Connie Kehoe. Illus. by Terry Denton. Literacy 2000. Rigby, 1989.

5. *Where's Spot?* by Eric Hill. Putnam, 1980.

6. *The Turnip* retold by Harriet Ziefert. Illus. by Laura Rader. Puffin Easy-To-Read. Puffin, 1996.

7. Tolstoy, Aleksei. *The Gigantic Turnip.* Illus. by Niamh Sharkey. Barefoot Books, 1998.

Expanded Narratives

1. *Sharing Danny's Dad* by Angela Shelf Medearis. Illus. by Jan Spivey Gilchrist. Little Celebrations. Celebration Press, 1993.

2. *Cookie's Week* by Cindy Ward. Illus. by Tomie dePaola. Putnam, 1988.

3. *Tiny's Bath* by Cari Meister. Illus. by Rich Davis. Puffin Easy-to-Read. Puffin, 1998.

4. *The Changing Caterpillar* by Sherry Shahan. Books for Young Learners. Richard Owen, 1997.

5. *I'm a Caterpillar* by Jean Marzollo. Illus. by Judith Moffatt. Hello Science Reader! Scholastic, 1997.

6. *More Spaghetti, I Say!* by Rita Golden Gelman. Illus. by Mort Gerberg. Hello Reader. Scholastic, 1993.

Small Stories

1. *Building a House* by Byron Barton. Greenwillow, 1981.
2. *Tarantula* by Jenny Feely. Photos by Michael Curtain. Alpha Kids. Sundance, 1999.
3. *Polar Bears* by Marcia Freeman. Pebble Books. Capstone Press, 1999.
4. *Old Grizzly* by Joy Cowley. Illus. by Jan van der Voo. Sunshine Books. Wright Group, 1987.
5. *Meet My Mouse* written by Fay Robinson. Photos by Dwight Kuhn. Little Celebrations. Celebration Press, 1993.
6. *Who Took the Farmer's Hat?* by Joan Nodset. Illus. by Fritz Siebel. Harper-Collins, 1963.

Other Children's Books

1. *Goldilocks and the Three Bears* by Paul Galdone. Houghton Mifflin, 1972.
2. *The Three Bears* by Byron Barton. HarperCollins, 1991.
3. *Deep in the Forest* by Brinton Turkle. Dutton, 1976.
4. *Chrysanthemum* by Kevin Henkes. Greenwillow, 1991.
5. *Swimmy* by Leo Lionni. Knopf, 1991.
6. *Charlotte's Web* by E.B. White. HarperCollins, 1952.
7. *Freight Train* by Donald Crews, Greenwillow, 1978.
8. *Brown Bear, Brown Bear, What Do You See?* by Bill Martin. Illus. by Eric Carle. Holt, 1992.
9. *Frog and Toad* books by Arnold Lobel. HarperCollins.
10. *Henry and Mudge* books by Cynthia Rylant. Illus. by Suçie Stevenson. Simon & Schuster.
11. *Huggles* books by Joy Cowley. Illus. by Elizabeth Fuller. Wright Group.
12. *Mrs. Wishy-Washy* books by Joy Cowley. Illus. by Elizabeth Fuller. Wright Group.
13. *Where's the Baby?* by Pat Hutchins. Greenwillow, 1988.
14. *Little Bear* books by Else Holmelund Minarik. Illus. by Maurice Sendak. HarperCollins.
15. *Bunnicula* by James and Deborah Howe. Simon & Schuster, 1979.
16. *Mouse Tales* by Arnold Lobel. HarperCollins, 1978.
17. *The Napping House* by Audrey Wood. Illus. by Don Wood. Harcourt, 1984.

18. *Owl at Home* by Arnold Lobel. HarperCollins, 1975.

19. *Ratty-tatty* by Joy Cowley. Illus. by Astrid Matijosevic. Sunshine Books. Wright Group, 1987.

20. *Hattie and the Fox* by Mem Fox. Illus. by Patricia Mullins. Simon & Schuster, 1987.

5

Small Chapter Books
for Transitional Readers

In the previous chapter, I wrote about books for emergent readers, beginning with texts written in short, patterned sentences, and concluding with small stories with predictable patterns, written in simple, story language. In this chapter, I write about books for transitional readers who can read many easy books on their own, without support from their teacher or librarian. They recognize many words in print and have a variety of ways to figure out unfamiliar words. They are like travelers who have learned their way around the neighborhood surrounding their hotel, and who are now ready to explore the city beyond. In this chapter, as in the previous chapter, I will discuss several books, pointing out features that have made them memorable for the Reading Explorers, the second-grade students who met with me in the library each week to read and talk about books. Keep in mind, however, that readers, like sightseers, have unique interests and each may prefer a different route to their destination.

In the library, next to the baskets of books for emergent readers, I have several shelves of books publishers produce for transitional readers that are marked with blue spine labels to help students quickly find them. The easiest of these are books like *A Kiss for Little Bear,* and the most challenging are books like the *Pinky and Rex* series, which has many characters and well-developed plots. Sometimes students call them "skinny chapter books," because they have the look and feel of a "big kid's book," but they are small enough for them to read independently.

My purpose in putting a selection of books together and marking them with easily recognizable labels is to help guide students in finding books they know they will like and be able to read on their own. I think of this special collection as a launching point for sending them off into deeper explorations of the library's collection. Many picture books they love, including Jonathan London's *Froggy* books, provide similar challenges as the small chapter books, and these are shelved with other picture books in the regular library collection. They also quickly learn how to find folktales, poetry, and other books about their favorite subjects. I make no attempt to level or label all the books in the library collection. That would be a perfectly dreadful thing to do.

For many students, these small chapter books are the perfect transition from "little books" to longer, more challenging texts. We take it for granted that any library or bookstore will have shelves of books created especially for new readers, but this style of writing has its roots in two classic series, each published in the same year. In 1957, Harper & Row (now HarperCollins) launched its line of *I Can Read Books*® with *Little Bear,* written by Else Holmelund Minarik and illustrated by Maurice Sendak. In the same year, Random House started the *I Can Read It All By Myself Beginner Books*® by publishing Dr. Seuss *The Cat in The Hat,* a character whose antics have tickled the funny bone of countless readers. Books like these have the look and feel of "grown-up" books and are easier to read than many picture books. Most are bountifully illustrated, and are between thirty-two and sixty-four pages long.

While each small chapter book usually has a few pages filled with print, most have print on less than half the page. Some books are arranged into short stories loosely focused on a broad theme, some have one story divided into several chapters, and some consist of one long story without chapter breaks. Most have two or three main characters, while other characters in the book play cameo roles. The main characters have unique personalities, but they do not ususally change or develop across the stories. Plot development is linear, with one event logically following another and without large gaps between events that force readers into figuring out what happened between events. Readers are not expected to interpret the meaning beyond what is stated in words and shown in the illustrations. Humor is a key ingredient of many stories. Many could be considered "realistic" fiction, where the characters, whether human or animal, behave as readers might in similar situations. Additionally, there are many superb books of nonfiction written especially for this audience.

Plot development is one key to understanding how easy readers, or small chapter books, are more challenging for children than books like *Hattie and the Fox* and *Who Took the Farmer's Hat?* The plot of each of these books develops from a series of very small episodes, so readers can follow the action easily and encounter rich, interesting language. Experienced readers, however, also look for more complexity and greater variety in what they read, whether seeking entertainment or information. With easier books, like those

I wrote about in Chapter 4, readers can grasp the meaning and flow of a text from reading just a few sentences or pages. More complex texts often require that readers read for several pages before they can put their hands around an event or a piece of information. Furthermore, some texts are not harder simply because they have more words and more pages. They are more difficult because writers include more details about characters and events and create plots that are not readily predictable at the start of a book. Nonfiction texts may be more difficult due to specialized vocabulary or because readers need to bring strong prior knowledge to the reading.

Not surprisingly, the Reading Explorers have never talked about genre, plot, or characterization. Almost always, they equate a good book with one that is funny. A few let it be known that they prefer stories about family and friends, but in talking about those they have read, they will often tell about a part that made them laugh. The Reading Explorers also like series books because they can read about their favorite characters over and over. They also like to read about subjects of interest to them. *Magic School Bus* books have an avid following, as do books about stars, volcanoes, and dinosaurs. Most like discovering new books, and while they tend to select books near their instructional level, they also enjoy talking about books an adult might consider too easy for them. Some also choose books too difficult for them to read alone, but they will tell about the story from illustrations, or from having heard someone else talk about the book. I have also observed that pictures are very important and contribute to the enjoyment of a book, and that readers move easily between illustrations and printed text while talking about a book.

To facilitate this discussion, I have clustered books with similar features at approximately the same reading level. Once again, I want to emphasize that there are no hard and fast boundaries between categories. As my friend and colleague Marilyn Carpenter says, the margins between such categories are permeable. For example, think of terms like *infant, toddler, child, adolescent,* and *adult* that are used to describe people along an age continuum. Most of us would readily agree on the differences between *infant* and *child* or *child* and *adult,* but think of the challenge in trying to differentiate between adjacent categories, like *toddler* and *child,* or *adolescent* and *adult.* One could argue that factors such as emotional maturity or physical maturity are important indicators, but individuals vary with respect to each. Similarly, with respect to books, it is much easier to describe differences in texts that are far apart in difficulty than those that are alike in many ways.

The phrases I use to describe the categories in this chapter highlight different styles of literature, as well as shifts in text complexity—one problem to solve, time marches on, the plot thickens, and a plethora of possibilities. The differences in text complexity between adjacent categories are small and not clear-cut, but the distinctions between the easiest and most difficult texts are easy to see. And, while I still talk about features of texts such as vocabulary and sentence structure, it is more meaningful to consider more complex texts with respect to larger units, particularly the structure of episodes or topics. Most of the books I discuss in this chapter are comparable to levels 16–20 in Reading Recovery.

One Problem to Solve

Summary of One Problem to Solve

- readers learn the focus of the book at the beginning of their reading
- each event shows another route to solving a problem
- reader's attention is always brought back to the problem
- language is conversational, chatty
- natural repetitions of words and phrases that occur in casual speech
- illustrations help readers understand and enjoy the story, but are not useful for identifying individual words

Focus Books

1. *Who's Afraid of the Dark?* by Crosby Bonsall. An I Can Read Book. HarperCollins, 1980.
2. *Rex and Lilly Family Time* by Laurie Krasny Brown. Illus. by Marc Brown. A Dino Easy Reader. Little Brown, 1995.
3. *Catch Me If You Can!* by Bernard Most. A Green Light Reader. Harcourt, 1999.
4. *Hiccups for Elephant* by James Preller. Illus. by Hans Wilhelm. Hello Reader! Scholastic, 1994.
5. *The Great Race* by David McPhail. Hello Reader! Scholastic, 1997.

At the beginning of the school year, a few Reading Explorers were just beginning to read small chapter books and needed books that looked like those the other students were reading, but which were easy enough for them to read independently. Of the several very easy, small chapter books I included in their basket, two were consistently popular with lower readers—*Who's*

Afraid of the Dark? and *Rex and Lilly Family Time.* Like most adult readers, children enjoy reading stories about the characters engaged in familiar activities of everyday life, and each of these books made connections to the Reading Explorer's personal lives, using language and events that seemed realistic to them.

Who's Afraid of the Dark?

Who's Afraid of the Dark? is a story about a boy who is afraid, but pretends that it is really his dog who is afraid of the dark. He tells a friend about everything that scares the dog, but instead of offering sympathy, the girl's response is to suggest that the dog isn't very smart. This comment leads to a round of exchanges in which the girl convinces the boy that he could teach the dog not to be afraid of the dark. On the last page, boy and dog are comfortably and happily tucked in bed for the night. Many Reading Explorers said this story reminded them of how they felt when they were much younger. They also understood that it was really the boy, not the dog, who was afraid of the dark, and that the girl's "trick" helped the boy.

There are several ways in which this book helps readers move into longer books with less patterned texts. The plot is simple, with only three events—the boy's telling about his dog's fear, the girl's offered advice, and the happy outcome. The text is brief—209 words, with no more than four lines of print per page. Half of the book's thirty-two pages has no printed text, but the illustrations contribute to the reader's understanding of what is happening. The story begins before the title page and continues for five pages with a simple illustration of a young boy talking to his dog. His friend comes along, and on page 6, he tells her, "Stella is afraid of the dark." Readers can tell right away who is truly afraid by looking at the next page, a wordless nighttime scene showing Stella sleeping peacefully, while the boy stands next to his bed, looking anxious and holding a baseball bat. For the next eight pages, the boy's words about Stella's behavior alternate with pictures that clearly demonstrate he is the one who is frightened.

> I have told her it is silly.
> I have told her I will protect her.
> But Stella is still scared. (8)
> When we go to bed she shivers.
> In the dark she shakes.
> She sees big scary shapes. (10)

While the illustrations are an integral part of the story, readers cannot depend on the pictures to identify particular words. Sentences are short (one to twelve words, with four to eight being typical), but sound natural because they mimic the way many children talk or hear their parents talk to them about fears. Readers recognize that everything the two characters say has been said to them at some point in their lives, so they have a strong basis for predicting meaning. Many of the words used are those children and their parents have used when talking about nighttime fears.

Rex and Lilly Family Time

Another book that grabbed the attention of many Reading Explorers was *Rex and Lilly Family Time,* one of three books featuring Rex and Lilly. Rex and Lilly are brother and sister dinosaurs whose zany, family-based activities brought forth plenty of laughter during book discussions. Like *Who's Afraid of the Dark?, Rex and Lilly Family Time* is an easy small chapter book that brought the lower level readers into equal participation with the higher readers. Additionally, it has been discussed enthusiastically by higher level readers, which tells me that it is a book with strong story appeal for many children.

There are three short chapters that are loosely connected, but which could also be read independently of one another without confusion about meaning. In the first, "Happy Birthday, Mom," Rex and Lilly have a grand time preparing a surprise party for Mom. When the party ends, there is a mess to clean up, so Dad declares in the beginning of the second chapter, "Robot Rob," that his present will be a housekeeper. Robot Rob causes problems when he gets carried away and cleans too much, so Rex and Lilly volunteer to take over the cleaning. In the third story, "The Best Pet," Dad tells Rex and Lilly that they have earned the right to adopt pets to take care of.

"Robot Rob" is a good story to write about because it is the story that tickled everyone's funny bones. "Robot Rob" begins with Rex and Lilly saying they have too much to do, and Dad announcing that his present will be a housekeeper. The housekeeper turns out to be Robot Rob, who announces "I am here to help!" He washes so much that the yard floods, he picks up so much that he creates another mess, and he cuts the grass and trees so much that the yard looks barren. Colorful, humorous pictures show the results of Robot Rob's work, filling in meaning that is not directly conveyed in words. Finally, Rex and Lilly decide they will clean the house and dismiss Robot Rob by telling him he is too much help.

To examine both the challenges and supports for readers of the easy small chapter books, it is useful to compare *Who's Afraid of the Dark?* and "Robot Rob." The overall text length of each is about the same—207 words and 38 sentences for "Robot Rob," and 209 words and 39 sentences for *Who's Afraid of the Dark?* More than 75 percent of the sentences in each range from four to eight words long. Short sentences do not necessarily make a text easier to read and understand, but in these examples, the sentence length mimics that of casual conversation, thus helping readers to make a connection between a written text and how they sometimes speak with friends. Each story has a clearly stated problem and the story works toward a resolution of that problem. The speech and the actions of the characters in each story are directly related to solving the problem. The dialogue in each story is brief and lively, quickly establishing the direction of the story. Readers of "Robot Rob" and the other stories in *Rex and Lilly Family Time* gain experience with quotation marks and other kinds of punctuation.

To help readers, the authors of both books repeat words and phrases. This redundancy is normal in most written and spoken language, but is harder to achieve in a natural sounding manner in books for beginning readers. In "Robot Rob," there are repeated phrases similar to refrains.

> Rob washed.
> Rob washed some more.
> Rob washed more and more and more. (17)
> Rob picked up.
> Rob picked up some more.
> Rob picked up more and more and more. (19)

Repetition such as this helps readers by providing a frame for the information just presented, and for new readers, serves as an anchor of knowledge and fluent reading. In addition to adding a touch of humor, this repetition gives readers a boost by letting them sail through a familiar section of text after they have worked to get meaning from unfamiliar parts of the story.

Catch Me If You Can!

The following three books were trailblazers for Alex, the student who read *Old Grizzly,* which I wrote about near the end of Chapter 4. I mentioned that when I gave him the book, he protested that it would be too hard for him. Well, he read it with a 93 percent accuracy, so I followed up by asking him to read *Hiccups for Elephant, The Great Race,* and *Catch Me If You Can!* Those he read with 92 percent, 92 percent, and 89 percent accuracy, respectively. He was astonished. "Now do you believe me," I asked, "when I say you are a good reader?" He did, at last, and this was a turning point for him because he became more adventurous in selecting and reading books.

Each of these books is similar in difficulty for readers, even though Alex's reading of *Catch Me If You Can!* was not as accurate as with the others. By the time he read this book, he had already read three other books and was getting tired; and, he was also getting ready to meet his class for a special program and expressed concern about the time. Several of his miscues were of the kind we all make when we are in a hurry—twice he substituted *didn't* for *did not,* for example. Another example is the word *biggest,* which is used five times in the story. The first time he read it accurately, the second and third times he substituted the word *big,* and he read it accurately the last two times. I have no doubt that had he read the book first thing the next morning when he was not fatigued from my asking him to read book after book, his accuracy would have more closely resembled that of the other books.

There are three parts to *Catch Me If You Can!*, all of which focus on the biggest dinosaur. First, readers find out that the other dinosaurs were afraid of his great big tail, his great big claws, his great big feet, and his great big teeth. Next, the littlest dinosaur is introduced:

> One little dinosaur wasn't afraid.
> She didn't run. She didn't hide.
> "Catch me if you can!" she called
> to the biggest dinosaur.

She taunts him by saying she is not afraid of his great big tail, his great big claws, his great big feet, and his great big teeth. Each time she calls to him, she ends with the refrain, "Catch me if you can!" Finally, the biggest dinosaur grabs the little one, but once readers turn the page, they find out he is her Grandpa. Like the text of "Robot Rob," there is a lot of repetition of words and phrases in *Catch Me If You Can!* that supports readers so they can focus their attention on unfamiliar words and variations in sentence patterns.

Hiccups for Elephant

Hiccups for Elephant has a clearly recognizable structure that gives readers a frame for predicting how the story will proceed. The opening scene announces that all the animals were fast asleep, except for Elephant, who had the hiccups. One by one, Chimp, Lion, and Zebra are awakened by the sound of hiccups, and one by one, each animal offers a solution to the problem. And, as any experienced reader would predict, none of those solutions work. Experienced readers also know that it is usually the smallest animal that solves the problem. Sure enough . . .

> Mouse looked Elephant
> in the eye.
> "BOO! he shouted.
> Everyone waited and waited.
> But there were no more hiccups!

Experienced readers also know there must be another surprise coming, and sure enough . . .

> All the animals
> fell back to sleep.
> Except for elephant.
> AH-CHOO!

What happens next is left to the imagination of the reader, for the book ends here. The best stories leave their readers with something to wonder about, and some readers might even notice a similarity between the close of *Hiccups for Elephant* and *Cookie's Week,* where the closing illustration shows Cookie with one eye opened, peering up at a flying bee. The words of the text say that Cookie might rest, but the picture shows otherwise. When young readers have plentiful opportunities to read all sorts of stories, they begin building literary pathways that enrich their future reading. When Jane Yolen (1981) wrote that "stories lean on stories," she was referring to the rich pantheon of myth and folk literature that underlies contemporary fantasies. Nevertheless, I think her phrase is also a vivid way of helping us remember that while our immediate purpose is to teach children *how* to read, our long term goal is to nurture their *becoming* readers.

The Great Race

David McPhail's *The Great Race,* is a comical narrative in which a whole cast of characters—cow, duck, rooster, goose, pig, and dog—are bored and decide to race around the barnyard. The race is so chaotic that readers never know how it will end until the last page. While reading, they feel more like participants than outsiders. Astute readers who notice the slapstick tone at the start of the race will enjoy many surprises along the way.

> "When do we start?" asked the duck.
> "When I say go,"
> said the dog.
> The rooster started to run.
> "You said go," he called,
> "so I'm going!"

Alex was so wrapped up in this story that his reading was peppered with his own responses. When the animals decided to have a race, one suggested they go around the world. "It's impossible," Alex said. When the pig falls behind, he noted, "That's cause pigs are slow."

Time Marches On

Summary of Time Marches On

- events of a story focus on one theme
- the events move along in time
- story events and nonfiction facts are developed in greater detail
- readers need to understand how each new event develops from the previous event
- written language structures and literary language
- vocabulary is more varied, but most words are familiar to readers
- illustrations provide useful information for enjoying and understanding the story
- readers need to understand that some story events take place in the characters' imaginations

Focus Books

1. *A Kiss for Little Bear* by Else Holmelund Minarik. Illus. by Maurice Sendak. An I Can Read Book. HarperCollins, 1996.
2. *One Saturday Afternoon* by Barbara Baker. Illus. by Kate Duke. Dutton, 1999.
3. *Danny and the Dinosaur* by Syd Hoff. An I Can Read Book. HarperCollins, 1986.
4. *Johnny Lion's Book* by Edith Thacher Hurd. Illus. by Clement Hurd. An I Can Read Book. HarperCollins, 1965.
5. *Stars* by Jennifer Dussling. Illus. by Mavis Smith. All Aboard Reading. Grosset & Dunlap, 1996.

Reading Explorers who were ready for more challenging stories than *Rex and Lilly,* delved into books like Syd Hoff's tales about Danny and his imaginary dinosaur companion. These books were enjoyed by a wide range of readers, but were especially popular with those excited about their newly discovered power to read a long book all the way to the end. They also explored nonfiction, including Jennifer Dussling's book *Stars.* A long time favorite of my children and me when they were young, *Johnny Lion's Book,* was out of print until recently, so I did not offer it to the Reading Explorers. Much to my delight, it is once again available, so I will include it with this discussion.

Several features make these and similar books more challenging for readers. First, they are longer, and greater length allows for more activities and adventures. The events that make up the plot are usually linear and closely sequenced, so the reader is not left to wonder what is happening. Some are books with single stories, while others consist of several stories about the same characters. Characters, whether animal or human, behave in ways predictable for young readers. They will find more variation in vocabulary in these and similar books, but most words will be known to them, and the style of telling is still close to that of interactive conversation. Readers will find more variation in sentence lengths, but most are fewer than fifteen words long. In contrast to the previous set of books, it is quite common at this level to have several pages with one-half to a full page of print. Illustrations are an important and delightful component of the books, but the printed text contains all of the information about the story.

A Kiss for Little Bear

I begin with *A Kiss for Little Bear,* a well-loved classic written by Else Holmelund Minarik and illustrated by Maurice Sendak. In my experience, every child able to read this book, loves it! It has also marked a rite of passage for many readers, launching them into longer books, such as the other *Little Bear* stories and Arnold Lobel's *Frog and Toad* books. It is a story with a circular plot that begins when Little Bear asks Hen to take a picture he has just made to his Grandmother. Hen agrees, and Grandmother is so happy that she asks Hen to take a kiss back to Little Bear. Hen agrees, but this time there are more steps to the journey. She stops to chat with friends and asks Frog to take the kiss. Frog stops to swim and asks Cat to deliver the kiss, who then asks Little Skunk to take over. Just when readers are wondering who will get the kiss next, Little Skunk meets a pretty girl skunk and they keep the kiss between themselves. Fortunately, Hen arrives on the scene, rescues the kiss and delivers it to Little Bear. The skunks decide to get married and the story closes with the wedding.

A *Kiss for Little Bear* is a memorable, multi-dimensional narrative that readers navigate and respond to on several levels. The experience of reading *A Kiss for Little Bear* extends well beyond identifying and understanding all of the words and events that take place. Literary theorist Wolfgang Iser gives insight to this kind of reading:

> A literary text must therefore be conceived in such a way that it will engage the reader's imagination in the task of working things out for himself, for reading is only a pleasure when it is active and creative (1974, 275).

A Kiss for Little Bear has the power to bring readers into an imaginary world to a much greater extent than any book I have discussed so far. Although the characters are animals, Minarik and Sendak have created a landscape rich with warm, loving relationships laced with gentle humor. Yet, like people, they can wander away from a task when something more interesting comes along. For example, in the following scene, Frog has the kiss, having agreed to take it from Hen, but then he sees a pond.

> But Frog saw a pond.
> He stopped to swim.
> "Hi, Cat.
> I have a kiss for Little Bear. (12)
> It is from his grandmother.
> Take it to him, will you?
> Cat—hi! Here I am, in the pond.
> Come and get the kiss." (13)

Who cannot empathize with Frog, who prefers a pond to a journey? The appeal and power of this book—the text and the illustrations—is that it sends readers beyond the print to their own imaginations and then back to the story. Furthermore, the illustrations are an integral part of the story. Consider Cat, for example, who is shown with his back to Frog, staring up a at bird flying close by. To fully appreciate the written text, readers must incorporate the images from the illustrations into the developing narrative.

One Saturday Afternoon

One way to prepare readers for extended stretches of text is to give them a collection of short stories, such as *One Saturday Afternoon*. The short stories in this book, like its companion, *One Saturday Morning*, are all about the Bear family—Mama and Papa, and their children, Lily, Rose, Daisy, and baby Jack. The stories range in length from just under 200 words to slightly over 300 words, so readers will feel accomplished, whether they read one at a time or all six in one sitting. There is even a table of contents to help them find the one they are looking for.

The time frame for the book is one Saturday afternoon. Mama's story is the first; she wants to go for a walk because she needs some time for herself. While she does this, Papa makes bread with all the children. Next, there is a story for each child and how they are spending the afternoon. Lastly, Papa's story tells about a hard-working Papa who decides to reward himself with some bread. The structure of the story helps readers make useful predictions about what will happen and at the same time, supports their reading of ten pages of text. First, there is an introduction telling about the wonderful cooking smells in the kitchen. Next, Papa declares he has worked hard and is ready for a piece of bread. He cuts himself a piece of bread, but decides it needs some butter. While he is gone, Rose eats his bread.

> Papa cut a piece of warm fresh bread.
> He sat down.
> "This bread needs butter,"
> said Papa.
> "Then it will be just right."
> He went to get the butter. (40)
> When he came back,
> the piece of bread was gone.
> "Yummy," said Rose.
> "That was *my* bread," said Papa. (41)

This cycle is repeated twice more. The next time, he leaves for jam and Daisy takes the bread, and the third time, he leaves for a glass of milk and returns to find that Lily has eaten the bread. Each time, there is some variation in vocabulary, but the pattern of sentences remains the same. There are 304 words in Papa's story, and 169 of those words, or a little more than half, are found in these three cycles of events. By the way, Papa does eventually get his bread and milk.

Danny and the Dinosaur

Being the first in the group to talk about *Danny and the Dinosaur* was a high point for one Reading Explorer, because the story is 838 words long and without chapter breaks. A closer look at the book will show how it makes a good reading link between books like *Rex and Lilly* and more challenging books. Both books feature dinosaur characters, an immediate attraction for contemporary children who seem to devour anything with a dinosaur-related theme. Danny's dinosaur is not a human person in dinosaur guise like Rex and Lilly's family, but his behavior is like that of every child's ideal of the perfect pet. The focus of the stories in each book is on action; readers can easily imagine themselves doing everything Rex and Lilly or Danny and his dinosaur do. And, while there may be several background characters, readers need only keep track of the actions of two or three of those characters.

Rex and Lilly is somewhat easier to read because events are divided into short chapters that can be understood independently from each other. The average sentence length in *Danny and the Dinosaur* is 6.8 words per sentence, while that in "Robot Rob" is 5.4 words. Several of the longer sentences in *Danny and the Dinosaur* are compound, challenging readers to comprehend two connected ideas at once.

He put his head down so Danny could get on him. (13)
The dinosaur was so tall Danny had to hold up the ropes for him. (16)
Danny and the dinosaur went all over town and had lots of fun. (26)

The overall length of *Danny and the Dinosaur* makes it look harder than it is, and while it is more challenging for readers than *Rex and Lilly,* it is easier than many other texts with a similar appearance. The best way to understand why this is so is to closely examine the events of the story and how they connect to each other.

1. Danny goes to the museum and sees many things.
2. He says it would be nice to play with the dinosaur, and the dinosaur talks and agrees.
3. They travel around town and see familiar sights: a policeman, a barking dog, tall buildings, people crossing streets, a baseball game, a river, the zoo.
4. He plays hide and seek with the children—a universal childhood game.
5. At the end of the day, Danny and the dinosaur each go to their own homes, and the adventure ends.

These events are loosely connected, somewhat like a child's account of summer vacation. One event did not cause another, nor does the reader have to think deeply to interpret the meaning of the events. The illustrations help readers with the setting, and the vocabulary is common to each of those settings. One advantage of a long text such as this is that many words are repeated in the natural flow of the story, but the structure of the sentences is varied so the text is not a series of repeated patterns. Reading Explorers also enjoyed reading *Danny and the Dinosaur Go to Camp* and *Happy Birthday, Danny and the Dinosaur.*

Johnny Lion's Book

Many children are enchanted by books that have a story within a story, and *Johnny Lion's Book* is just that. The outer layer, or the "real" characters in the story, are Johnny Lion and his parents, Mother and Father Lion. Mother Lion gives Johnny Lion a book about a baby lion called "The Little Lion," which he promises to read all day long while they go out hunting. The "fictional" lion is Oscar P. Lion, who does not stay home while his parents go out hunting. Instead, he wanders out into the world, has a close encounter with a crocodile, and then gets lost. Fortunately, his parents find him; they are happy to see him, but he is sent to bed right after supper. Johnny Lion finishes his book just before *his* parents return home, and *he* gets to stay up late because *he* was a good lion. This is a text of almost 1,200 words, so readers who finish it all by themselves feel justifiably proud of their accomplishment. If you look closely at the language, you can see how cleverly the Hurds wrote for newly independent readers. Many phrases are repeated, but this repetition is artfully used to create suspense, as during Oscar P. Lion's very scary encounter with a crocodile. To leave you wondering what happens, I will not finish the episode; you will have to get the book and read it yourself.

> All this time
> something lay still and quiet,
> looking at Oscar P. Lion. (42)
> The something had two little eyes.
> The something had big white teeth.
> The something had a long tail.
> The tail went
> swish — swish — swish
> in the dark, cool river. (43)

Stars

While the Reading Explorers like good stories, they are also very curious about the world around them. They borrow voraciously from the nonfiction books in the library, but the texts of many of these books are too difficult for independent reading. *Stars* gave several readers a text they could read and understand, and prompted an enthusiastic discussion about the information in the book and other facts known by the readers. The narrative begins with contemporary children gazing at the stars; it tells how some people of long ago told about stars through stories; and it describes what is known about stars, the reason why stars look small, the importance of the sun, eclipses, and the Big Dipper.

When trying to determine how challenging a nonfiction book will be for readers, it is important to consider how the author presents information about concepts that may confuse readers. For example, how big are stars?

> Think of the biggest star
> and Earth like this.
> You have a soccer ball
> in one hand.
> That is the big star!
> You have one little
> grain of sand in your
> other hand.
> That is Earth. (17)

The Plot Thickens

Summary of The Plot Thickens

- Plots are simple and straightforward, but episodes have shape and dimension.
- Characters have distinctive names and memorable personalities.
- Vocabulary varies greatly, but most words are familiar to readers.
- Dialogue advances the plot.
- Illustrations are important for the book as a literary work, but not essential in helping readers understand the stories.

Focus Books

1. *Three by the Sea* by Edward Marshall. Illus. by James Marshall. Puffin Easy-to-Read. Puffin Books, 1981.
2. *Owl at Home* by Arnold Lobel. An I Can Read Book. HarperCollins, 1975.
3. *Father Bear Comes Home* by Else Holmelund Minarik. Illus. by Maurice Sendak. An I Can Read Book. HarperCollins, 1987.
4. *Addie's Bad Day* by Joan Robins. Illus. by Sue Truesdell. An I Can Read Book. HarperCollins, 1993.
5. *Johnny Appleseed* by Patricia Demuth. Illus. by Michael Montgomery. All Aboard Reading. Grosset & Dunlap, 1996.
6. *Johnny Appleseed* by Steven Kellogg. Morrow, 1988.

Readers who can easily read from a variety of works of fiction such as those previously discussed have developed the ability to follow a plot with several events, broadened their reading vocabularies, and come to know different literary characters. When reading from informational books, they know how to follow a writer's explanation of a topic of interest, and to make connections to what they previously knew about the subject. They are now capable of reading and understanding writing that is more descriptive and more expansive. The characters they will encounter are slightly more complex, the plots more involved, the vocabulary more distinctive, and the humor more subtle. When students reach the point of being able to read books I write about in this section, they become confident and thrilled about their ability to read anything that comes their way.

Three by the Sea

Three by the Sea has long been a favorite of Tully students, but it was Vincent, a second year Reading Explorer, who made it his mission to see that all of his classmates discovered this book and its sequels, *Three Up a Tree* and *Four on the Shore.* Each of these books is a testament to the power of plot in grabbing and holding a reader's attention. Lolly, Sam, and Spider are three friends who take turns telling stories. In *Three by the Sea,* the three friends are trying to decide what to do after a tasty picnic lunch when Lolly volunteers to read a story from her reader. It is a very short story written in mostly decodable words.

> The dog and the cat saw the rat.
> "We see the rat," they said.
> And that was that. (13)

While countless children have been taught that texts like Lolly's were the keys to making them readers, Sam and Spider were not impressed.

> "Dull," said Spider. (15)

Next, Sam declares he can tell a better story. He begins.

> A rat went for a walk. (20)

While that sounds like the start of another Lolly-like story, Sam is a bit better at plot construction than the writer of Lolly's reader. On his walk, the rat looks in a shop window and purchases a cat.

> "Are you sure you want a *cat?*"
> asked the owner. (23)

The rat insists he is sure, and buys the cat. They seem to get along well, but suspense rises as the conversation turns to the cat's favorite food. Lolly and Spider and readers of *Three by the Sea* are ready, of course, for disaster, because everyone is certain the cat will say his favorite food is rats. However, this is what the cat really likes best.

> "What I like," said the cat, "is . . ." (33)
> ". . . CHEESE!" (34)

Spider declares the ending "dumb" and says he will tell a scary story. His story begins with a monster who comes out of the sea very hungry. He looks around the beach, but rejects the cheese, rat, and cat he sees along the way.

> Monsters really like kids.
> On toast! (43)

Well, Spider's story is so believable that when he describes the monster creeping closer to three yummy looking children . . .

> Lolly and Sam jumped ten feet.
> "Help!" they cried.

Of course, there was no monster, only the one planted in their minds by Spider, the consummate story teller. *Three by the Sea* lets children know that good stories are page-turners, not just strings of easy-to-read words.

Owl at Home

Arnold Lobel's inimitable *Frog and Toad* stories are widely known and loved, but Lobel also created other memorable characters worthy of readers' attention. One of these, *Owl at Home,* is a collection of six stories about an earnest but somewhat eccentric fellow. In the first story, "The Guest," he hears winter knocking at the door and invites it in. Winter, however, does not behave like a proper guest. Readers can well imagine what havoc Winter could wreak inside a house, and Lobel delivers some of the expected consequences, like cold wind and snow whirling everywhere. However, only a writer with Lobel's creative ear for story and language could surprise readers with unexpected images.

> It made the window shades
> flap and shiver.
> It turned the pea soup
> into hard, green ice. (13)

Owl is successful in ridding his house of Winter, but he never does figure out what to do with the two strange bumps he sees at the foot of his bed just as he is ready to go to sleep in the next story, called "Strange Bumps." Poor Owl is most distressed.

> "What if those
> two strange bumps
> grow bigger and bigger
> while I am asleep?"
> said Owl. (21)

He moves one foot up and down, and then the other. He pulls the covers off his bed, and the bumps are gone. Seeing only his feet, he covers up again, and, of course, the bumps reappear. (This was the Reading Explorers' favorite story in the book, and by this point in the story, they were either falling off their chairs or rolling on the floor with laughter.)

"Those bumps are back!"
shouted Owl.
"Bumps, bumps, bumps!
I will never sleep tonight!" (24)

Father Bear Comes Home

The *Little Bear* books have many aficionados among the Reading Explorers. These are warm-hearted stories about Little Bear, Mama Bear, Father Bear, and their friends, and while many of the stories are grounded in recognizable family activities like having birthday parties, others gently explore the world of imaginative make believe. One story that enters this realm is "Little Bear and Owl," the first chapter of *Father Bear Comes Home*. Mother Bear asks Little Bear to go to the river to catch a fish. Once there, he meets Owl, catches a fish, and tells Owl that his father is away catching bigger fish in the ocean. Next, Little Bear suggests to Owl they make believe that the log Owl is sitting on is a boat and that they are fishing on the ocean. Readers are transported to a pretend world, where Owl catches an octopus and Little Bear catches a whale. To help readers know they have entered this imaginary world, artist Sendak shows the pair in a boat wearing sailor hats, and has changed the background color, for this page only, from white to light peach.

Books that are easier to read usually do not contain very much descriptive writing because it is easy for readers to get tangled up in descriptions and lose track of what is happening in the story. However, in the *Little Bear* books, there are many fine examples of how a writer can support a reader's developing ability to read descriptive language. In the second story in the book, also called "Father Bear Comes Home," Little Bear tries to convince his friends that his father will bring home a mermaid. Duck asks what a mermaid is like.

"A mermaid!" said Little Bear.
"Why, a mermaid is very pretty.
A mermaid's hair is blue and green.
Like the ocean,
blue and green." (26)

Addie's Bad Day

For readers who prefer books about "real kids like me," the Addie and Max books are just perfect. In the first, *Addie Meets Max*, Addie is reluctant to meet the new boy next door. When they do meet, they literally run into each other—on their bikes. In the second book, *Addie Runs Away*, Addie decides that her parents do not want her because they are sending her to camp for two weeks, where she will not know anyone. Running away with her suitcase packed seems like the only answer, but Max intervenes and convinces her camp would be fun.

The third book, *Addie's Bad Day*, brought the biggest laughs from the Reading Explorers. Addie arrives at Max's house for his birthday party, hands him his present, then says she must leave. She is very evasive about why, but readers who look closely at the illustrations will see that Addie is wearing a hat with a broad bill and earflaps. Once they are in the house ("I will only stay a minute," said Addie.), Addie continues wearing her hat. This is one chapter book where the illustrations play an important role in telling the story. Finally, Addie tells Max about her trip to the barber and how ALL her hair ended up on the floor. Anyone who has ever had a "bad hair day" will empathize with Addie, but Max, the ever-encouraging friend, tells her it will grow back.

> "Your hair will grow back."
> "Not in time for the party,"
> said Addie.
> "I look funny.
> Everyone will laugh at me." (18)

Addie and Max are so busy they forget about Max's dog Ginger, whom they find chewing up his birthday present. A comical scene follows when Max rescues his present—a jungle suit—and Addie tells him she has one just like it. She runs home to get her jungle suit, and there are no more worries about haircuts.

Johnny Appleseed

When I moved to Arizona, I was surprised to discover that stories about Johnny Appleseed are as popular here as they are in the midwest. Our school library has three superb picture books about him, which many teachers borrow to read to their students in the fall. Steven Kellogg's book *Johnny Appleseed* relates biographical information and some of the tall tales told about his life. Margaret Hodges' *The True Tale of Johnny Appleseed*, illustrated by Kimberly Bulcken Root, is also written in biographical form. Reeve Lindbergh's *Johnny Appleseed*, illustrated by Kathy Jakobsen, is a fictionalized narrative poem based on his life story. Each is popular with the students, but the texts are too difficult for most first and second graders to read on their own, although they love the books and their unique illustrations. Consequently, I was pleased to discover Patricia Demuth's easy-to-read biography, *Johnny Appleseed*, because it is the perfect companion for the picture books. Note how she begins his story by succinctly telling readers who he was and why he was an important person. Note also that while her language is simple and direct, it creates a clear image for readers to plant in their minds as the story unfolds.

Who was Johnny Appleseed?
Was he just in stories?
No.
Johnny was a real person.
His name was John Chapman.
He planted apple trees—
lots and lots of them. So people called him
Johnny Appleseed. (5)

Let's contrast this with Steven Kellogg's introduction, which also clearly describes the person that readers are going to read more about. Compare the two passages, which have approximately the same number of words.

John Chapman, who later became known as Johnny Appleseed, was born on September 26, 1774, when the apples on the trees surrounding his home in Leominster, Massachusetts, were as red as the autumn leaves.

Demuth's introduction consists of seven sentences; Kellogg's introduction is one sentence. Both styles of writing can play an important role in children's reading development. The easier text gives readers immediate access to the facts, while the more challenging text packs a lot of information into a small space. Students not ready to independently read Kellogg's more literary style can learn a lot about Johnny Appleseed from Demuth's easier text. In turn, what they learn from Demuth's text will provide them with a strong foundation for exploring and learning from the more difficult Kellogg version.

A Plethora of Possibilities

Summary of A Plethora of Possibilities

- elaborated episodes
- more descriptive detail fleshes out the plot, giving readers more to follow between the high points of the action
- characters have more depth to their personalities
- outcome or endings are less predictable to readers
- vocabulary varies; most words are part of readers' spoken vocabulary, but many many be new to them in print
- more sophisticated use of dialogue
- nonfiction topics are more detailed, with some specialized vocabulary

Focus Books

1. *Frog and Toad Are Friends* by Arnold Lobel. An I Can Read Book. HarperCollins, 1970.

2. *Henry and Mudge Take the Big Test* by Cynthia Rylant. Illus. by Suçie Stevenson. Ready-to-Read. Simon & Schuster, 1991.

3. *Henry and Mudge and the Happy Cat* by Cynthia Rylant. Illus. by Suçie Stevenson. Ready-to-Read. Simon & Schuster, 1990.

4. *Snakes* by Patricia Demuth. Illus. by Judith Moffatt. All Aboard Reading. Grosset & Dunlap, 1993.

5. *Oliver Pig at School* by Jean Van Leeuwen. Illus. by Ann Schweninger. Puffin Easy-to-Read, 1990.

6. *Growing Ideas (Meet the Author)* by Jean Van Leeuwen. Richard Owen Publishers, 1998.

7. *Fox on Stage* by James Marshall. Puffin Easy-to-Read. Puffin Books, 1996.

The Reading Explorers liked to mark their favorite pages with Post-It™ notes—or "sticker bumps," as they came to be known, thanks to Brad. At first, their purpose in doing this was to highlight pages they wanted to read to the rest of the group. For one group in particular, reading aloud to their classmates was embraced as enthusiastically as reading the books to themselves. Not only had they joined Frank Smith's "literacy club" (1988); they created their own organization. Gradually, they made a shift from reading to talking about the books, or doing a little bit of each. They seemed to make this move at the time they could read most anything that came their way. Their reading vocabularies developed immensely, as had their ability to solve new words "on the fly." Nothing could stop them!

There is an abundance of good literature for these readers, and splendid opportunities for teachers to introduce their students to different characters and different styles of writing. Reading Explorers who read books like those I am going to discuss in this section will tell you they love *Henry and Mudge,* or that *Frog and Toad* are the greatest. Others insist they prefer reading about *Oliver and Amanda Pig, Amelia Bedelia,* or *Addie and Max.* Still others read the same book about snakes over and over, and tell me I should buy more copies. "I read *Snakes* **again!**" proclaimed Ian. Dave announces that Ian has been making *everyone* read *Magic School Bus Books.* "Fox makes me laugh," announced Jerry after he read several of Edward and James Marshall's *Fox* books. Annie contributes, "Henry and Mudge remind me of people I know, like my cousin. She likes her dog the way Henry likes Mudge."

I learned to listen closely. Students like Ian are intellectually adventurous and delve into a great many books. Annie's interests are more focused—
she prefers stories about families and friendships, although she is happy to
follow recommendations of others. Jerry was more of a challenge for me. He
is a strong and capable reader, but not an eager reader. One day he began talking about James Marshall's *Fox Outfoxed,* and he talked on and on about the
pictures and one of the stories in the book. In my notes, I wrote, "This is the
most animated Jerry has been in the group when talking about a book." Besides the *Fox* stories, the only other book I saw him truly enjoy was *Sweets and
Treats,* a collection of dessert poems compiled by Bobbye Goldstein. Week after week, he read several poems to the group, stopping only because someone
else wanted a turn. He was not deterred by a great many words in those poems that were new to his vocabulary. He just asked for help, then moved on.
The lessons I learned from the Reading Explorers were innumerable, but the
most valuable is how vitally important it is to provide children access to a
great many books, and give them abundant opportunities to read and talk
with their friends about reading.

I call this section "a plethora of possibilities" because there are far more
wonderful books for readers than I have room to write about. Elaborated episodes, more intricate plotting, and more descriptive and detailed writing are
some of the hallmarks of these books. And, as with the other categories of
books I have written about, not all books possess the same characteristics.

Frog and Toad Are Friends

One of the most memorable and enduring literary friendships for early readers is that of Frog and Toad. Arnold Lobel wrote and illustrated four books of
their adventures: *Frog and Toad Are Friends,* which was named a Caldecott
Honor book in 1971; *Frog and Toad Together,* which was named a Newbery
Honor book in 1973; *Frog and Toad All Year;* and *Days with Frog and Toad.*

When I first met with the Reading Explorers and asked about their favorite books, *Frog and Toad* books were a consistent choice. Their teacher had
been reading them aloud in class, so they were available to all students, not
only to those able to read them independently. There are five stories in *Frog
and Toad Are Friends*—"Spring," "The Story," "A Lost Button," "A Swim,"
and "The Letter." In the first story, Frog and Toad wake up in April, after a
long winter's sleep. Frog is ready to greet the world, but Toad wants to sleep
some more.

> "Think of it," said Frog.
> "We will skip through the meadows
> and run through the woods

and swim in the river.
In the evenings we will sit
right here on this front porch
and count stars." (8)
"You can count them, Frog,"
said Toad. "I will be too tired.
I am going back to bed."
Toad went back into the house.
He got into the bed
and pulled the covers
over his head again. (9)

This point-counterpoint interaction is typical of the two characters, and a style readers need to grasp in order to fully enjoy the stories. It is a demand placed beyond the need to read the words and follow the plot. Toad insists he be allowed to sleep until mid-May, but Frog, who does not want to be lonely, tears the pages off the calendar, leaving the May page on top. He wakes up Toad, who is surprised the time has passed so quickly, but who, nevertheless, climbs out of bed and joins Frog to see the world in spring.

Reading is more than knowing the words and understanding the meaning of individual sentences, as is exemplified by the next story, "The Story." In this one, Frog is not feeling well ("Today you look very green, even for a Frog," said Toad.). Frog asks for a story, and Toad tries to think of one to tell. First, he thinks and thinks. Next, he walks up and down the porch. Still, no luck, so he stands on his head, pours water on his head, and finally bangs his head on the wall. By this time, Frog feels better, but Toad is not well and goes to bed. Frog proceeds to tell the story, beginning with "Once upon a time," of what has just happened to the two friends.

At first glance, these two characters seem more alike than different, but readers who pick up the subtlety of the characterizations come to realize they have unique personalities and, consequently, play different roles in the stories. Frog is the wise, steady, ever-knowing figure. When Toad loses his button in the story "A Lost Button," Frog suggests simply that they retrace the steps of their walk. He listens patiently as the agitated Toad rejects each button they find along the way; he is not reproachful when the missing button is found at home. He might laugh at his friend's silly behavior, as he did when Toad insisted on wearing a bathing suit for swimming in the story "The Swim," but he cheers him up with a letter when Toad feels sad because no one writes him in the story "The Letter." In contrast, Toad's mercurial temperament makes life interesting. There would be no stories to tell without his willingness to be so human.

Henry and Mudge Take the Big Test

Equal in popularity to the *Frog and Toad* books are the *Henry and Mudge* books, stories about a young boy, Henry, his big dog, Mudge, and his mother and father. While Frog and Toad are animal characters living in an imaginary world, Henry and Mudge are contemporary characters doing things their readers might be doing with their own dogs. The style and organization of the writing in the two series differ as well. Most Henry and Mudge books are single stories, divided into three or four chapters. Dialogue is the main vehicle for telling *Frog and Toad* stories, but most of the Henry and Mudge stories are told in third-person narrative, with occasional segments of dialogue.

One of the Reading Explorers' favorite books in this series is *Henry and Mudge Take the Big Test*. The first three pages of the book provide a good example of how a text challenges readers beyond word recognition and sentence comprehension. On the first three pages (4–6), Henry, his mother, and Mudge are sitting on their front porch when a man with a collie walks by. The man stops and gives his dog instructions to sit, then lie down. The collie performs both of those actions. On page 7, the text says:

> Henry looked at Mudge.
> Mudge looked at Henry.
> They both looked at the collie. (7)

These are easy sentences to read, but unless a reader can anticipate the direction of the story from only having read a few pages, the significance of those words will not be appreciated. Readers who already know Henry and Mudge from their other books will readily interpret those sentences because they know that while Mudge is very lovable, he does not follow directions well. The focus of the next two pages shifts back to the man and his collie's perfect behavior. Not until page 11 of the text does attention turn to Mudge's behavior. However, it is not until page 14 that the reader will find stated in print the purpose and direction of the story.

> "Maybe Mudge needs to go to school,"
> Henry said to his mother. (14)

The next chapter, called "School," shows Henry's preparations for Mudge's first day. Reading Explorers laughed the most on pages 23–26 when Mudge danced with the instructor. At the beginning of the third chapter, "The Big Test," the reader is not sure how Mudge will do at this school business. Mudge liked sniffing students and thinking about things other than his school work.

A reader who is reading beyond the sentence level will be able to interpret the three sentences as a hopeful sign that Mudge will do all right in the end.

> But he always showed up.
> And he always wagged his tail.
> And he always gave his teacher a kiss. (30)

In the end, Mudge does pass the test, but as if to assure the reader that Mudge has not lost his endearing personality, Rylant closes the story showing Mudge drooling on his teacher's foot "one last time."

Henry and Mudge and the Happy Cat

Another favorite Henry and Mudge book for the Reading Explorers was *Henry and Mudge and the Happy Cat,* which begins with the discovery of a stray cat on the doorstep. Notice how vividly Cynthia Rylant describes this unexpected visitor.

> Henry's father opened
> the door. Sitting
> on the steps was
> the shabbiest cat
> Henry had ever seen. (7)
> It had a saggy belly,
> skinny legs,
> and fur that looked like
> mashed prunes. (8)

Whenever the Reading Explorers talked about this book, they laughed and repeated the phrase "mashed prunes," a sure sign that author Rylant has done more than merely string words together. Her imaginative way of looking at the world has led her to show readers something ordinary in an extraordinary way. Artist Suçie Stevenson's portrait of the shabby cat also captured the Reading Explorers' attention, and, for a long time, it was their favorite page to show everyone.

Snakes

Many readers at this time are capable of reading nonfiction books, particularly those designed with developing readers in mind. The snake book I referred to earlier is *Snakes,* written by Patricia Demuth. The text takes readers through topics of interest, including comparative sizes, where snakes live, their body temperature, shedding, eating, and camouflage. Each topic is described in short paragraphs in a style, vocabulary, and syntax that is typical of other books at this level. The text and attractive collage illustrations work closely together to help readers learn more. For example, on pages 26 and 27 there is information about how snakes swallow food. There is a close-up cut-out picture of the jaws, with short captions that read "jaws unhook here," and "elastic muscle that can stretch wide open." The narrative reads:

> Snakes do not chew their food.
> They swallow it whole
> by "unhooking" their jaws.
> A python can swallow
> a whole pig in one bite (27).

Oliver Pig at School and Growing Ideas

There are many other fine books for readers that provide similar challenges and opportunities. The Reading Explorers who were avid readers of the *Little Bear* books moved into the stories of *Oliver and Amanda Pig* by Jean Van Leeuwen. The main characters are Oliver Pig, his baby sister Amanda, Mother, Father, and Grandmother. The stories are as varied as any family's activities and moods, and each book contains four or five short stories. Van Leeuwen explains the origin of the Oliver and Amanda stories in *Growing Ideas*, her autobiography written especially for children.

> About half the books I have written were inspired by my own children. When David and Elizabeth were little, I started writing down the funny and interesting things they said and did. (8) There was the time they put too much bubble bath in the tub, and we had a bubble disaster. There was David's first day of kindergarten. There was the "monster bush" in a nearby yard that scared Elizabeth. Later it became a monster clock in a story I wrote. (9)

Oliver Pig at School is the book about David's first day of kindergarten, and alert readers will notice the author's dedication, "For David, who didn't cry on his first day." Of all the Amanda and Oliver stories, this has proved to be the favorite of the Reading Explorers', although as second graders they are a few years past entering kindergarten. I am sure that Van Leeuwen's description of Oliver's feelings are so universal that she stirred up vivid memories of the Reading Explorers' own first days of school. Who among us cannot empathize with Oliver, remembering our first day at a new school or new job?

> Oliver was all alone.
> Suddenly his eyes felt funny,
> like they wanted to cry.
> What was the matter with them?
> Oliver looked around. (14)

For the first sixteen pages of the book, readers follow Oliver's fear and anguish. Then, on page 16, his bus arrives at school. Oliver wants to go home, but he gathers his courage. Notice how beautifully and subtly Van Leeuwen lets Oliver and the readers know that all will be well.

> Slowly he climbed down the tall steps.
> Waiting at the bottom was his teacher.
> "I am Miss Jessie Pig," she said.
> She looked just like Grandmother. (17)

Fox on Stage

Several Reading Explorers have told me that James Marshall's *Fox* stories are "just a little bit harder than Henry and Mudge," so I will end this chapter by discussing why this might be so for most readers. The tone of the *Fox* stories is zanier than Henry and Mudge; more characters are involved at one time, and dialogue is a main component of the story telling. Each book has three stories loosely tied to a theme and name of the book title, but the stories are independent of each other. *Fox on Stage* contains three stories about being performers.

In the last story, "Fox on Stage," Fox suggests to his friends that they put on a play when the television set is broken. The challenges to readers in *Fox* stories are the shifting points of view and keeping track of the six named and two unnamed characters who always have something to say. The story develops from their responses to Fox through fast-paced dialogue expressing different points of view.

> "Let's put on a play!" he said.
> "We can charge everyone a dime."
> "We'll get rich!" said Dexter.
> "I'll buy a new car," said Carmen. (36)

In addition to shifts in conversation, there are several twists and turns in the plot that readers must follow to comprehend the story.

1. the problem with the broken TV
2. Fox's great ideas and his friends enthusiastic responses
3. borrowing a book of plays from the library
4. practicing the play
5. making the scenery
6. putting up posters
7. making the costumes

8. getting ready to begin
9. things going wrong during the play and the play being ruined
10. finding out the next day that everyone thought it was the funniest play they had ever seen
11. ending with Fox thinking about his next play

So Many Books, So Little Time

Readers of *Oliver and Amanda* stories also liked the stories about Arthur and his family by Lillian Hoban, such as *Arthur's Birthday Party* and *Arthur's Back to School Day.* Page by page, the Arthur stories provide similar degrees of challenge in vocabulary and sentence syntax as the *Oliver and Amanda* stories, but Arthur books contain one story that develops over the entire book, without chapter breaks. This characteristic is helpful in getting readers to develop their ability to follow a sequence of events in which each new event is a result of the previous event. Also, part of growing as a reader is following and sustaining interest in a plot that develops as much from interior thoughts and feelings as it does from significant events. For example, *Oliver Pig at School* is more than 1,300 words long, and the four chapters of the book are devoted to just one day at school. If a reader is not interested in a subject, it makes no difference if the words are easy for him to read, or if she can understand the meaning of each of the sentences in the book.

Reading Explorers who liked stories of friendship and camaraderie, such as the *Addie and Max* books, went on to enjoy the *Beezy* books, written by Megan McDonald and illustrated by Nancy Poydar. Hurricanes, honeybees, and baseball games are just a few of the stories about Beezy, her friends Merlin and Sarafina, her Gran, and their neighbor Mr. Gumm. Some readers have discovered mystery and magic through *Detective Dinosaur,* written by James Skofield and illustrated by R.W. Alley, *Aunt Eater Loves a Mystery* by Doug Cushman, and *Wizard and Wart,* written by Janice Lee Smith and illustrated by Paul Meisel. A favorite of many is *Rollo and Tweedy and the Ghost at Dougal Castle* by Laura Jean Allen, popular in part because of its exotic setting (exotic for desert dwellers, that is) in a castle in Scotland. Others have relished each new adventure of *Nate the Great,* written by Marjorie Weinman Sharmat and illustrated by Marc Simont.

Reading Explorers who prefer funny books devoured the fast-paced *Fox* books. They chuckled at the gentle, self-mocking humor in *A Friend for Dragon* and the other *Dragon* books by Dav Pilkey. They loved the word play in Bernard Wiseman's *Morris Goes to School* and *Morris the Moose.* They laughed and laughed at *Amelia Bedelia*'s obliviousness to her own misunderstandings of common words. Who else but Peggy Parish's well-loved housekeeper would assume that instructions to "change the towels in the guest bathroom" would mean to physically change them in some manner, and proceed to take scissors and snip a little here and there? Who else but Amelia Bedelia would interpret "dust the furniture" as sprinkling dusting powder *on* the furniture? The comical antics of *The Golly Sisters,* written by Betsy Byars and illustrated by Sue Truesdell, were must-reads for many. There are three books in this series: *Hooray for the Golly Sisters, The Golly Sisters Go West,* and *The Golly Sisters Ride Again.* More than any other books, these three were constantly passed around, with one person telling the next to "read this book!"

Reading Explorers who read these books were also amazed to discover that more and more of the library's other books were within their reach as readers. Books such as *Froggy Goes to School* and the other *Froggy* stories, written by Jonathan London, were impossible to keep on the shelves. Some were surprised to discover that Frank Asch's books about Bear that they had listened to their teachers read aloud when they were in kindergarten and first grade, such as *Bear Shadow* and *Happy Birthday, Moon,* were now just right for independent reading.

Summary

Readers who can read the books I have written about have many choices at their fingertips. I discovered that they are developing preferences for particular styles of writing and characters. I also came to realize how important it is not to rush readers into "harder" books simply because they seem capable of handling more complex text. The Reading Explorers read widely from books with similar challenges and resisted my attempts to put longer books in their hands. They particularly liked books in series, which is not so different from adults, who have favorite authors and like to read about the same characters in new situations. After working with two classes of Reading Explorers, I also came to realize how important my role, and the role of their teachers, is in introducing them to books they might not otherwise notice. One day I brought a review copy of Lillian Hoban's most recent *Arthur* book, *Arthur's Birthday Party,* to a meeting. Until that time, the *Arthur* books were not widely read by this class, but once they were given the privilege of seeing a brand new book "hot off the press," they started reading every single book in the series on the library shelves.

Closing Points

KEEP IN MIND . . . Reading is more than just knowing the words and understanding the meaning of individual sentences.

Transitional readers are readers who no longer need to attend closely to print, except to solve for unknown words. Consequently, they can shift their attention to longer, more interesting stories and nonfiction books. Transitional readers can:

- read many easy books on their own
- recognize many words in print
- figure out many of the words they do not recognize
- enter imaginary literary worlds

Teachers and librarians can support transitional readers by:
- setting aside a small collection of books they can read on their own
- showing them how to find other books they can read in school and classroom libraries
- not rushing them into harder books before they are ready
- encouraging them to try something new
- giving them abundant opportunities to read and talk with their friends about their reading

Characteristics of transitional texts include:
- stories with straightforward, linear plots
- narrative structures readers can quickly see
- words readers usually use in their speaking vocabularies
- characters (human or animal) who act like "real people"
- memorable characters
- nonfiction narratives that carefully help readers link new information with prior knowledge

Bibliography

Children's Literature Books

One Problem to Solve

1. *Who's Afraid of the Dark?* by Crosby Bonsall. An I Can Read Book. Harper-Collins, 1980.

2. *Rex and Lilly Family Time* by Laurie Krasny Brown. Illus. by Marc Brown. A Dino Easy Reader. Little, Brown, 1995.

3. *Catch Me If You Can!* by Bernard Most. A Green Light Reader. Harcourt, 1999.

4. *The Great Race* by David McPhail. Hello Reader! Scholastic, 1997.

5. *Hiccups for Elephant* by James Preller. Illus. by Hans Wilhelm. Hello Reader! Scholastic, 1994.

Time Marches On

1. *A Kiss for Little Bear* by Else Holmelund Minarik. Illus. by Maurice Sendak. An I Can Read Book. HarperCollins, 1996.

2. *One Saturday Afternoon* by Barbara Baker. Illus. by Kate Duke. Dutton, 1999.

3. *Danny and the Dinosaur* by Syd Hoff. An I Can Read Book. HarperCollins, 1986.

4. *Johnny Lion's Book* by Edith Thacher Hurd. Illus. by Clement Hurd. An I Can Read Book. HarperCollins, 1965.

5. *Stars* by Jennifer Dussling. Illus. by Mavis Smith. All Aboard Reading. Grosset & Dunlap, 1996.

The Plot Thickens

1. *Three by the Sea* by Edward Marshall. Illus. by James Marshall. Puffin Easy-to-Read. Puffin Books, 1981.

2. *Owl at Home* by Arnold Lobel. An I Can Read Book. HarperCollins, 1975.

3. *Father Bear Comes Home* by Else Holmelund Minarik. Illus. by Maurice Sendak. An I Can Read Book. HarperCollins, 1987.

4. *Addie's Bad Day* by Joan Robins. Illus. by Sue Truesdell. An I Can Read Book. HarperCollins, 1993.

5. *Johnny Appleseed* by Patricia Demuth. Illus. by Michael Montgomery. All Aboard Reading. Grosset & Dunlap, 1996.

6. *Johnny Appleseed* by Steven Kellogg. Morrow, 1988.

A Plethora of Possibilities

1. *Frog and Toad Are Friends* by Arnold Lobel. An I Can Read Book. HarperCollins, 1970.

2. *Henry and Mudge Take the Big Test* by Cynthia Rylant. Illus. by Suçie Stevenson. Ready-to-Read. Simon & Schuster, 1991.

3. *Henry and Mudge and the Happy Cat* by Cynthia Rylant. Illus. by Suçie Stevenson. Ready-to-Read. Simon & Schuster, 1990.

4. *Snakes* by Patricia Demuth. Illus. by Judith Moffatt. All Aboard Reading. Grosset & Dunlap, 1993.

5. *Oliver Pig at School* by Jean Van Leeuwen. Illus. by Ann Schweninger. Puffin Easy-to-Read, 1990.

6. *Growing Ideas (Meet the Author)* by Jean Van Leeuwen. Richard Owen Publishers, 1998.

7. *Fox on Stage* by James Marshall. Puffin Easy-to-Read. Puffin Books, 1996.

Other Children's Books

1. *Pinky and Rex* books by James Howe. Illus. by Melissa Sweet. Simon & Schuster.

2. *Froggy* books by Jonathan London. Illus by Frank Remkiewicz. Viking.

3. *Arthur* books by Marc Brown. Little Brown.

4. *Little Bear* by Else Holmelund Minarik. Illus. by Maurice Sendak. Harper-Collins, 1957.

5. *The Cat in the Hat* by Dr. Seuss. Random House, 1957.

6. *Hattie and the Fox* by Mem Fox. Illus. by Patricia Mullins. Simon & Schuster, 1987.

7. *Who Took the Farmer's Hat?* by Joan Nodset. Illus. by Fritz Siebel. Harper-Collins, 1963.

8. *Magic School Bus* books by Joanna Cole. Illus. by Bruce Degen. Scholastic.

9. *Old Grizzly* by Joy Cowley. Illus. by Jan van der Voo. Wright Group, 1987.

10. *Cookie's Week* by Cindy Ward. Illus. by Tomie dePaola. Putnam, 1988.

11. *Danny and the Dinosaur Go to Camp* by Syd Hoff. HarperCollins, 1996.

12. *Happy Birthday, Danny and the Dinosaur* by Syd Hoff. HarperCollins, 1997.

13. *One Saturday Morning* by Barbara Baker. Illus. by Kate Duke. Dutton, 1994.

14. *Three Up a Tree* by James Marshall. Puffin, 1985.

15. *Four on the Shore* by Edward Marshall. Illus. by James Marshall. Puffin, 1985.

16. *Addie Meets Max* by Joan Robins. Illus by Sue Truesdell. HarperCollins, 1988.

17. *Addie Runs Away* by Joan Robins. Illus. by Sue Truesdell. HarperCollins, 1989.

18. *The True Tale of Johnny Appleseed* by Margaret Hodges. Illus. by Kimberly Bulcken Root. Holiday House, 1997.

19. *Johnny Appleseed* by Reeve Lindbergh. Illus. by Kathy Jakobsen. Little Brown, 1990.

20. *Fox Outfoxed* by James Marshall. Puffin, 1996.

21. *Sweets and Treats: Dessert Poems* by Bobbye Goldstein. Illus. by Kathy Couri. Hyperion, 1998.

22. *Frog and Toad Together* by Arnold Lobel. HarperCollins, 1971.

23. *Frog and Toad All Year* by Arnold Lobel. HarperCollins, 1976.

24. *Days with Frog and Toad* by Arnold Lobel. HarperCollins, 1979.

25. *Arthur's Back to School Day* by Lillian Hoban. HarperCollins, 1996.

26. *Arthur's Birthday Party* by Lillian Hoban. HarperCollins, 1999.

27. *Beezy* books by Megan McDonald. Illus. by Nancy Poydar. Orchard Books, 1997.

28. *Detective Dinosaur* by James Skofield. Illus. by R. W. Alley. HarperCollins, 1996.

29. *Aunt Eater Loves a Mystery* by Doug Cushman. HarperCollins, 1987.

30. *Wizard and Wart* by Janice Lee Smith. Illus. by Paul Meisel. HarperCollins, 1994.

31. *Rollo and Tweedy and the Ghost at Dougal Castle* by Laura Jean Allen. HarperCollins, 1992.

32. *Nate the Great* books by Marjorie Weinman Sharmat. Illus. by Marc Simont. Dell Yearling.

33. *A Friend for Dragon* by Dav Pilkey. Orchard Books, 1991.

34. *Morris Goes to School* by Bernard Wiseman. HarperCollins, 1970.

35. *Morris the Moose* by Bernard Wiseman. HarperCollins, 1989.

36. *Amelia Bedelia* books by Peggy Parish. Illus. by Fritz Siebel and Wallace Tripp. HarperCollins.

37. *The Golly Sisters Go West* by Betsy Byars. Illus. by Sue Truesdell. Harper-Collins, 1994.

38. *The Golly Sisters Ride Again* by Betsy Byars. Illus. by Sue Truesdell. Harper-Collins, 1985.

39. *Hooray for the Golly Sisters* by Betsy Byars. Illus. by Sue Truesdell. Harper-Collins, 1992.

40. *Froggy Goes to School* by Jonathan London. Illus. by Frank Remkiewicz. Viking, 1996.

41. *Bear Shadow* by Frank Asch. Simon & Schuster, 1985.

42. *Happy Birthday, Moon* by Frank Asch. Simon & Schuster, 1982.

6

Literary Genres for Proficient Readers

In the previous chapter, I wrote about small chapter books for transitional readers, beginning with stories shaped by a single problem, and concluding with books having well-developed plots. In this chapter, I write about books for proficient readers, who can read almost any book written for children their age. The dictionary uses words like *expert* and *adept* to define *proficiency*. Proficient readers are highly independent readers who read with a deep level of understanding. They can talk about what they are reading by summarizing a story, without giving a detailed description of the plot. I am reminded of Carl, who one day told the other Reading Explorers that he was tired of hearing them talk about everything that happened in a book; he just wanted to hear what a book was about. Carl had become a proficient reader who only wanted to find out if a book was interesting enough for him to read himself.

Nancy was another Reading Explorer who became a proficient reader near the end of second grade. She is the student I wrote about in Chapter 3 who, early in the school year, read *Poppleton and His Friends,* but told me that *Bear's Hiccups* had "too many hard words." At the end of the school year, I asked her if she would try reading *Bear's Hiccups* one more time. This time, she was engrossed in the story. When she came to words she had never heard before, such as *wilted* and *quivered,* she could sound them out, but had to ask me what they meant. Our side conversations about the meanings of words did not interfere with her understanding or enjoyment of the story. Marina, one of the students who read the frog books I wrote about in Chapter 3, was another proficient reader. She could read any book I gave her, and she often stopped reading to reflect on what she had just read and relate that information to what she already knew about frogs.

As the Reading Explorers became more proficient readers, their reading preferences became less predictable to me. No one series captured everyone's attention the way *Henry and Mudge* or the *Fox* books had, and I realized their interests had become very diverse. Many discovered they could read Marc Brown's *Arthur* picture books such as *Arthur Lost and Found.* All continued reading widely from the library's collection of picture books, folktales, and a whole array of nonfiction subjects. A few made the leap into longer chapter books, such as *Bunnicula,* while most looked for well-illustrated, but longer books than they had been reading. They read easy books along side difficult books.

Elena, for example, brought her copy of C.S. Lewis' *The Magician's Nephew* to read during several Reading Explorer meetings, but other times, she selected beautifully illustrated picture books such as Eric Carle's *The Very Busy Spider.* And, no matter how advanced James became in his reading, he never gave up his love for Jonathan London's *Froggy* books. He read them over and over, and all year long, there was usually a *Froggy* book in his stack of library books. If we truly wish to nurture children's love of reading, it is very important that we never ask them to give up beloved books.

I also found out, too late, there were some serious gaps in my library collection to meet the needs of the more advanced, second year Reading Explorers. This group loved having multiple copies of books because two or three always wanted to be reading the same book. In contrast to students like Elena and James who confidently forged ahead, others needed extra support and encouragement to extend their reading to more challenging books. One trio of girls, Vicki, Diana, and Marlene, were happiest when I could give them each a copy of a book I encouraged them to read. They found a table by themselves and took turns reading to each other. In this way, they discovered many books they might never have read on their own.

However, my collection of book sets jumped from illustrated series like *Fox* and *Nate the Great,* to short first novels such as *Freckle Juice* by Judy Blume, *Scaredy Dog* by Jane Resh Thomas, and *Dinosaurs Before Dark: A Magic Tree House Book* by Mary Pope Osborne. These are books many of the Reading Explorers were capable of reading, but their preferences were for shorter, abundantly illustrated stories. Although I had single and double copies of the books I write about in this chapter, I think they would have been more adventurous in reading new books if I could have given copies of the same book to four or five children.

Children who can read the books I write about in this chapter are at a critical juncture in their reading lives. They can read longer and longer stretches of text fluently and have large reading vocabularies. They have gotten to know many literary characters, can follow different kinds of story plots, and appreciate small stretches of descriptive writing. Reading comes easily to them and they have a wide selection of books to choose from. Some readers are adventurous risk takers, willing to try books that look different from their old favorites. Others, however, need encouragement from teachers and librarians to continue reading widely, beyond their comfort zones. We need to continually remind ourselves that knowing *how* to read does not make a person a reader.

Some of the books I write about in this chapter are similar in style to those I discussed in the previous chapter, while others take readers into unfamiliar literary territory. Some stories have complex plots with many twists and turns for readers to follow. The characters in some books have unique personalities that influence how they act toward other characters. Sometimes, events of a story happen as a result of decisions made by these characters, so readers must be sensitive to aspects of a character's nature that may not be explained explicitly in print. Some genres of writing, such as historical fiction and fantasy, are challenging to read because they are set in a time or place far from our own. Nonfiction can be difficult for readers who do not have background knowledge about the subject they want to learn about.

As in previous chapters, I have selected a small number of books to write about to demonstrate the wide variety of texts available. Unlike the focus books in Chapters 4 and 5, which covered several levels, those I discuss in this chapter are approximately the same reading level. Consequently, I have grouped them by category or genre. The categories are: stories of family and friends, humorous stories, poetry, and nonfiction. I also created a category called "stories with unique challenges," which includes historical fiction and science fiction. Keep in mind that this is not a comprehensive list, but one to use as a springboard for further exploration. The following chart summarizes features that may be characteristic of some books, but not all books include the same features.

Summary of Text Features

- course of action or plot not readily apparent at the start of the narrative
- well-developed episodes, with increased distance between each event
- characters' interior thoughts and motivations influence the direction of the story
- meaning of many stories is deeper than the surface level of events
- rich literary, descriptive language in stories and poetry
- specialized vocabulary in nonfiction books
- greater variety of words in fiction and nonfiction
- intentional manipulation of language to create humorous effects

(continued)

> **Summary of Text Features (continued)**
>
> - fiction and nonfiction rooted in a particular time or place requires more extensive reader background or prior knowledge
> - illustrations are entertaining and important for the enjoyment of a story
> - illustrations are accurate, detailed, and clearly labeled with signs or captions in nonfiction books
> - illustrations are an important source of information in nonfiction books

Stories of Family and Friends

Focus Books

1. *Lionel in the Spring* by Stephen Krensky. Illus. by Susanna Natti. Puffin Easy-to-Read. Puffin Books, 1990.
2. *Frog and Toad Together* by Arnold Lobel. An I Can Read Book. Harper-Collins, 1971.
3. *Gus and Grandpa and Show-and-Tell* by Claudia Mills. Illus. by Catherine Stock. Farrar, Straus and Giroux, 2000.
4. *Edgar Badger's Balloon Day* by Monica Kulling. Illus. by Carol O'Malia. MONDO, 1997.
5. *Little Bear* by Else Holmelund Minarik. Illus. by Maurice Sendak. An I Can Read Book. HarperCollins, 1957.
6. *Pinky and Rex and the School Play* by James Howe. Illus. by Melissa Sweet. Ready-to-Read. Simon & Schuster, 1998.
7. *Alison's Puppy* by Marion Dane Bauer. Illus. by Laurie Spencer. Hyperion Chapters. Hyperion, 1997.

Many Reading Explorers continued to a have strong preference for stories about families and friends, and they liked series books because they could keep reading about their favorite characters. When readers start a book from a familiar series, they begin by entering a world they have visited before. They already know the characters and their personalities, so the readers feel like they are meeting up with old friends.

Lionel in the Spring and *Frog and Toad Together*

Lionel in the Spring is one of a half dozen books about Lionel, his family, and friends. There are four stories in the book—"In the Garden," "The Anniversary," "The Mad Scientist," and "Spring Cleaning." If you skim the book, you will see that it doesn't look much more challenging than the books I discussed near the end of the previous chapter. Remember, in looking at a progression of texts along a gradient, those near each other will be more alike than different with respect to difficulty; the differences are subtle.

For example, let's look more closely at "The Garden," a story of just over 300 words in length. Quickly skimming the text, I only see a handful of words that might be new to readers in print—*imagined, stubborn, scoop,* and *enough,* for example. Even if you toss in a few more, such as *bowling, cucumbers,* and *crowded,* the vocabulary in the story would not intimidate children who have already read books like *Frog and Toad.* The illustrations are colorful and attractive, showing Lionel busy planting his garden. On the first page is a full-color picture of smiling Lionel standing with a rake in his fenced-in garden. The second sentence gives a clue as to the challenge facing Lionel.

> He had big plans. (5)

While adults know that "big plans" are often trimmed along the way, Lionel has only the perspective of youth and unlimited optimism.

> Lionel imagined how much
> the vegetables would grow
> in a few months. (6)

This is not only a grammatically complex sentence; it is one that leaves the reader uncertain about what direction the story will take because, at this point, Lionel is just using his imagination. The next couple of pages show him imagining what everyone in his family could do with all the vegetables he plans on growing. Thus, the direction of the story is conditional, not definite, something readers need to understand or they will miss the humor in the story. After visualizing how the garden could turn out, Lionel starts thinking about all the work a garden requires. Faced with many stubborn weeds to pull, Lionel gradually reduces the number of vegetables he will plant, until he decides to only plant pumpkins; then, pumpkins become one pumpkin. After planting his one pumpkin seed, his father looks outside.

> "I hope you didn't plant too much,"
> said Father.
> "It's easy to get carried away,
> you know." (15)

Experienced readers will catch the irony of Father's statements, but it is easy for young readers to interpret this on a literal level. While no harm will come to readers who miss this element of humor, those who catch it also receive an untaught lesson in how some stories work, a small lesson that may serve a reader well in future years with more complex literature.

If readers of *Lionel in the Spring* had read Arnold Lobel's *Frog and Toad Together,* they would have encountered another untaught lesson in the nature of stories. Some stories go hand in hand. Alert Reading Explorers told me that one of their favorite *Frog and Toad* stories is also called "The Garden." In this one, Toad walks by Frog's house and admires his garden. Frog acknowledges that it is a nice garden, but also one that took a lot of hard work. He gives some seeds to Toad, saying that if he plants them, he "will soon have a garden." Well, Toad, like Lionel, has his own brand of impatience with hard work. He plants the seeds, but when they do not immediately start growing, he shouts at them. Still, when they do not grow, he reads them a story. Finally, they do grow, and when Frog mentions his new garden, Toad's closing comment is enough to make any reader's mouth drop open in amazement. Irony at work!

> "Yes," said Toad,
> "but you were right, Frog.
> It was very hard work." (29)

Gus and Grandpa and Show-and-Tell

The tone of the *Gus and Grandpa* series is more serious than the tone in the *Lionel* books. The six books about Gus and Grandpa focus on their close, loving relationship. Gus is seven and Grandpa seventy, but they share many experiences together. In one, *Gus and Grandpa and Show-and-Tell,* Gus is stumped when his teacher tells her students to bring something to class on Colorado history. When Gus looks around Grandpa's house for a possibility, the perfect idea comes to him when Grandpa says:

> "I've got nothing here
> *but* Colorado history,"
> Grandpa told Gus.
> "I've lived seventy years
> of Colorado history." (31)

Alert readers realize at this point that Gus will take Grandpa to school for show-and-tell. And, this is exactly what happens.

> Grandpa showed them
> his long-ago pictures
> and told them
> his long-ago stories. (45)

Edgar Badger's Balloon Day and *Little Bear*

The *Edgar Badger* books were also popular with Reading Explorers. *Edgar Badger's Balloon Day* is reminiscent of the story "Birthday Soup" in *Little Bear*. In that story, Little Bear knows it is his birthday but cannot find Mother Bear, so he proceeds to make birthday soup for his friends. They are all getting ready to eat birthday soup when Mother Bear suddenly appears with a birthday cake for Little Bear. The story closes simply, with words from Mother Bear.

> "This Birthday Cake is a surprise for you.
> I never did forget your birthday,
> and I never will." (34)

Edgar Badger's tale begins much as Little Bear's, with the main character expecting recognition on his birthday. However, Edgar Badger must work through much more sadness and frustration than Little Bear, because each of his friends stops by his house for a reason, but none of those reasons has anything to do with his birthday; poor Edgar Badger. He checks the calendar to see if he has the date wrong, but no, today is his birthday; poor Edgar Badger.

> "My birthday is today
> and no one knows it."
> Edgar sighed again and slumped
> into a chair. He stared out the
> window. He forgot about lunch.
> He forgot about his afternoon nap.
> He just sat and stared out the
> window. (40)

Alas, all is well that ends well. Suddenly, all of his friends show up at his door laden with bunches of brightly colored balloons, a colorful sign with "Happy Birthday Edgar Badger," and his favorite cake—banana grub. In order to feel connected with this story, readers not only need to understand what happens; they need to be in tune with Edgar Badger's roller coaster of emotions and empathize with his plight. Finally, they need to celebrate the joyous close to the story.

Pinky and Rex and the School Play

Once they had read widely from books like the *Henry and Mudge* and *Fox* books, many Reading Explorers moved into the *Pinky and Rex* series. Far more challenging than other books they read, the *Pinky and Rex* books proved to be a good transition to longer chapter books. Most range from between 2,300 and 2,500 words, quite a lot of reading, which required some students to read a portion of the text, mark their place, and return at a later time. To do this, children must be strong, fluent readers in order to follow the events and pick up the story line when they return to the book. The child-oriented, "slice-of-life" focus of each *Pinky and Rex* book usually hooks readers, who can see themselves or their friends engaged in the same amusements, trials, and tribulations as best friends Pinky and Rex, the main characters. The physical design of the books was comforting for the Reading Explorers, who liked the colorful illustrations on each page.

Pinky and Rex and the School Play is a good example of two characters who cope with an unexpected conflict that jeopardizes their friendship. The story opens with Pinky and Rex talking about tryouts for the school play. Pinky announces he's going to audition because he intends to be an actor when he grows up. Rex, on the other hand, expresses a different point of view.

> "You wouldn't get *me* up
> on a stage in front of all those people,"
> she said. "I'd forget what I was supposed
> to say and make a total fool of myself." (4)

As luck would have it, Rex, without telling Pinky, tries out and is given the lead role. Pinky, however, gets the part of a monkey—a non-speaking part. The resulting rift in their friendship is a powerful theme running throughout the rest of the story.

> Later in class, Pinky wouldn't even
> look at Rex.
> "I'm never going to speak to you
> again," he told her when she tried to join
> him walking home. "You're supposed
> to be my friend!" (10)

Fortunately, they mend their friendship before the play. Rex does a fine job in her lead role, but Pinky does get his chance to shine. During the production, when some of the other children do not respond to their cue and remain frozen in place, Pinky uses monkey antics to get them to move. He also earns the esteem of the director, who asks Pinky to be his assistant in the next school play.

Alison's Puppy

Some Reading Explorers eagerly jumped into short, lightly illustrated chapter books, but others were reluctant to try anything that was not heavily illustrated. Ironically, the language in many of these short chapter books is less complex and easier to read than the language in some of the books labeled "easy readers." Author Bonnie Graves (1998) uses the phrase "first novels" to characterize short chapter books that have more words than pictures, a story with a narrow focus, and a main character readers can easily understand.

Alison's Puppy by Marion Dane Bauer, turned out to be the perfect first novel for Vicki, Diana, and Marlene. Fortunately, I had enough copies for each of them, and they took turns reading the book to each other. Physically, the book looks like the chapter books their older friends were reading, but with larger type and black-and-white illustrations on every page. The story line was easy for them to follow and they liked that the main character was a girl close to their own age. Alison tells her family she wants a puppy for her birthday—more than anything else. Even when her mother and father say "no puppies," Alison still wants a puppy. She looks at all kinds of dogs, wondering how each would be for a pet. She even goes to the library and borrows books about dogs, including *Henry and Mudge*. She imagines having her own Mudge.

> Alison went to the library. "My birthday is coming," she told the librarian. "I want books about dogs. Books I can read myself. Lots of them." (23)

Her longed-for puppy turns out to be a kitten, and gradually her disappointment turns to happiness as she discovers everything her new pet can do. And the kitten's name? She calls him "Puppy"!

Humorous Stories

Focus Books

1. *George and Martha* by James Marshall. Houghton Mifflin, 1972.
2. *Minnie and Moo Go to the Moon* by Denys Cazet. DK, 1998.
3. *Mud Flat Spring* by James Stevenson. Greenwillow, 1999.
4. *Doctor DeSoto* by William Steig. Farrar, Straus and Giroux, 1982.
5. *The True Story of the 3 Little Pigs! by A. Wolf,* as told to Jon Scieszka. Illus. by Lane Smith. Viking, 1989.

The Reading Explorers continued to enjoy books that made them laugh. They had fun with the slapstick, silly humor in books like *Minnie and Moo Go to the Moon,* but they also learned to understand the dry humor in books like *George and Martha* and *Mud Flat Spring*. Additionally, they discovered that picture books once read aloud to them, such as *Doctor De Soto* and *The True Story of the 3 Little Pigs!,* were now easy for them to read independently.

George and Martha

Three series appealed to the Reading Explorers' funny bones. James Marshall, author and illustrator of the *Fox* books, also created the *George and Martha* series. Each book is a collection of little stories, or vignettes, about two hippo friends who always seem to find themselves in ludicrous situations. "The Flying Machine" is the second story in the *George and Martha* book. The scene opens with a picture of George sitting in the basket of a hot air balloon, making the following announcement.

"I'm going to be the first of my species to fly!" said George. (16)

Martha asks the obvious question.

"Then why aren't you flying?" asked Martha. (16)

Thinking that the basket might be too heavy, George gets out. Sure enough, the balloon lifts into the air! Martha consoles him, saying she would rather have him with her than up in the air somewhere. The humor in the *George and Martha* books is subtle because much of it comes from who they are and not what they do, and Marshall's droll pictures of them are as important as the written text in revealing their personalities.

Minnie and Moo Go to the Moon

The humor in Denys Cazet's *Minnie and Moo* series grows out of the antics of the main characters, and is a little easier for readers to follow than the *George and Martha* books. Minnie and Moo are two cows who always manage to get themselves into some very silly situations. In *Minnie and Moo Go to the Moon*, Moo gets a hankering to drive the farmer's tractor. Minnie reminds Moo that cows give milk and farmers drive tractors. After a long discussion, Moo convinces her that the reason the farmer can drive a tractor is because he has boots and a hat. Seeing the farmer's hat and boots on his porch, they put them on and get ready to take off. Finally, they get the tractor going and it crashes, first into the pigsty, then into the chicken coop. The tractor becomes airborne.

"We're flying!" shouted Moo.
"We're in outer space!"
shouted Minnie. (26)

When they crash land, Minnie declares they've landed on the moon. Moo, on the other hand, knows the moon is made of cheese and she does not see any cheese. Minnie contradicts her, noting that the farmer's tractor and hay baler are sitting in a crater, and there are craters on the moon. Next, Minnie declares she sees moon people, or Moonsters. Moo says they are just chickens. The story just keeps getting sillier and sillier, but Minnie and Moo eventually return home, leaving a perplexed farmer to figure out why his tractor is stuck in the pond.

Mud Flat Spring

James Stevenson's quirky *Mud Flat* books, copiously illustrated with his signature black ink and watercolor illustrations, were a hit with one Reading Explorer, who took them home to read to his younger sister. There are seven short stories in *Mud Flat Spring.* Mud Flat is populated with an array of interesting characters. The first opens with two of them, Archie and Lois, tricking Morgan the bear into thinking it is still winter so he will sleep longer, because he is always grumpy when he wakes up. In the next story, Bentley the mole unintentionally uproots the first crocus of spring, and when he puts it back in the ground, he starts telling everyone he planted it. The humor is subtle and sophisticated. His friends, Parker and Zooty, have this to say about Bentley's claim that he planted the flower.

> "Bentley has been down in the dark
> much too long," said Parker.
> "He thinks he plants crocuses,"
> said Zooty.
> "Spring will do Bentley a world
> of good," said Parker. (13)

Doctor De Soto

Doctor De Soto is a mouse and a dentist who serves the animal community well. He has one rule—he will not treat dangerous animals. He and his wife face a dilemma when a fox suffering from a dreadful toothache seeks their help. Reluctantly, Doctor DeSoto agrees to treat the fox. However, once the fox is feeling better, he starts thinking about eating his benefactor. In the meantime, Doctor De Soto has a plan of his own to thwart the fox. This funny story is just right for reading aloud or independent reading by proficient readers.

The True Story of the 3 Little Pigs! by A. Wolf

Children love to hear their favorite folktales with a modern twist; *The True Story of the 3 Little Pigs!* is one of the funniest stories of this kind. Alexander T. Wolf tells the story, and claims he was framed. He just wanted to borrow a cup of sugar from his nearest neighbor, who happened to be a pig. He did not huff and puff to blow the straw house down—he had a terrible cold and sneezed. The house fell down, and the pig was dead, and he could not pass up a perfectly good dinner. Readers know how this one will turn out, but read it over and over because it is so funny.

Stories with Unique Challenges

Focus Books

1. *The Smallest Cow in the World* by Katherine Paterson. Illus. by Jane Clark Brown. An I Can Read Book. HarperCollins, 1991.
2. *The Josefina Story Quilt* by Eleanor Coerr. Illus. by Bruce Degen. An I Can Read Book. HarperCollins, 1986.
3. *Buttons for General Washington* by Peter and Connie Roop. Illus. by Peter Hanson. Carolrhoda, 1986.
4. *Commander Toad in Space* by Jane Yolen. Illus. by Bruce Degen. Putnam, 1980.

The four books I write about in this section feature stories and styles of writing that stretch readers, because each takes readers to an unfamiliar world, asking them to enter a reality very different from their everyday lives. Children often need extra support to follow the action in these stories, and teachers and librarians can help by providing an introduction to a book's setting, characters, and plot. By preparing children in this way, that is, giving them a framework of how to proceed, their attention will be freed to more fully enjoy the story.

The Smallest Cow in the World

Katherine Paterson, one of the most acclaimed writers for children, has written two short chapter books for readers not yet ready for her longer novels. Both are about a boy named Marvin and his family. In the first, *The Smallest Cow in the World,* Marvin's family works on the farm of Mr. Brock. Marvin loves the cow Rosie, even though she is the meanest cow in the world. Then, one day, Mr. Brock decides to sell his farm, and Marvin's dad must look for another job. The whole family will be uprooted, and worse for Marvin, he will miss Rosie the cow. They find a new home, and everyone settles in happily, except Marvin. One day, dad finds drawings on the side of their trailer, Mom's garden is uprooted, and sister May's books are scattered all over the floor. They converge upon Marvin, who tells them, "Rosie did it." He points to a spot in the grass, and claims it is Rosie, the meanest cow in the world. Instead of mocking him, they simply say they thought she was the most beautiful cow in the world. Then, they listen. Sensitive readers will understand that Marvin's words about Rosie are a reflection of his own feelings about his family's move.

> "She didn't want to move,"
> said Marvin.
> "It's no fun to move.
> And she doesn't like being little.
> It's no fun being little. (39)

Next, the conversation turns to how Rosie got so small. Marvin explains that her new owner was a witch whom Rosie did not like. Rosie butted her and pushed her up against the barn wall, so the witch turned her into the smallest cow in the world. With gentle wisdom, Mom suggests that Rosie needs a barn of her own.

> "You are right," said Marvin.
> "Someone might step on her."
> "Or she might pull up
> more flowers," said Mom. (42)
> "She might draw on more walls,"
> said Dad.
> "She might tear more books,"
> said May.
> "Yes," said Marvin.
> "She is very mean." (43)

Marvin is happy when Dad makes Rosie a barn. Then there is a new problem, because Marvin plays with her all summer. When Mom suggests that he leave Rosie home when he starts school, he says he will take her so she can become the smartest cow in the world. He does, and all the children taunt him. Jenny sticks up for him and tells everyone he has a great imagination. That gives May the idea to tell Marvin that Rosie can't go to school any more because she's going to have a calf. He then makes sure that everyone will take care of her and not harm her, and he is given assurances that if they ever move again, Rosie will go with them.

The Josefina Story Quilt and Buttons for General Washington

The Josefina Story Quilt provides an artful entry into the world of historical fiction. The theme of steadfast love is one that is found in many of the world's stories. In this case, the setting is somewhere in the eastern United States in 1850, as a young girl, Faith, is about to leave with her family to travel by wagon train to California. While excited about the adventure, Faith cannot bear to leave her pet hen Josefina behind, but her father is adamant that there is no room for an old hen who can no longer lay eggs. Finally, on the day of the journey, he relents, and Faith promises there will be no trouble from Josefina. Besides keeping Josefina calm, Faith's job on the journey is to make patchwork quilt squares for remembering their adventures.

Woven throughout the story is factual information about the rigors of wagon train travel. Adventure and emotions are important aspects of *The Josefina Story Quilt,* and readers can see themselves in Faith, the unexpected heroism of an old hen, and the recording and storing of memories from remnants of cloth and imagination.

While *The Josefina Story Quilt* is a story grounded in an era of American history, the events are not linked to a specific time or place. *Buttons for General Washington*, on the other hand, is a retelling in story form of documented events from the American Revolution. According to an authors' note, the Darragh family of Philadelphia served as spies for General Washington. In this story, fourteen-year-old John carries a message to the General hidden in his coat buttons. The text is slightly longer than *The Josefina Story Quilt*, but presents more challenges for the readers.

A reader needs minimal knowledge of wagon trains traveling west to follow the plot of *The Josefina Story Quilt*, and to understand and empathize with Faith's passion for her pet hen and her determination to have the hen go with them on their journey. The details of the historical setting can be acquired and understood during the reading. On the other hand, readers of *Buttons for General Washington* would have a difficult time with reading without prior knowledge of the American Revolution. While the sentences are only slightly longer, and the vocabulary not appreciably harder, the structure and dialogue of *Buttons for General Washington* make it more challenging for a reader to grasp.

The opening of *The Josefina Story Quilt* sets the stage for the entire narrative, telling the reader everything needed to follow the action of the story, in thirty-three words.

> It was May 1850.
> Father was excited.
> They were going to California
> in a covered wagon.
> "Please," Faith asked Ma,
> "can I take Josefina?" (5)
> Josefina was her pet hen and Faith loved her. (6)

In contrast, the first thirty-three words of *Buttons for General Washington* are likely to leave the inexperienced reader confused about the purpose of the story. The first sixty-one words establish the direction of the narrative, but they are in the form of a conversation among three people, a form of dialogue that can be hard for readers to follow. An author's note that precedes the story provides the essential information about the American and British sides and the identity of Generals Howe and Washington, but the writing in the note is more complex than the writing in the story.

> "Are any soldiers in the street, John?"
> his mother asked.
> "Only the guard at General Howe's
> headquarters," John answered.
> "Remember, John.

Keep away from the British soldiers,"
his mother said.
"And go the way I told thee."
"But I know a faster way,"
John said.
"Do as thy mother asks,"
his father said.
"She has sent messages to
General Washington before." (6)

The dialogue among these three people does not specifically tell the reader what to expect. The significance of their words is not immediately made clear, but the reader must be able to recognize that something secretive and dangerous is about to take place. John is described as being nervous and in a hurry, but the reasons are implied. Two pages (8–9) of writing describe the preparations of the buttons, but the reason is not made explicit until the end of page 9. "Secret messages for General Washington were hidden in those holes." Suspense builds up in small increments—warnings about avoiding British guards, the consequence of prison if caught, that friends could be for the British side. There are twists and turns to the plot, and, in spite of reading words easily understood, it is not always easy to understand the significance of what is happening. When John is captured, readers don't find out for several pages that he is being taken to an American camp, and is safe.

Commander Toad in Space

Jane Yolen's *Commander Toad* stories give readers an entertaining introduction to the world of science fiction. As the titles indicate, the characters in the *Commander Toad* books are toads. Their names, however, have their roots in popular culture. Commander Toad's ship is called the "Star Warts," and his crew consists of Mr. Hop, Lieutenant Lily, and Jake Skyjumper. On their first adventure, *Commander Toad in Space,* they discover a brand new planet in their spaceship screen, so they prepare to take their space skimmer to explore it. When a computer scan reveals the destination planet is made up of water, Commander Toad has a perfect solution—an inflatable lily pad. Jane Yolen poetically describes the descent of the sky skimmer to the unknown planet.

It floats down
light as milkweed fluff,
noiseless as a feather in the wind.
It hovers over
the watery world. (19)

One characteristic of science fiction is a surprise encounter with a fierce adversary. When the crew lands, they hear a humming sound. That sound grows into a buzz and then a roar.

> "I AM DEEP WADER,"
> says the roar.
> "AND THIS PLANET
> BELONGS TO ME!" (28)

For a short while, Deep Wader continues his territorial display, but then all is quiet. Tension builds, but Yolen gives readers—and her characters—a brief time to relax and gather their wits. Deep Wader disappears and all is quiet, for a while. The following three sentences indicate why the act of reading is much more than a matter of word recognition. In the context of the story, these words create a mood of tension and anticipation.

> And now it is silent.
> Too silent.
> The silence is fear. (32)

Experienced readers know this silence will be followed by a battle. If we were discussing a complex work of science fiction or fantasy intended for older readers, it would be difficult to predict the outcome. However, in a work for younger children, it is likely the main characters will triumph in the end. Sure enough, there is a confrontation between Deep Wader and the space crew, and in another twist of the plot, the sky skimmer falls off the lily pad and sinks into the water. All ends well, thanks to a clever device. Commander Toad surprises his crew with a candle with a flame that cannot blow out. He uses it to heat up the air of the lily pad, causing it to rise like a hot air balloon, taking it to the safety of the Star Warts.

The *Commander Toad* books are also filled with humorous turns of phrase that readers find immensely funny. When Commander Toad tells Deep Wader that his crew "came in peace," Deep Wader's response is, "I'd like you better in pieces" (57). The answer to a riddle about a monster's favorite ballet is "Swamp Lake," and Lieutenant Lily once acted in a play called "Warts and Peace" (51–52).

Poetry

Focus Books

1. *Dinosaur Dinner (With a Slice of Alligator Pie)* by Dennis Lee. Selected by Jack Prelutsky. Illus. by Debbie Tilley. Knopf, 1999.
2. *Sweets and Treats: Dessert Poems.* Compiled by Bobbye Goldstein. Illus. by Kathy Couri. Hyperion Chapters. Hyperion, 1998.

3. *Never Take a Pig to Lunch and Other Poems About the Fun of Eating.* Selected and illustrated by Nadine Bernard Westcott. Orchard, 1995.

4. *Splish Splash* by Joan Bransfield Graham. Illus. by Steve Scott. Houghton Mifflin, 1994.

5. *Flicker Flash* by Joan Bransfield Graham. Illus. by Nancy Davis. Houghton Mifflin, 1999.

6. *Antarctic Antics: A Book of Penguin Poems* by Judy Sierra. Illus. by Jose Areugo and Ariane Dewey. Harcourt, 1998.

7. *Beast Feast: Poems and Paintings* by Douglas Florian. Harcourt, 1994.

8. *The Llama Who Had No Pajama: 100 Favorite Poems* by Mary Ann Hoberman. Illus. by Betty Fraser. Harcourt, 1998.

9. *Little Dog Poems* by Kristine O'Connell George. Illus. by June Otani. Clarion, 1999.

10. *The Dragons Are Singing Tonight* by Jack Prelutsky. Illus. by Peter Sis. Greenwillow, 1993.

11. *Blast Off! Poems About Space.* Selected by Lee Bennett Hopkins. Illus. by Melissa Sweet. An I Can Read Book. HarperCollins, 1995.

12. *Sports! Sports! Sports!: A Poetry Collection.* Selected by Lee Bennett Hopkins. Illus. by Brian Floca. An I Can Read Book. HarperCollins, 1999.

13. *Nathaniel Talking* by Eloise Greenfield. Illus. by Jan Spivey Gilchrist. Black Butterfly Books, 1988.

14. *It's Raining Laughter* by Nikki Grimes. Photos by Myles C. Pinkney. Dial, 1997.

15. *Gathering the Sun: An Alphabet in Spanish and English* by Alma Flor Ada. English translation by Rosa Zubizarreta. Illus. by Simón Silva. Lothrop, Lee and Shepard, 1997.

16. *Laughing Tomatoes and Other Spring Poems/Jitomates risueños y otros poemas de primavera* by Francisco X. Alarcón. Illus. by Maya Christina Gonzalez. Children's Book Press, 1997.

17. *Confetti: Poems for Children* by Pat Mora. Illus. by Enrique O. Sanchez. Lee & Low, 1996.

In addition to the Reading Explorers, a group of eight second graders from another class met with me weekly to read and talk about books. They wanted to read some of the library's poetry books, and they decided to call themselves the Poetry Stars. At first, they read from the selection of books I keep on a poetry table in the library, but gradually they became more adventurous and moved to the library's main poetry collection. Michael Opitz and Tim Rasinski (1998) recommend the reading aloud of poetry as one way for children to expand their vocabularies and increase their reading fluency. Poetry can be difficult for readers to understand because the language of poetry is compact, and poets strive to use interesting and unusual words to create memorable images. When working with both groups of students, I found that their tastes in stories carried over to poetry—they all liked poems that made them laugh.

The books I write about in this section are filled with poems that children of all ages take pleasure in listening to, whether or not they can read them independently. At the beginning of one school year, I taught all of my preschool through second grade students the words to Dennis Lee's poem "Alligator Pie." While many of the second graders could read the poem independently or with assistance, all of the children learned all three verses from memory and had a rollicking time chanting it out loud with their classmates. Poetry should not be reserved just for children to read on their own, but should be read aloud to them everyday for the sheer pleasure. As with every other group of books I have written about, I only have space to include a sampling of wonderful poetry for primary grade children. Use this list as a springboard for making more discoveries.

I met with the Poetry Stars for about an hour each week. They began by choosing a book and reading alone or with a friend or two. Next, they chose one poem to record and illustrate in their poetry journals (giving proper credit to the poet and the book). Each session closed with reading a favorite poem out loud, individually or in a group. Usually, this was the time the students enjoyed most, and their laughter filled the library for a little while every Thursday morning. By far, their favorite poetry book was *Dinosaur Dinner (With a Slice of Alligator Pie)*, a collection of poems by Canadian poet Dennis Lee, illustrated by Debbie Tilley, and selected by Jack Prelutsky. The poems are wacky and the rhythms bouncy, an irresistible combination for getting everyone to join in and chant along. Anna Banana, Big Bad Billy, Little Miss Dimble, Mabel, and Tony Baloney are characters in some of the poems they liked best—not names of the Poetry Stars.

Several other poetry collections tickled the funnybones of Poetry Stars and Reading Explorers alike. Bobbye Goldstein's collection of dessert poems called *Sweets and Treats*, illustrated by Kathy Couri, includes poems by noted poets, such as X. J. Kennedy, Karla Kuskin, Eve Merriam, Jack Prelutsky, and Shel Silverstein. There are poems about fruit, ice cream, cookies, candy, and cake. Another popular collection of funny poems about food is Nadine Bernard Westcott's *Never Take a Pig to Lunch and Other Poems About the Fun of Eating*. The students quickly recognized Westcott's zany style of illustration because, as kindergartners, they had developed a love for her illustrated versions of *The Lady with the Alligator Purse, I Know an Old Lady Who Swallowed a Fly,* and *Peanut Butter and Jelly: A Play Rhyme*. Like *Sweets and Treats, Never*

Take a Pig to Lunch is a compilation of the works of many poets. Included is one of my all time favorite poems, "O Sliver of Liver" by Myra Cohn Livingston. A wordsmith beyond compare, Livingston painted a picture in words to explain why so many people dislike liver.

Another book that consistently held the attention of Poetry Stars and Reading Explorers is Joan Bransfield Graham's *Splish Splash*, a collection of twenty-one poems she wrote celebrating water in its various forms. The opening poem is entitled, "Water." Others include: "Crocodile Tears," "Waterfall," "Ice Cubes," "Rain," and "River." Inseparable from the language of the poems is the graphic artistry of Steve Scott, who uses bold colors and different fonts to shape the words into pictures. For example, he used red, black, and white to illustrate the poem "Steam." A black pot sits on top of a burner of an electric stove, filled with words about water turning to vapor. The background color, representing the wall behind the stove, is solid red. Rising vertically from the pot are the letters that form the word *steam*. Students loved saying the words out loud and delighted in studying their arrangement on the page. They were also happy to see a new book of picture poetry by Joan Bransfield Graham, *Flicker Flash*, a collection of poems about light, illustrated by Nancy Davis.

Books about animals, whether fact or fiction, have always been popular with Tully kids; many delighted in discovering books of animal poetry. Judy Sierra's *Antarctic Antics: A Book of Penguin Poems* was a must read for many. Another was Douglas Florian's *Beast Feast*, where they read about animals as diverse as chameleons, barracudas, and boas. Florian, who illustrates his poetry with his own watercolor paintings, has created several other collections of animal poems. Animals are also the subject of many of Mary Ann Hoberman's poems in *The Llama Who Had No Pajama*, illustrated by Betty Fraser. Poet Kristine O'Connell George wrote a whole collection of poems about her own little dog for the book *Little Dog Poems*, illustrated by June Otani.

Dragons are celebrated in Jack Prelutsky's *The Dragons Are Singing Tonight*, illustrated by Peter Sis, a book that captivated Gilbert's attention for several weeks. I was particularly impressed with his tenacity in working through the poem "My Dragon Wasn't Feeling Good," filled with words he had never heard before, such as *fizzle, pallid,* and *phosphorous,* as well as words he knew the meaning of, but had never seen in print, such as *specialist, pulse,* and *turpentine*. I helped by telling him words he had questions about. When he already knew the meaning of a word, I read it aloud and drew his attention to the spelling and parts of the word. With unknown words, we first talked about their meaning, and then focused on their spelling. Watching Gilbert dive into new poems week after week was pure delight for me, because each new encounter was an adventure for him, and he always chose something different from the rest of the group.

The Poetry Stars and Reading Explorers also liked several of poet and anthologist Lee Bennett Hopkins' collections for newer readers, which include the poems of many poets. By far, the favorite of these was *Sports! Sports! Sports!*, illustrated by Brian Floca. *Blast Off! Poems About Space*, illustrated by Melissa Sweet, also attracted a cadre of readers. Popular, too, were books of poetry about the lives of other children, such as Eloise Greenfield's *Nathaniel Talking*, illustrated by Jan Spivey Gilchrist. Miles Pinkney's delightful photographs of children became the inspiration for Nikki Grimes' poems in *It's Raining Laughter*, a joyous celebration of the many faces of childhood.

Several of the Poetry Stars could read both English and Spanish, and they especially enjoyed reading from bilingual poetry collections. Alma Flor Ada celebrates the lives of farmworkers and the bounty of the harvest in *Gathering the Sun: An Alphabet in Spanish and English*, translated by Rosa Zubizarreta and illustrated by Simón Silva. Poet Francisco X. Alarcón writes exuberantly about a whole array of life experiences in *Laughing Tomatoes and Other Spring Poems/Jitomates risueños y otros poemas de primavera*, illustrated with the vibrant, colorful paintings of Maya Christina Gonzalez. The poems in Pat Mora's book *Confetti*, illustrated by Enrique O. Sanchez, are written in English, but sprinkled with words in Spanish, which are translated at the end of the book.

Nonfiction

Focus Books

1. *The Magic School Bus at the Waterworks* by Joanna Cole. Illus. by Bruce Degen. Scholastic, 1986.
2. *The Emperor's Egg* by Martin Jenkins. Illus. by Jane Chapman. Candlewick, 1999.
3. *Polar Bears* by Sarah Palmer. Sea Mammal Discovery Library. Rourke, 1989.
4. *Polar Bears* by Dorothy Hinshaw Patent. Photos by William Muñoz. A Carolrhoda Nature Watch Picture Book. Carolrhoda, 2000.
5. *Ice Bear and Little Fox* by Jonathan London. Illus. by Daniel San Souci. Dutton, 1998.
6. *Barrio: José's Neighborhood* by George Ancona. Harcourt Brace, 1998.
7. *Celebrating Chinese New Year* by Diane Hoyt-Goldsmith. Photos by Lawrence Midgale. Holiday House, 1998.
8. *I Am Rosa Parks* by Rosa Parks, with Jim Haskins. Illus. by Wil Clay. Puffin Easy-to-Read. Penguin Putnam, 1997.

Students who can read the books I write about in this chapter have large reading vocabularies and strong word-analysis skills. They read fluently; they are able to link ideas from several paragraphs together to comprehend the message in the written text. They consult pictures, diagrams, or other visual information to get at the meaning of the text before them. Like Gilbert, who doggedly worked his way through Jack Prelutsky's poem "My Dragon Wasn't Feeling Good," they are not deterred by a few unknown words. They are capable of taking in new information and incorporating it into the bigger picture of the subject they are working on. Nevertheless, these readers still require the support of carefully designed texts and visual materials. The world of nonfiction for children is just as diverse as fiction, so I will highlight books that use different styles of writing and art to present information.

The Magic School Bus at the Waterworks

The Reading Explorers, like most Tully students, were avid fans of Joanna Cole's and Bruce Degen's *The Magic School Bus* books. I have multiple copies of each title in English and Spanish, and they occupy a shelf in the library that is highly visible from all directions. Students of all ages borrow them. They are designed for many levels of readers, though, in order to read and comprehend the main narrative on their own, students must be able to read quickly and fluently enough to manage large stretches of text without becoming confused. However, the format of *The Magic School Bus* books provides many entry points for readers of differing abilities to enjoy and learn from them. The pictures are informative; some characters' comments are printed in speech bubbles; brief facts about the subject are printed on composition paper and placed in the corners of some pages; some information is recorded briefly onto charts made by the students; a longer narrative, with more detailed information, runs throughout the book; the author adds special notes at the end for interested readers.

The Magic School Bus at the Waterworks was the first in this unique series of science books. Unlike the old adage, "You can't tell a book by its cover," the covers of children's books often reveal important information about what readers will find inside. On the cover of this book is a picture of the famous school bus, getting ready to go over a dam. Ms. Frizzle and her students are dressed in swimsuits and scuba gear. Remember how many times I have said that young children like books that make them laugh? Well, they start to laugh even before they open the book. Inside, readers see a lot of activity—Ms. Frizzle and the magic school bus head for the clouds, and she tells them to get out of the bus. They shrink to the size of raindrops and start on a long journey that takes them through the cycle of water flow that eventually returns them to the faucet in the girls' bathroom at school.

Children who cannot read the text learn something about the water cycle by following the narrative developed through the illustrations. Those able to read only a little bit can read some of the speech bubbles coming from some of the characters' mouths. "We can't get through." "We'll be stuck in the waterworks forever!" (24). More advanced readers will be able to read the water facts written on composition paper and posted in the corners of some pages.

WATER FACT #7

by Molly

<u>Clear</u> water is not
always <u>clean</u> water.
It may still contain
disease germs
that can make
you sick. (26)

Still other readers will be able to work their way through all the bits and pieces in the text and illustrations. Some of the language of the text is densely packed with high content words and ideas. Notice how the following information on the water purification system complements and extends Water Fact #7.

In the pipe from the filter
to a storage tank, a chemical called
chlorine was added to the water.
Chlorine kills any remaining disease germs. (26)

Finally, on the last two pages of the book are some notes from the author, "for serious students only," to help them sort out the jokes from the facts. Savvy readers find the humor in these notes. They learn that plants do not have hands, that a school bus cannot rise into the air, and that children cannot shrink and enter raindrops.

The Emperor's Egg

When I first brought my copy of *The Emperor's Egg* to Tully, so many students and teachers wanted to borrow it that I was afraid I might never see it again! (The library now has its own copy.) I wasn't worried that someone would add it to their own book collection, but that so many people would want it, I wouldn't have it back in time to introduce it to my two third-grade habitat study groups. Fortunately, this was not the case, and I read it aloud to both groups.

This beautifully illustrated picture book frames factual information about the development of an emperor penguin, from egg to chick, within a lively, entertaining narrative. As soon as I would finish reading the text on a double-page spread, students would jump in with questions or comments; as soon as I started the next page, the writer answered their questions. As a teacher and librarian, I was grateful for the opening paragraph.

> Down at the very bottom of the
> world, there's a huge island that's
> almost completely covered in snow
> and ice. It's called Antarctica, and
> its the coldest, windiest place
> on Earth. (6)

The reason I appreciate this introduction is that I have known many students who confuse the poles, and who think penguins and polar bears live in the same place! I start reading the book with a globe next to me, and before continuing, I ask students to show me Antarctica. Two-thirds of the first double-page spread shows this landscape, with a small figure in the distance. The text says:

> But wait . . .
> what's that shape over there?
>   It can't be.
>   Yes! (6)

This book is so much fun to read aloud because the reader can be dramatic, and the listeners love to jump in. All the kids yelled, "Yes!" with me, and before I could turn the page, they yelled, "It's a penguin!" They were right. That's what the words say at the top of the next page. My students already knew that the male penguin sits on the egg while the mother goes off to sea in search of food, so they felt quite smart as I read aloud. Most of them had also read Judy Sierra's book of penguin poems, *Antarctic Antics,* and some remembered the poem "My Father's Feet," which tells of a baby penguin keeping warm under his father's feet.

They loved how the author gave them information, but made them laugh at the same time. On page 9, the artist painted a full-page portrait of the father penguin, with his back to the reader, protecting his egg. The text says:

> He didn't lay it himself, of course. (9)

By itself, that sentence looks ordinary, but in the context of the book and in the company of a group of children, it is very funny! In addition to the main narrative, author Jenkins, a conservation biologist, has also included more facts about the emperor penguin, printed in a smaller typeface and different font than the rest of the text. For example:

> Female Emperor penguins lay one egg in May or June,
> which is the beginning of winter in Antarctica. (15)

Polar Bears (Palmer); *Polar Bears* (Patent); *Ice Bear and Little Fox*

Books written in the style of *The Emperor's Egg* engage readers by putting them right in the middle of the action. Sometimes, however, readers want facts to be immediately accessible to them. The format of Sarah Palmer's book *Polar Bears* is similar to Marcia Freeman's book *Polar Bears,* which I wrote about in Chapter 4. It has a table of contents, an index, and a glossary. Every double-page spread has text on one page and a color photograph on the other. Thus, in addition to learning about the subject at hand, readers receive clear signals about how the information is organized, an "untaught lesson" that will support their access to other similar books in the future. Sarah Palmer's *Polar Bears* is one of many books published by Rourke that have helped Tully second and third graders gather information for animal reports.

Each subject covered in the book has its own title, in child-friendly words, such as: How They Look, Where They Live, and What They Eat. Each section is organized like a chapter, but is short enough to fit on half a page. Notice how the following two sentences provide a simple, but vivid description of a polar bear's fur.

> Polar bears are covered in thick, creamy white
> fur. This fur keeps them warm and gives them
> good **camouflage** in the snowy landscape. (6)

The photograph next to this text shows a polar bear lying down. The caption describes the image and also supports the information in the main text.

> Well camouflaged in the snow, this
> polar bear lies down to rest. (6)

Books that are more challenging than this one provide more detail and used more specialized vocabulary. To illustrate, I will quote from a paragraph in Dorothy Hinshaw Patent's book *Polar Bears.* The text of this book would be too difficult for children reading at the level of books I write about in this chapter, but I include it to show how two texts that are organized in a similar way can provide different degrees of challenge for readers. Like Sarah Palmer's book, this one is organized in to several chapters. However, each of the chapters in Patent's book is several pages long. The title of the chapter that corresponds to Palmer's "What They Look Like" is called "Physical Characteristics." Note how the sentences that roughly correspond to Palmer's text use a more varied and specialized vocabulary, which allows for a more detailed description. Note, also, the more complex sentence structures in this text.

> Polar bears are suited for their life in
> the cold, icy North in many ways. The
> polar bear has a thick coat of fur, with
> soft, dense underfur and long, coarse
> **guard hairs.** The guard hairs are hollow,
> which helps insulate, or protect, the bear
> from the cold. (17)

Teachers and librarians are wise to give young researchers books from a range of levels. If a subject is new to a student, an easy book can provide a quick overview of the subject to support further searching. Texts written at the student's approximate reading level are likely to be the most helpful, but such books can also provide a frame of reference to help them understand more challenging texts. Well-chosen fiction can also enhance a student's understanding of a subject. Take for example, Jonathan London's picture book *Ice Bear and Little Fox.* The characters are given names and the narrative is fictionalized, but readers come away with an emotional connection to their lives. To illustrate, read the following sentence from Sarah Palmer's book *Polar Bears.*

> Polar bears **stalk** seals quietly and carefully. (14)

Now, compare that sentence with the dramatic, poetic language from *Ice Bear and Little Fox.*

> Downwind, he waits and waits,
> flat to the ice—his patience matched
> by the young fox, who curls up
> in a hollow scooped out of snow.
> Floes crack, hours pass.

Each book contributes to the readers' knowledge and understanding of polar bears, but in different ways. One provides factual information in the form of written text and photographs; the other uses facts to create a dramatic scene, illustrated with panoramic paintings that put the reader close to the action. Additionally, author London includes a lengthy glossary of terms at the beginning of the book.

Barrio: José's Neighborhood and Celebrating Chinese New Year

There are many splendid books combining text and photographs that show contemporary children and adults celebrating their cultures through their daily lives and traditional festivities. Among writer and photographer George Ancona's many books is *Barrio: José's Neighborhood,* a photographic essay about many of the people who live in San Francisco's Mission District. Glorious color photographs show José and his friends at Cesar Chavez Elementary

School, the artistic murals painted on many buildings in the barrio, and many other community fiestas and activities. The written narrative vividly weaves in richly textured descriptions of the events captured in the photographs. The text is a little more challenging than other books I write about in this chapter but, with a helpful introduction from a teacher or librarian, should be within the reach of these readers. For example, some of the words in the following two sentences may be new for some readers, but a brief discussion of the text, along with the photograph, will make the reading easy.

> Many of the houses in the barrio are very old.
> Some have beautifully carved doors and archways
> and window moldings, and are painted in bright colors.

Diane Hoyt-Goldsmith has teamed with photographer Lawrence Midgale to produce many colorful, lively books about families and their celebration of traditional, cultural events. *Celebrating Chinese New Year* focuses on one family's preparations, as a mother, father, and their two children prepare the household, buy special foods and flowers, visit the graves of ancestors, and attend San Francisco's Chinese New Year's Parade. Readers who spend time with this book will feel as though they, too, are in the middle of the festivities. Children who can read other books described in this chapter will understand the narrative without difficulty, though an adult may have to explain the meaning of some words, such as *symbol* and *prosperity*. A glossary at the end of the book explains many English and Chinese words that may be new to readers.

> Oranges represent money and wealth, while tangerines are symbols of good luck. People believe that displaying both fruits will bring good luck and prosperity in the year ahead. (8)

I Am Rosa Parks

Learning about the lives of important historical figures is part of every school curriculum, but biographies can be difficult for newer readers to manage. Writers of biographies tell about their subjects' lives, but they also write about the historical events surrounding those lives. Thus, readers must not only be able to read and comprehend the individual words, sentences, and paragraphs. They must put all of the ideas together in order to learn about someone's life, but they must also develop an understanding of why that person is considered important. In order to understand the significance of a life, readers must also know something of history and the times in which the person lived.

Rosa Parks' autobiography for children, *I Am Rosa Parks,* written with Jim Haskins and illustrated by Wil Clay, is a good example of a text that guides readers in learning personal history in the broader context of social history.

The book is divided into four chapters. The first, entitled "I Get Arrested," tells about the event for which Rosa Parks is most widely known, her refusal to give up her seat on the bus for a white person. In order to help today's children understand the significance of something that happened nearly fifty years ago, the narrative begins with a description of what life was like for black people at that time.

> Many years ago
> black people in the South
> could not go to the same schools
> as white people. (5)

Mrs. Parks continues by saying that black people had to eat in different restaurants and drink from different water fountains than white people.

> This was called segregation.
> Segregation was the law in the South. (6)

This simple, but clear description explains the meaning of the term and paves the way for telling readers about segregation on the city buses, which, in turn, provides the information readers need in order to grasp the significance of Rosa Parks' refusal one day to give up her seat on the bus to a white person. The first chapter closes with a description of her arrest for this action.

By the close of the first chapter, readers have learned more about why Rosa Parks became famous. The second chapter focuses on her personal and family history, helping readers learn more about how her own beliefs led to her decision. The third chapter describes how her actions helped lead to the Montgomery bus boycott, and introduces Martin Luther King, Jr. and other key figures. The last chapter briefly summarizes the civil rights movement and her life following the boycott. Thus, in approximately 1,500 words, Rosa Parks gives readers a clear understanding of her actions and the impact they had on history. It is an account that stands by itself, but also one that supports a reader's future encounters with other books about the history of civil rights in the United States.

Summary

Readers who can read the books I discuss in this chapter are like drivers who know a large city well enough to navigate its streets with ease, regardless of unexpected detours they meet along the way. These readers do not need to begin a book and know with certainty what direction it will take, so long as they have a general understanding of the kind of story or information they expect to find inside. Intuitively, they shape their expectations by drawing on their accumulated encounters with all kinds of books. They read quickly and fluently so they are able to comfortably read several pages of a book without quite knowing the direction a story will take. Because they read with ease, their attention can be focused on understanding and reflecting on the whole text, and not on isolated words or sentences. Like any one of us, most of these readers like working in the comfort zone of their favorite authors and genres. The challenge for teachers and readers is to nurture and nudge them to expand their reading horizons by reading books like those I have profiled in this chapter.

Closing Points

KEEP IN MIND . . . We need to continually remind ourselves that knowing *how* to read does not make a person a reader.

Proficient readers are highly independent and read with a deep level of understanding. They can:
- read large stretches of text quickly and fluently
- integrate new information from their reading into their previous knowledge
- stop to reflect on what they have read without interfering with the flow of their reading
- find the meaning of unfamiliar words without being distracted from their reading

Proficient readers continue to need support from their teachers and librarians, who can:
- provide multiple copies of favorite books
- encourage students to read the same book with a friend or two
- encourage students to read books from a range of reading levels
- support students in developing strategies for understanding complex texts
- encourage students to read widely, beyond their comfort zones

Characteristics of complex texts include:
- plots with many twists and turns
- characters with distinctive personalities and feelings
- conflicts between some characters
- detailed descriptions in nonfiction writing
- traditional literary genres, such as fantasy, historical fiction, and biography

Bibliography

Children's Books

Stories of Family and Friends

1. *Lionel in the Spring* by Stephen Krensky. Illus. by Susanna Natti. Puffin Easy-to-Read. Puffin Books, 1990.
2. *Frog and Toad Together* by Arnold Lobel. An I Can Read Book. HarperCollins, 1971.
3. *Gus and Grandpa and Show-and-Tell* by Claudia Mills. Illus. by Catherine Stock. Farrar, Straus and Giroux, 2000.
4. *Edgar Badger's Balloon Day* by Monica Kulling. Illus. by Carol O'Malia. MONDO, 1997.
5. *Little Bear* by Else Holmelund Minarik. Illus. by Maurice Sendak. An I Can Read Book. HarperCollins, 1957.
6. *Pinky and Rex and the School Play* by James Howe. Illus. by Melissa Sweet. Ready-to-Read. Simon & Schuster, 1998.
7. *Alison's Puppy* by Marion Dane Bauer. Illus. by Laurie Spencer. Hyperion Chapters. Hyperion, 1997.

Humorous Stories

1. *George and Martha* by James Marshall. Houghton Mifflin, 1972.
2. *Minnie and Moo Go to the Moon* by Denys Cazet. DK, 1998.
3. *Mud Flat Spring* by James Stevenson. Greenwillow, 1999.
4. *Doctor De Soto* by William Steig. Farrar, Straus and Giroux, 1982.
5. *The True Story of the 3 Little Pigs! by A. Wolf,* as told to Jon Sciezska. Illus. by Lane Smith. Viking, 1989.

Stories with Unique Challenges

1. *The Smallest Cow in the World* by Katherine Paterson. Illus. by Jane Clark Brown. An I Can Read Book. HarperCollins, 1991.
2. *The Josefina Story Quilt* by Eleanor Coerr. Illus. by Bruce Degen. An I Can Read Book. HarperCollins, 1986.
3. *Buttons for General Washington* by Peter and Connie Roop. Illus. by Peter Hanson. Carolrhoda, 1986.
4. *Commander Toad in Space* by Jane Yolen. Illus. by Bruce Degen. Putnam, 1980.

Poetry

1. *Dinosaur Dinner (With a Slice of Alligator Pie)* by Dennis Lee. Selected by Jack Prelutsky. Illus. by Debbie Tilley. Knopf, 1999.

2. *Sweets and Treats: Dessert Poems.* Compiled by Bobbye Goldstein. Illus. by Kathy Couri. Hyperion Chapters. Hyperion, 1998.

3. *Never Take a Pig to Lunch and Other Poems About the Fun of Eating.* Selected and illustrated by Nadine Bernard Westcott. Orchard, 1995.

4. *Splish Splash* by Joan Bransfield Graham. Illus. By Steve Scott. Houghton Mifflin, 1994.

5. *Flicker Flash* by Joan Bransfield Graham. Illus. by Nancy Davis. Houghton Mifflin, 1999.

6. *Antarctic Antics: A Book of Penguin Poems* by Judy Sierra. Illus. by Jose Areugo and Ariane Dewey. Harcourt, 1998.

7. *Beast Feast: Poems and Paintings* by Douglas Florian. Harcourt, 1994.

8. *The Llama Who Had No Pajama* by Mary Ann Hoberman. Illus. by Betty Fraser. Harcourt, 1998.

9. *Little Dog Poems* by Kristine O'Connell George. Illus. by June Otani. Clarion, 1999.

10. *The Dragons Are Singing Tonight* by Jack Prelutsky. Illus. by Peter Sis. Greenwillow, 1993.

11. *Blast Off! Poems About Space.* Selected by Lee Bennett Hopkins. Illus. by Melissa Sweet. An I Can Read Book. HarperCollins, 1995.

12. *Sports! Sports! Sports!: A Poetry Collection.* Selected by Lee Bennett Hopkins. Illus. by Brian Floca. An I Can Read Book. HarperCollins, 1999.

13. *Nathaniel Talking* by Eloise Greenfield. Illus. by Jan Spivey Gilchrist. Black Butterfly Books, 1988.

14. *It's Raining Laughter* by Nikki Grimes. Photos by Myles C. Pinkney. Dial, 1997.

15. *Gathering the Sun: An Alphabet in Spanish and English* by Alma Flor Ada. English translation by Rosa Zubizarreta. Illus. by Simón Silva. Lothrop, Lee and Shepard, 1997.

16. *Laughing Tomatoes and Other Spring Poems/Jitomates risueños y otros poemas de primavera* by Francisco X. Alarcón. Illus. by Maya Christina Gonzalez. Children's Book Press, 1997.

17. *Confetti: Poems for Children* by Pat Mora. Illus. by Enrique O. Sanchez. Lee & Low, 1996.

Nonfiction

1. *The Magic School Bus at the Waterworks* by Joanna Cole. Illus. by Bruce Degen. Scholastic, 1986.

2. *The Emperor's Egg* by Martin Jenkins. Illus. by Jane Chapman. Candlewick, 1999.

3. *Polar Bears* by Sarah Palmer. Sea Mammal Discovery Library. Rourke, 1989.

4. *Polar Bears* by Dorothy Hinshaw Patent. Photos by William Muñoz. A Carolrhoda Nature Watch Picture Book. Carolrhoda, 2000.

5. *Ice Bear and Little Fox* by Jonathan London. Illus. by Daniel San Souci. Dutton, 1998.

6. *Barrio: José's Neighborhood* by George Ancona. Harcourt Brace, 1998.

7. *Celebrating Chinese New Year* by Diane Hoyt-Goldsmith. Photos by Lawrence Midgale. Holiday House, 1998.

8. *I Am Rosa Parks* by Rosa Parks, with Jim Haskins. Illus. by Wil Clay. Puffin Easy-to-Read. Penguin Putnam, 1997.

Other Children's Books

1. *Henry and Mudge* books by Cynthia Rylant. Illus. by Suçie Stevenson. Simon & Schuster.

2. *Fox* books by James Marshall. Puffin.

3. *Bunnicula* by James and Deborah Howe. Simon & Schuster, 1979.

4. *The Magician's Nephew* by C.S. Lewis. Illus. by Chris Van Allsburg. HarperCollins, 1994.

5. *The Very Busy Spider* by Eric Carle. Philomel, 1984.

6. *Froggy* books by Jonathan London. Illus. by Frank Remkiewicz. Viking.

7. *Freckle Juice* by Judy Blume. Simon & Schuster, 1984.

8. *Scaredy Dog* by Jane Resh Thomas. Hyperion, 1997.

9. *Dinosaurs Before Dark: A Magic Tree House Book* by Mary Pope Osborne. Random House, 1992.

10. *I Know an Old Lady Who Swallowed a Fly*, retold and illustrated by Nadine Bernard Westcott. Little Brown, 1988.

11. *The Lady with the Alligator Purse.* Retold and illustrated by Nadine Bernard Westcott. Little Brown, 1990.

12. *Peanut Butter and Jelly: A Play Rhyme.* Retold and illustrated by Nadine Bernard Westcott. Dutton, 1992.

7

Extending Literary Pathways

Becoming a reader is a lifelong journey that can take many pathways. Teachers and librarians play an important role in teaching children how to read and how to be a reader. We need to encourage children to explore many kinds of books on their own, but we also need to give them books at their instructional level so they can become better readers. When carefully chosen with readers in mind, "little books" and small chapter books can give them experience with many styles of writing in fiction and nonfiction. They do not have to wait until they are "better" readers to be able to read all of the "good books." They can learn how to read with interesting, authentic texts that engage their imaginations and extend their understanding of the world around them.

Through books, children can meet literary characters with distinctive personalities. They can meet a dog named Tiny who jumps in the mud just after he has had a bath. They can meet a lively cat named Tabby Cat who chases everything in sight. They can meet a funny lady named Amelia Bedelia, or a big lovable dog named Mudge. Through books, children can read about children doing things they do in their own lives. They can read about kids who play soccer, a boy who spends the day with a friend and his dad, or a girl who wants a puppy for her birthday.

Through books, children can enter imaginary worlds. They can read about a fox who tries to catch a tasty hen, and an owl who can't sleep because there are strange bumps at the bottom of his bed. They can read about a dinosaur who briefly comes to life and takes a boy on a grand tour of the city. Through books, children can learn more about the natural world. They can read books about caterpillars and butterflies and books about the stars. They can learn about the lives of famous people who have changed the course of history.

180

We want reading to be easy for children, but we also want to give them books that will make a difference in their lives. To do this well, we must be voracious readers ourselves. Children must see us reading and taking delight in the very books we give them to read. There are many ways teachers and librarians can help children become excited about reading. Here are a few suggestions for extending their literary pathways.

- *Multiple copies.* Try to have five or six copies of the same book on hand so children can encourage and support each other. If a book is part of a series, try to have as many titles as possible. Work out a long-range plan in your school for building collections of literature sets.
- *Conversation.* Encourage children to talk about their books to each other. It is usually more effective for them to meet in small interest groups or literature circles where the talk sounds like natural conversation.
- *Reading time.* Set aside a block of time every day for reading, without interruptions. Some children like to read with friends, while others prefer a space to themselves.
- *Book talks.* The phrase "book talk" sounds like a quaint phrase in this age of cyberspace, but I still find book talks to be a good way to introduce books to children. The best book talks are designed to spring from readers' current interests and take them just a little further.
- *Literary partners.* Encourage children to find books that are alike in some way. Talk about the different ways books can be like each other. Show how an easy "little book" can have a lot in common with a picture book. Have them create book displays or charts of literary partners. Make this an ongoing project so that finding literary partners is more like making a pleasant discovery than doing an assignment. Don't try to find a partner for every book.
- *Read alouds.* Read books aloud that children might not pick up and read on their own. Invite them to help you decide if it is a good book. Be sure to include picture books, poetry, and nonfiction. Read a non-fiction book and a fiction book about the same subject to let children hear how writers use different styles of language to express ideas.
- *Genre read-ins.* Lynda Brady, the Reading Explorers classroom teacher, and I sometimes planned library "read-ins" for the whole class. Our main reason for doing this was for everyone to have a good time reading, but we also looked at these sessions as a way to stretch reading interests. One time we focused on historical fiction. We introduced the

topic and talked with the class about what history is, and then I gave book talks about a stack of books that included *The Josefina Story Quilt* and *Buttons for General Washington*. Next, everyone selected a book and found a good place in the library to read. It was near the end of the school year, so most everyone could read at least one of the books I recommended, and Lynda and I read to those who needed assistance. As people finished reading, we gathered together and talked about the stories we had read.

In my two years of working with the Reading Explorers, I found out how important talk and friendship are to nurturing readers. They liked reading books together and talking about their favorites. Sometimes, they wanted to read aloud to each other, and other times they preferred reading quietly to themselves. Some liked sitting at tables, while others liked sprawling out on the floor. They reminded me of the pig, the duck, and the cow in Becky Bloom's book *Wolf!*, a very funny book with very funny illustrations by Pascal Biet.

In this story, a hungry wolf finds a farm where he plans to get a good meal. He looks over the fence and is astounded to see a pig, a duck, and a cow reading! He is so hungry he is sure his eyes are playing tricks on him. When he makes his move to grab a meal, the reading animals do not move. In fact, they are very annoyed at this interruption to their reading. Well, the wolf decided he had better learn how to read, and off to school he went. Friendship and camaraderie inspired the wolf to become a reader, just as the Reading Explorers became better readers by sharing books together.

At the beginning of *Literary Pathways*, I suggested that good literature, attention to text complexity, and the children we teach are an inseparable trio. Our goal should be to provide students with books that will make them so enthusiastic about reading, they will read as easily and as willingly as they turn on television. We should make reading so irresistable that they go to libraries and borrow stacks of books. At the same time, we need to provide them with books they can read while they are learning more about reading. There are so many superb books for new readers, it is not necessary to sacrifice literary quality to find readable texts for them. For every one of our students, our ultimate goal is to find the right book for the right child at the right time.

PROFESSIONAL REFERENCES

Adams, M. J. 1990. *Beginning to Read: Thinking and Learning About Print.* Cambridge, MA: MIT Press.

Allington, R. and H. Woodside-Jiron. 1998. "Decodable Text in Beginning Reading: Are Mandates and Policy Based on Research?" *ERS Spectrum* 16: 3–11.

American Heritage Dictionary of the English Language, 3rd ed., 1996. Boston: Houghton Mifflin.

Applebee, A. N. 1978. *The Child's Concept of Story: Ages Two to Seventeen.* Chicago: Univ. of Chicago Press.

Bruner, J. S. 1973. "Going Beyond the Information Given." In *Beyond the Information Given,* ed. J. S. Bruner and J. M. Anglin. New York: Norton.

Bussis, A. M., E. A. Chittenden, M. Amarel, and E. Klausner. 1985. *Inquiry into Meaning: An Investigation of Learning to Read.* Hillsdale, NJ: Erlbaum.

Calkins, L. M. 2001. *The Art of Teaching Reading.* New York: Longman.

Carey, S. 1978. "The Child as Word Learner." In *Linguistic Theory and Psychological Reality,* ed. M. Halle, J. Breslin, and G. A. Miller. (Cited in F. Smith. 1994. *Understanding Reading.* 5th ed. Hillsdale, NJ: Erlbaum). Cambridge, MA: MIT Press.

Chall, J. S. and E. Dale. 1995. *Readability Revisited: The New Dale-Chall Readability Formula.* Cambridge, MA: Brookline Books.

Clay, M. M. 1968. "A Syntactic Analysis of Reading Errors." *Journal of Learning and Verbal Behaviour* 7 (2): 434–438.

———. 1982. *Observing Young Readers: Selected Papers.* Portsmouth, NH: Heinemann.

———. 1991. *Becoming Literate: The Construction of Inner Control.* Portsmouth, NH: Heinemann.

———. 1993a. *An Observation Survey of Early Literacy Achievement.* Portsmouth, NH: Heinemann.

———. 1993b. *Reading Recovery: A Guidebook for Teachers in Training.* Portsmouth, NH: Heinemann.

———. 2000. *Running Records for Classroom Teachers.* Portsmouth, NH: Heinemann.

Dollar, T. 1999. "Focus on Nature." *Arizona Highways* 75 (7): 32–33.

Ferreiro, E. and A. Teberosky. 1979. *Literacy Before Schooling.* Trans. K. G. Castro. Portsmouth, NH: Heinemann.

Freedman, R. 1992. "Fact or Fiction?" In *Using Nonfiction Trade Books in the Elementary Classroom: From Ants to Zeppelins,* ed. E. Freeman and D. Person. Urbana, IL: National Council of Teachers of English.

Fresch, M. J. 1995. "Self-selection of Early Literacy Learners." *The Reading Teacher* 49 (3): 220–227.

Giorgis, C. and B. Peterson. 1996. "Teachers and Librarians Collaborate to Create a Community of Learners." *Language Arts* 73 (7): 477–482.

Goodman, K. S. 1965. "A Linguistic Study of Cues and Miscues in Reading." *Elementary English* 42 (6): 639–643.

———. 1996. *On Reading.* Portsmouth, NH: Heinemann.

Goodman, Y. 1996. "The Roots of Literacy." In *Notes from a Kidwatcher: Selected Writings of Yetta M. Goodman,* ed. S. Wilde. Portsmouth, NH: Heinemann.

Gourley, J. W. 1984. "Discourse Structure: Expectations of Beginning Readers and Readability of Text." *Journal of Reading Behavior* 16 (3): 169–188.

Graves, B. 1998. "First Novels." *Book Links* 7 (5): 51–55.

Guice, S., R. Allington, P. Johnston, K. Baker, and N. Michelson. 1996. "Access?: Books, Children, and Literature-Based Curriculum in Schools." *The New Advocate* 9 (3): 197–207.

Gunning, T. G. 1996. *Best Books for Beginning Readers.* Needham Heights, MA: Allyn & Bacon.

Halliday, M. A. K. 1975. *Learning How to Mean: Explorations in the Development of Language.* London: Edward Arnold.

Harris, V. J. 1997. *Using Multiethnic Literature in the K–8 Classroom.* Norwood, MA: Christopher-Gordon.

Harwayne, S. 2000. *Lifetime Guarantees: Toward Ambitious Literacy Teaching.* Portsmouth, NH: Heinemann.

Hepler, S. I. and J. Hickman.1982. "'The Book Was Okay. I Love You'—Social Aspects of Response to Literature." *Theory into Practice* 22 (4): 278–283.

Hiebert, E. H. 1999. "Text Matters in Learning to Read." *The Reading Teacher* 52 (6): 552–566.

Holland, K. E. and L. A. Shaw. 1993. "Dances Between Stances." In *Journeying: Children Responding to Literature,* ed. K. E. Holland, R. A. Hungerford, and S. B. Ernst. Portsmouth, NH: Heinemann.

Huck, C. S. 1989. "In the Words of Charlotte S. Huck." In *Children's Literature in the Classroom: Weaving Charlotte's Web,* ed. J. Hickman and B. Cullinan. Norwood, MA: Christopher-Gordon.

———. 1990. "The Power of Children's Literature in the Classroom." In *Talking About Books: Creating Literate Communities,* ed. K. G. Short and K. M. Pierce. Portsmouth, NH: Heinemann.

Huck, C. S., S. Hepler, J. Hickman, and B. Z. Kiefer. 2000. *Children's Literature in the Elementary School.* 7th ed. New York: McGraw Hill.

Iser, W. 1974. *The Implied Reader.* Baltimore, MD: Johns Hopkins Univ. Press.

Johnston, P. and M. M. Clay. 1997. "Interpreting Oral Reading Records." In *Knowing Literacy: Constructive Literacy Assessment,* by P. Johnston. York, ME: Stenhouse.

Karolides, N. J. 1999. "Theory and Practice: An Interview with Louise M. Rosenblatt." *Language Arts* 77 (2): 158–170.

Kerper, R. 1998. "Choosing Quality Nonfiction Literature: Features for Accessing and Visualizing Information." In *Making Facts Come Alive: Choosing Quality Nonfiction Literature K–8,* ed. R. A. Bamford and J. V. Kristo. Norwood, MA: Christopher-Gordon.

Kiefer, B. Z. 1995. *The Potential of Picture Books: From Visual Literacy to Aesthetic Understanding.* Columbus, OH: Merrill.

Kingsolver, B. 1995. *High Tide in Tucson: Essays from Now or Never.* New York: HarperCollins.

Krashen, S. D. 1995. "School Libraries, Public Libraries, and the NAEP Reading Scores." *School Library Media Quarterly* 23 (Summer): 235–237.

———. 1997/98. "Bridging Inequity with Books." *Educational Leadership* 55 (4): 18–22.

Leal, D. 1993. "Storybooks, Information Books and Informational Storybooks: An Explication of the Ambiguous Grey Genre." *The New Advocate* 6 (1): 61–70.

Lindfors, J. W. 1987. *Children's Language and Learning.* 2nd ed. Englewood Cliffs, NJ: Prentice-Hall.

Lloyd, B. 1999. "Sailor Plots the Revenge of the Tomatoes." *New York Times,* May 2, 1999, Sports section, p. 54.

MacMahon, J. A. 1985. *Deserts: Audubon Society Nature Guides.* New York: Knopf.

McQuillan, J. 1998. *The Literacy Crisis: False Claims, Real Solutions.* Portsmouth, NH: Heinemann.

Meek, M. 1988. *How Texts Teach What Readers Learn.* Lockwood, England: Thimble Press.

———. 1996. *Information and Book Learning.* Lockwood, England: Thimble Press.

Messmer, H. A. 1999. "Scaffolding a Crucial Transition Using Text with Some Decodability." *The Reading Teacher* 53 (2): 130–142.

Moore, P. 1998. "Choosing Quality Nonfiction Literature: Aspects of Selection for Emergent Readers." In *Making Facts Come Alive: Choosing Quality Nonfiction Literature K–8,* ed. R. A. Bamford and J. V. Kristo. Norwood, MA: Christopher-Gordon.

Morrow, L. M., D. H. Tracey, D. G. Woo, and M. Pressley. 1999. "Characteristics of Exemplary First-Grade Literacy Instruction." *The Reading Teacher* 52 (5): 462–476.

Opitz, M. F. 1998. *Flexible Grouping in Reading: Practical Ways to Help All Students Become Stronger Readers.* New York: Scholastic.

Opitz, M. F. and T. V. Rasinski. 1998. *Good-Bye Round Robin: 25 Effective Oral Reading Strategies.* Portsmouth, NH: Heinemann.

Peterson, B. 1988. *Characteristics of Texts That Support Beginning Readers.* Ph.D. dissertation. The Ohio State University, Columbus.

———. 1991. "Selecting Books for Beginning Readers." *In Bridges to Literacy: Learning from Reading Recovery,* ed. D. E. DeFord, C. Lyons, and G. S. Pinnell. Portsmouth, NH: Heinemann.

———. 1998. "Children's Literature Leads to Collaboration in Action." *Journal of Children's Literature* 24 (1): 84–89.

Pierce, K. M. 1999. "'I Am a Level 3 Reader': Children's Perceptions of Themselves as Readers." *The New Advocate* 12 (4): 359–375.

Rasinski, T. 2000. "Speed Does Matter in Reading." *The Reading Teacher* 54 (2): 146–151.

Rhodes, L. 1979. "Comprehension and Predictability: An Analysis of Beginning Reading Materials." *Monographs in Language and Reading Studies*

No. 3 (*New Perspectives on Comprehension,* J. C. Harste & R. F. Carey, eds.), 100–131.

Rosenblatt, L. M. 1978. *The Reader the Text the Poem: The Transactional Theory of the Literary Work.* Carbondale, IL: Southern Illinois University Press.

———. 1993. "The Literary Transaction: Evocation and Response." In *Journeying: Children Responding To Literature,* ed. K. E. Holland, R. A. Hungerford, and S. B. Ernst. Portsmouth, NH: Heinemann.

Routman, R. 1996. *Literacy at the Crossroads.* Portsmouth, NH: Heinemann.

Short, K. G. 1997. *Literature as a Way of Knowing.* York, ME: Stenhouse.

Smith, F. 1988. *Joining the Literacy Club.* Portsmouth, NH: Heinemann.

———. 1994. *Understanding Reading.* 5th Ed. Hillsdale, NJ: Erlbaum.

Strickland, D. and L. M. Morrow. 1989. *Emerging Literacy: Young Children Learn to Read and Write.* Newark, DE: International Reading Association.

Taberski, S. 2000. *On Solid Ground: Strategies for Teaching Reading K–3.* Portsmouth, NH: Heinemann.

Wells, G. 1986. *The Meaning Makers: Children Learning Language and Using Language to Learn.* Portsmouth, NH: Heinemann.

Yolen, J. 1981. *Touch Magic: Fantasy, Faerie and Folklore in the Literature of Childhood.* New York: Philomel.

CHILDREN'S LITERATURE BIBLIOGRAPHY

Ada, Alma Flor. 1997. *Gathering the Sun: An Alphabet in Spanish and English.* Trans. by Rosa Zubizarreta. Illus. by Simón Silva. Lothrop, Lee & Shepard.

Alarcón, Francisco X. 1997. *Laughing Tomatoes and Other Spring Poems/Jitomates risueños y otros poemas de primavera.* Illus. by Maya Christina Gonzalez. San Francisco: Children's Book Press.

Allen, Laura Jean. 1992. *Rollo and Tweedy and the Ghost at Dougal Castle.* New York: HarperCollins.

Ancona, George. 1998. *Barrio: José's Neighborhood.* San Diego: Harcourt.

Asch, Frank. 1982. *Happy Birthday, Moon.* New York: Simon & Schuster.

———. 1985. *Bear Shadow.* New York: Simon & Schuster.

———. 1981. *Just Like Daddy.* New York: Simon & Schuster.

Bang, Molly. 1996. *Wiley and the Hairy Man.* New York: Simon & Schuster.

Baker, Barbara. 1999. *One Saturday Afternoon.* Illus. by Kate Duke. New York: Dutton.

———. 1994. *One Saturday Morning.* Illus. by Kate Duke. New York: Dutton.

Barton, Byron. 1981. *Building a House.* New York: Greenwillow.

———. 1991. *The Three Bears.* New York: HarperCollins.

Bauer, Marion Dane. 1997. *Alison's Puppy.* Illus. by Laurie Spencer. New York: Hyperion.

———. 1998. *Bear's Hiccups.* Illus. by Diane Dawson Hearn. New York: Holiday House.

Bebop Books for Emergent Readers. New York: Lee & Low Books.

Berenstain, Stan and Jan. 1971. *Bears in the Night.* New York: Random House.

Bloom, Becky. 1999. *Wolf!* Illus. by Pascal Biet. New York: Orchard Books.

Blume, Judy. 1984. *Freckle Juice.* New York: Simon & Schuster.

Bonsall, Crosby. 1974. *And I Mean It, Stanley.* New York: HarperCollins.

———. 1980. *Who's Afraid of the Dark?* New York: HarperCollins.

Boss, Kittie. 1999. *Cat Tails.* Illus. by Erin Marie Mauterer. Katonah, NY: Richard Owen.

Brown, Arthur. 1998. *Arthur Lost and Found.* Boston: Little Brown.

Brown, Laurie Krasny. 1995. *Rex and Lilly Family Time.* Illus. by Marc Brown. Boston: Little Brown.

Brown, Ruth. 1992. *A Dark Dark Tale.* New York: Dutton.

Byars, Betsy. 1992. *Hooray for the Golly Sisters.* Illus. by Sue Truesdell. New York: HarperCollins.

———. 1994. *The Golly Sisters Go West.* Illus. by Sue Truesdell. New York: HarperCollins.

———. 1985. *The Golly Sisters Ride Again.* Illus. By Sue Truesdell. New York: HarperCollins.

Carle, Eric. 1987. *Have You Seen My Cat?* New York: Simon & Schuster.

———. 1984. *The Very Busy Spider.* New York: Philomel.

Catling, Patrick. 1979. *The Chocolate Touch.* Illus. by Margot Apple. New York: Morrow.

Cazet, Denys. 1998. *Minnie and Moo Go to the Moon.* New York: DK Ink.

Chin, Teresa. 1997. *I Am a Cat.* Photos by Graham Meadows. Crystal Lake, IL: Rigby.

Coerr, Eleanor. 1986. *The Josefina Story Quilt.* Illus. by Bruce Degen. New York: HarperCollins.

Cole, Joanna. 1986. *The Magic School Bus at the Waterworks.* Illus. by Bruce Degen. New York: Scholastic.

Cowley, Joy. 1983. *The Ghost.* Illus. by Robyn Belton. Bothell, WA: Wright Group.

———. 1986. *Huggles' Breakfast.* Illus. by Elizabeth Fuller. Bothell, WA: Wright Group.

———. 1987. *I'm Bigger Than You!* Illus. by Jan van der Voo. Bothell, WA: Wright Group.

———. 1980. *Mrs. Wishy-Washy.* Illus. by Elizabeth Fuller. Bothell, WA: Wright Group.

————. 1987. *Old Grizzly.* Illus. by Jan van der Voo. Bothell, WA: Wright Group.

————. 1987. *Ratty-tatty.* Illus. by Astrid Matijosevic. Bothell, WA: Wright Group.

Crewe, Sabrina. 1997. *The Frog.* Austin, TX: Raintree Steck-Vaughan.

Crews, Donald. 1978. *Freight Train.* New York: Greenwillow.

Cushman, Doug. 1987. *Aunt Eater Loves a Mystery.* New York: HarperCollins.

Cutting, Jillian. 1992. *The Sausage.* Illus. by Peter Stevenson. Bothell, WA: Wright Group.

Demuth, Patricia. 1996. *Johnny Appleseed.* Illus. by Michael Montgomery. New York: Grosset & Dunlap.

————. 1993. *Snakes.* Illus. by Judith Moffatt. New York: Grosset & Dunlap.

Driscoll, Laura. 1998. *Frogs.* Illus. by Judith Moffatt. New York: Grosset & Dunlap.

Dussling, Jennifer. 1996. *Stars.* Illus. by Mavis Smith. New York: Grosset & Dunlap.

Feely, Jenny. 1999. *Butterfly.* Photos by Michael Curtain. Littleton, MA: Sundance.

————. 1999. *Tadpoles and Frogs.* Photos by Michael Curtain. Littleton, MA: Sundance.

————. 1999. *Tarantula.* Photos by Michael Curtain. Littleton, MA: Sundance.

Florian, Douglas. 1994. *Beast Feast: Poems and Paintings.* San Diego: Harcourt.

Fowler, Allan. 1992. *Frogs and Toads and Tadpoles, Too.* Chicago: Children's Press.

Fox, Mem. 1987. *Hattie and the Fox.* Illus. by Patricia Mullins. New York: Simon & Schuster.

Freedman, Russell. 1987. *Lincoln: A Photobiography.* New York: Clarion.

Freeman, Marcia. 1999. *Polar Bears.* Mankato, MN: Capstone Press.

Galdone, Paul. 1972. *Goldilocks and the Three Bears.* Boston: Houghton.

————. 1979. *The Three Billy Goats Gruff.* Boston: Houghton.

Gelman, Rita Golden. 1993. *More Spaghetti, I Say!* Illus. By Mort Gerberg. New York: Scholastic.

George, Kristine O'Connell. 1999. *Little Dog Poems.* Illus. by June Otani. New York: Clarion.

Gibbons, Gail. 1993. *Frogs.* New York: Holiday House.

Ginsburg, Mirra. 1972. *The Chick and the Duckling.* Illus. by Jose Aruego and Ariane Dewey. New York: Simon & Schuster.

Goldstein, Bobbye, compiler. 1998. *Sweets and Treats: Dessert Poems.* Illus. by Kathy Couri. New York: Hyperion.

Graham, Joan Bransfield. 1999. *Flicker Flash.* Illus. by Nancy Davis. Boston: Houghton Mifflin.

———. 1994. *Splish Splash.* Illus. by Steve Scott. Boston: Houghton Mifflin.

Greenfield, Eloise. 1988. *Nathaniel Talking.* Illus. by Jan Spivey Gilchrist. New York: Black Butterfly Children's Books.

Grimes, Nikki. 1997. *It's Raining Laughter.* Photos by Myles C. Pinkney. New York: Dial.

Harris, Jenny. 1997. *Amy Goes to School.* Illus. by Phyllis Pollema-Cahill. Crystal Lake, IL: Rigby.

Henkes, Kevin. 1991. *Chrysanthemum.* New York: Greenwillow.

Hill, Eric. 1980. *Where's Spot?* New York: Putnam.

Hoban, Lillian. 1996. *Arthur's Back to School Day.* New York: HarperCollins.

———. 1999. *Arthur's Birthday Party.* New York: HarperCollins.

Hoberman, Mary Ann. 1998. *The Llama Who Had No Pajama: 100 Favorite Poems.* Illus. by Betty Fraser. San Diego: Harcourt.

Hodges, Margaret. 1997. *The True Tale of Johnny Appleseed.* Illus. by Kimberly Bulcken Root. New York: Holiday House.

Hoff, Syd. 1986. *Danny and the Dinosaur.* New York: HarperCollins.

———. 1996. *Danny and the Dinosaur Go to Camp.* New York: HarperCollins.

———. 1997. *Happy Birthday, Danny and the Dinosaur.* New York: HarperCollins.

Hopkins, Lee Bennett, selector. 1986. *Surprises.* Illus. by Megan Lloyd. New York: HarperTrophy.

———. 1995. *Weather: Poems for All Seasons.* Illus. by Melanie Hall. New York: HarperTrophy.

———. 1995. *Blast Off! Poems About Space.* Illus. by Melissa Sweet. New York: HarperCollins.

———. 1999. *Sports! Sports! Sports! A Poetry Collection.* Illus. by Brian Floca. New York: HarperCollins.

Howe, James. 1998. *Pinky and Rex and the School Play.* Illus. by Melissa Sweet. New York: Simon & Schuster.

Howe, James and Deborah. 1979. *Bunnicula.* New York: Simon & Schuster.

Hoyt-Goldsmith, Diane. 1998. *Celebrating Chinese New Year.* Photos by Lawrence Midgale. New York: Holiday House.

Hurd, Edith Thacher. 1965. *Johnny Lion's Book.* Illus. by Clement Hurd. New York: HarperCollins.

Hutchins, Pat. 1971. *Titch.* New York: Simon & Schuster.

———. 1991. *Tidy Titch.* New York: Greenwillow.

———. 1983. *You'll Soon Grow Into Them, Titch.* New York: Greenwillow.

———. 1988. *Where's the Baby?* New York: Greenwillow.

Hyman, Trina Schart, 1983. *Little Red Riding Hood.* New York: Holiday House.

Jenkins, Martin. 1999. *The Emperor's Egg.* Illus. by Jane Chapman. Cambridge, MA: Candlewick.

Kahl, Virginia. 1955. *The Duchess Bakes a Cake.* New York: Scribner.

Kehoe, Connie. 1989. *Green Footprints.* Illus. by Terry Denton. Crystal Lake, IL: Rigby.

Keller, Holly. 1999. *What I See.* San Diego: Harcourt.

Kellogg, Steven. 1988. *Johnny Appleseed.* New York: Morrow.

———. 1999. *The Three Sillies.* Cambridge, MA: Candlewick.

Kraus, Robert. 1970. *Whose Mouse Are You?* Illus. by Jose Aruego. New York: Simon & Schuster.

Krauss, Ruth. 1945. *The Carrot Seed.* Illus. by Crockett Johnson. New York: HarperCollins.

Krensky, Stephen. 1990. *Lionel in the Spring.* Illus. by Susanna Natti. New York: Puffin.

Kulling, Monica. 1997. *Edgar Badger's Balloon Day.* Illus. by Carol O'Malia. Greenvale, NY: MONDO.

Kwitz, Mary DeBall. 1992. *Little Chick's Friend Duckling.* Illus. by Bruce Degen. New York: HarperCollins.

Lawrence, Lucy. 1989. *Ouch!* Illus. by Graham Porter. Crystal Lake, IL: Rigby.

Lee, Dennis. 1999. *Dinosaur Dinner (With a Slice of Alligator Pie).* Selected by Jack Prelutsky. Illus. by Debbie Tilley. New York: Knopf.

Lewis, C. S. 1994. *The Magician's Nephew.* Illus. by Chris Van Allsburg. New York: HarperCollins.

Lindbergh, Reeve. 1990. *Johnny Appleseed: A Poem.* Illus. by Kathy Jakobsen. Boston: Little Brown.

Lionni, Leo. 1991. *Swimmy.* New York: Knopf.

Lobel, Arnold. 1976. *Frog and Toad All Year.* New York: HarperCollins.

———. 1979. *Days with Frog and Toad.* New York: HarperCollins.

———. 1970. *Frog and Toad Are Friends.* New York: HarperCollins.

———. 1971. *Frog and Toad Together.* New York: HarperCollins.

———. 1978. *Mouse Tales.* New York: HarperCollins.

———. 1975. *Owl at Home.* New York: HarperCollins.

London, Jonathan. 1996. *Froggy Goes to School.* Illus. by Frank Remkiewicz. New York: Viking.

———. 1998. *Ice Bear and Little Fox.* Illus. by Daniel San Souci. New York: Dutton.

Louie, Ai-Ling. 1982. *Yeh-Shen: A Cinderella Story from China.* Illus. by Ed Young. New York: Philomel.

Lynch, Patricia Ann. 1996. *Fix It, Fox.* Illus. by Jane Caminos. Needham Heights, MA: Silver Burdett Ginn.

Marshall, Edward. 1985. *Four on the Shore.* Illus. by James Marshall. New York: Puffin.

Marshall, James. 1981. *Three by the Sea.* Illus. by James Marshall. New York: Puffin.

———. 1996. *Fox on Stage.* New York: Puffin.

———. 1996. *Fox Outfoxed.* New York: Puffin.

———. 1972. *George and Martha.* Boston: Houghton Mifflin.

———. 1985. *Three Up a Tree.* New York: Puffin.

Martin, Bill. 1992. *Brown Bear, Brown Bear, What Do You See?* Illus. by Eric Carle. New York: Holt.

Marzollo, Jean. 1997. *I'm a Caterpillar.* Illus. by Judith Moffatt. New York: Scholastic.

Matthias, Catherine. 1982. *Too Many Balloons.* Illus. by Gene Sharp. Chicago: Children's Press.

Mayer, Mercer. 1984. *There's a Nightmare in My Closet.* New York: Dial.

McDonald, Megan. 1997. *Beezy.* Illus. by Nancy Poydar. New York: Orchard.

McMillan, Bruce. 1993. *Mouse Views: What the Class Pet Saw.* New York: Holiday House.

McPhail, David. 1997. *The Great Race.* New York: Scholastic.

Medearis, Angela Shelf. 1993. *Sharing Danny's Dad.* Illus. by Jan Spivey Gilchrist. Upper Saddle River, NJ: Celebration Press.

Meister, Cari. 1998. *Tiny's Bath.* Illus. by Rich Davis. New York: Puffin.

Melser, June. 1982. *Look for Me.* Illus. by Lynette Vondruska. Bothell, WA: Wright Group.

Mills, Claudia. 2000. *Gus and Grandpa and Show-and-Tell.* Illus. by Catherine Stock. New York: Farrar, Straus and Giroux.

Minarik, Else Holmelund. 1996. *A Kiss for Little Bear.* Illus. by Maurice Sendak. New York: HarperCollins.

———. 1987. *Father Bear Comes Home.* Illus. by Maurice Sendak. New York: HarperCollins.

———. 1957. *Little Bear.* Illus. by Maurice Sendak. New York: HarperCollins.

Mora, Pat. 1996. *Confetti: Poems for Children.* Illus. by Enrique O. Sanchez. New York: Lee & Low.

Most, Bernard. 1999. *Catch Me If You Can!* San Diego: Harcourt.

Moyes, Leslie. 1983. *Saturday Morning.* Wellington, New Zealand: Learning Media.

Nodset, Joan. 1963. *Who Took the Farmer's Hat?* Illus. by Fritz Siebel. New York: HarperCollins.

Osborne, Mary Pope. 1992. *Dinosaurs Before Dark: A Magic Tree House Book.* New York: Random House.

Palmer, Sarah. 1989. *Polar Bears.* Vero Beach, FL: Rourke.

Parish, Peggy. 1963. *Amelia Bedelia.* Illus. by Fritz Siebel. New York: Harper-Collins.

Parks, Rosa and Jim Haskins. 1997. *I Am Rosa Parks.* Illus. by Wil Clay. New York: Penguin Putnam.

Patent, Dorothy Hinshaw. 2000. *Polar Bears.* Photos by William Muñoz. Minneapolis, MN: Carolrhoda.

Paterson, Katherine. 1991. *The Smallest Cow in the World.* Illus. by Jane Clark Brown. New York: HarperCollins.

Peek, Merle. 1985. *Mary Wore Her Red Dress, Henry Wore His Green Sneakers.* Boston: Houghton Mifflin.

Pfeffer, Wendy. 1994. *From Tadpole to Frog.* Illus. by Holly Keller. New York: HarperCollins.

Pilkey, Dav. 1991. *A Friend for Dragon.* New York: Orchard.

Piñata and *Mas Piñata* books. Upper Saddle River, NJ: Celebration Press.

Preller, James. 1994. *Hiccups for Elephant.* Illus. by Hans Wilhelm. New York: Scholastic.

Prelutsky, Jack. 1993. *The Dragons Are Singing Tonight*. Illus. by Peter Sis. New York: Greenwillow.

Robins, Joan. 1993. *Addie's Bad Day*. Illus. by Sue Truesdell. New York: Harper-Collins.

———. 1988. *Addie Meets Max*. Illus. by Sue Truesdell. New York: Harper-Collins.

———. 1989. *Addie Runs Away*. Illus. by Sue Truesdell. New York: Harper-Collins.

Robinson, Fay. 1993. *Meet My Mouse*. Photos by Dwight Kuhn. Upper Saddle River, NJ: Celebration Press.

Roop, Peter and Connie. 1986. *Buttons for General Washington*. Illus. by Peter Hanson. Minneapolis, MN: Carolrhoda.

Root, Phyllis. 2000. *The Chase (Hey, Tabby Cat)*. Illus. by Katharine McEwen. Cambridge, MA: Candlewick.

Rylant, Cynthia. 1990. *Henry and Mudge and the Happy Cat*. Illus. by Suçie Stevenson. New York: Simon & Schuster.

———. 1991. *Henry and Mudge Take the Big Test*. Illus. by Suçie Stevenson. New York: Simon & Schuster.

———. 1997. *Poppleton and His Friends*. Illus. by Mark Teague. New York: Scholastic.

Salem, Lynn and Josie Stewart. 1992. *It's Game Day*. Illus. by Tim Collins. Columbus, OH: Seedling Publications.

———. 1992. *The Cat Who Loved Red*. Illus. by Holly Pendergast. Columbus, OH: Seedling Publications.

Scieszka, Jon. 1989. *The True Story of the 3 Little Pigs! by A. Wolf*. Illus. by Lane Smith. New York: Viking.

Seuss, Dr. 1960. *Green Eggs and Ham*. New York: Random House.

———. 1957. *The Cat in the Hat*. New York: Random House.

Shahan, Sherry. 1997. *The Changing Caterpillar*. Katonah, NY: Richard Owen.

Sharmat, Marjorie Weinman. 1981. *Nate the Great and the Sticky Case*. Illus. by Marc Simont. New York: Dell Yearling.

———. 1990. *Nate the Great and the Halloween Hunt*. Illus. by Marc Simont. New York: Dell Yearling.

Sierra, Judy. 1998. *Antarctic Antics: A Book of Penguin Poems*. Illus. by Jose Aruego and Ariane Dewey. San Diego: Harcourt.

Skofield, James. 1996. *Detective Dinosaur*. Illus. by R. W. Alley. New York: HarperCollins.

Sloan, Peter and Sheryl Sloan. 1995. *Animal Homes.* Littleton, MA: Sundance.

Smith, Janice Lee. 1994. *Wizard and Wart.* Illus. by Paul Meisel. New York: HarperCollins.

Steig, William. 1982. *Doctor DeSoto.* New York: Farrar, Straus and Giroux.

Stevens, Janet. 1990. *The Three Billy Goats Gruff.* San Diego: Harcourt.

Stevenson, James. 1999. *Mud Flat Spring.* New York: Greenwillow.

Taylor, Kim and Jane Burton. 1997. *Frog (See How They Grow).* New York: Dutton.

Thomas, Jane Resh. 1997. *Scaredy Dog.* New York: Hyperion.

Tolstoy, Aleksei. 1998. *The Gigantic Turnip.* Illus. by Niamh Sharkey. Brooklyn, NY: Barefoot Books.

Turkle, Brinton. 1976. *Deep in the Forest.* New York: Dutton.

Tyler, Michael. 1997. *Frogs.* Greenvale, NY: MONDO.

Van Leeuwen, Jean. 1998. *Growing Ideas (Meet the Author).* Katonah, NY: Richard Owen.

————. 1990. *Oliver Pig at School.* Illus. by Ann Schweninger. New York: Puffin.

Visions™ Books. Bothell, WA: The Wright Group.

Walsh, Jill Paton. 1982. *The Green Book.* New York: Farrar, Straus and Giroux.

Ward, Cindy. 1988. *Cookie's Week.* Illus. by Tomie dePaola. New York: Putnam.

Westcott, Nadine Bernard. 1988. *I Know an Old Lady Who Swallowed a Fly.* Boston: Little Brown.

————. 1992. *Peanut Butter and Jelly: A Play Rhyme.* New York: Dutton.

————. 1990. *The Lady with the Alligator Purse.* Boston: Little Brown.

Westcott, Nadine Bernard, selector. 1995. *Never Take a Pig to Lunch and Other Poems About the Fun of Eating.* New York: Orchard.

White, E. B. 1952. *Charlotte's Web.* Illus. by Garth Williams. New York: HarperCollins.

Wildsmith, Brian. 1983. *All Fall Down.* New York: Oxford.

Williams, Sue. 1989. *I Went Walking.* Illus. by Julie Vivas. San Diego: Harcourt.

Wiseman, Bernard. 1970. *Morris Goes to School.* New York: HarperCollins.

————. 1989. *Morris the Moose.* New York: HarperCollins.

Wood, Audrey. 1984. *The Napping House.* Illus. by Don Wood. San Diego: Harcourt.

Yolen, Jane. 1980. *Commander Toad in Space.* Illus. by Bruce Degen. New York: Putnam.

Young, Ed. 1989. *Lon-Po-Po: A Red-Riding Hood Story from China.* New York: Philomel.

———. 1992. *Seven Blind Mice.* New York: Philomel.

Ziefert, Harriet. 1995. *The Gingerbread Man.* Illus. by Emily Bolam. New York: Puffin.

———. 1995. *The Little Red Hen.* Illus. by Emily Bolam. New York: Puffin.

———. 1996. *The Turnip.* Illus. by Laura Rader. New York: Puffin.

APPENDIX A

Literary Partners for Extending Literary Pathways

Some books are natural partners. Alex, a student I introduced in Chapter 3, made this discovery for himself when I gave him a copy of *The Terrible Tiger*, a lively, easy-to-read story of two children who are going to hunt the terrible tiger. " 'We're not scared of the terrible tiger. We're not scared of anything." Alex looked through the book and read the first page. "This book is just like *We're Going on a Bear Hunt!*" he announced in an excited voice. He noticed that the story line and language patterns are very similar. *The Terrible Tiger* is a "little book" written for emergent readers. *We're Going on a Bear Hunt* is a large picture book with delightful pictures and memorable language that is a wonderful story for reading aloud. I think of books that go together as *literary partners*.

Pairing books like *The Terrible Tiger* and *We're Going on a Bear Hunt* is an effective and enjoyable away to help children extend their literary pathways. Reading *The Terrible Tiger* on his own was a springboard for Alex to tackle the more challenging language of *We're Going on a Bear Hunt*. Not all books have literary partners, but teachers and librarians can encourage their students to discover them. Classes could keep lists of literary partners they find throughout the year. Literary partners can be books close in reading level, but they can also be a very easy book paired with a more challenging book. There are several possible kinds of literary partners.

- books with similar story structures, such as cumulative tales or "all fall down" stories
- books with memorable characters who act in similar ways
- a fiction book with a nonfiction book on the same subject

199

- books written by the same author
- books illustrated by the same artist

Here are a few literary partners for some of the books I have written about in *Literary Pathways*. After each title, I indicate whether the book is appropriate for emergent, transitional, or proficient readers. Keep in mind that any book can be a good read aloud for a wide range of students, and that the illustrations in picture books deserve as much attention as the written text.

Going on a Hunt

The Terrible Tiger by Joy Cowley. Illus. by John Francis. Sunshine Books. The Wright Group, 1987.

Although written in repeated patterns to support emergent readers, it is a lively narrative that captures their attention. (emergent)

We're Going on a Bear Hunt by Michael Rosen. Illustrated by Helen Oxenbury. Margaret McElderry Books, 1989.

Rich vocabulary and humorous, cartoon-like pictures make this a splendid book for reading aloud or independently. (emergent)

We're Going on a Lion Hunt by David Axtell. Holt, 1999.

This version features "real" children setting out for a day of play and lion hunting. (emergent)

"Sneaking Up" Stories with Surprise Endings

The Ghost by Joy Cowley. Story Box. The Wright Group, 1983.

A very easy "sneaking up" story with a surprise ending. (emergent)

A Dark Dark Tale by Ruth Brown. Dial, 1981.

A classic "sneaking up story" with a mysterious tone that begins in a dark, dark moor and ends with a surprise. (emergent)

A Beasty Story by Bill Martin. Illus. by Steven Kellogg. Harcourt, 1999.

Similar to Ruth Brown's story, but a rollicking version that opens in a dark, dark wood and ends with a surprise. (emergent)

Fishing with Dad

Just Like Daddy by Frank Asch. Simon & Schuster, 1981.

A young bear does everything "just like daddy," until his family goes fishing. He catches a fish, but this time, it is "just like mommy." (emergent)

Gone Fishing by Earlene Long. Illus. by Richard Brown. Houghton Mifflin, 1984.

A warm-hearted story about a father and son who spend the day fishing together. (emergent)

Father Bear Comes Home by Else Holmelund Minarik. Illus. by Maurice Sendak. HarperCollins, 1987.

Little Bear goes fishing while he waits for Father Bear to come home from his ocean fishing trip. (transitional)

Trying to Catch a Tasty Hen

Hattie and the Fox by Mem Fox. Illus. by Patricia Mullins. Simon & Schuster, 1987.

A worried hen thinks she sees a fox in the bushes, but her barnyard friends pay no heed to her warnings. (emergent)

Rosie's Walk by Pat Hutchins. Simon & Schuster, 1968.

Rosie the Hen takes a pleasant walk through the barnyard, oblivious to the hungry fox who is trying to catch her. (emergent)

Across the Stream by Mirra Ginsburg. Illus. by Nancy Tafuri. Greenwillow, 1982.

The book opens with a picture of a dreaming, curled-up fox, and a hen and her chicks are having a bad dream. (emergent)

All Fall Down

All Fall Down by Brian Wildsmith. Oxford, 1983.

A simple cumulative narrative of one animal climbing on top of another until they "all fall down." (emergent)

The Napping House by Audrey Wood. Illus. by Don Wood. Harcourt, 1984.

It's a rainy day in this napping house, and one by one, all of the characters pile on top of the snoring granny. When a wakeful flea bites the mouse, they "all fall down." (emergent)

Mr. Gumpy's Outing by John Burningham. Holt, 1970.

When Mr. Gumpy gets ready to take his boat out on the river, a whole cast of characters, from children to goats, asks to come along. The ride goes smoothly for a while, but then everyone starts to squabble and they "all fall down." (transitional and for reading aloud)

Who Sank the Boat? by Pamela Allen. Putnam, 1996.

A cow, a donkey, a sheep, a pig, and a tiny little mouse decide to go for a ride in their boat. Guess which causes the boat to sink and "all fall down?" (transitional and for reading aloud)

Lively Cats

The Chase (Hey, Tabby Cat!) by Phyllis Root. Illus. by Katharine McEwen. Candlewick, 2000.

A simple narrative about the lively Tabby Cat who chases everything in sight. (emergent)

Cat on the Mat by Brian Wildsmith. Oxford Univ. Press, 1982.

One by one, a dog, a goat, a cow, and an elephant join the cat on his mat. The cat takes action and sends them all running. (emergent)

Cookie's Week by Cindy Ward. Illus. by Tomie dePaola. Putnam, 1988.

The adventurous Cookie causes trouble every day of the week. (emergent)

Feathers for Lunch by Lois Ehlert. Harcourt, 1990.

A hungry cat looking for lunch climbs higher and higher in a tree, looking for a tasty bird, but all he gets are "feathers for lunch." (transitional and for reading aloud)

Lovable Dogs

Where's Spot? by Eric Hill. Putnam, 1980.

Where's Spot? is just one of the many lift-the-flap books featuring this popular dog. (emergent)

Biscuit by Alyssa Satin Capucilli. Illus. by Pat Schories. HarperCollins, 1996.

Stories about the lovable Biscuit are written in two formats—"My First I Can Read Book" for emergent readers, and picture books for transitional readers. However, both may be read aloud to the same audience. (emergent and transitional)

Martha Speaks by Susan Meddaugh. Houghton Mifflin, 1992.

This is one of several books about an amazing dog who eats alphabet soup and can talk! (transitional and for reading aloud)

McDuff Moves In by Rosemary Wells. Illus. by Susan Jeffers. Hyperion, 1997.

There are four books about McDuff, a dog who escapes from the dogcatcher's truck and finds a home with a loving young couple. (transitional and for reading aloud)

Little Dog Poems by Krisitne O'Connell George. Illus. by June Otani. Clarion, 1999.

A series of small poems tell about the days of a little girl and her Little Dog. (transitional and for reading aloud)

School Days

Oliver Pig Goes to School by Jean Van Leeuwen. Illus. by Anne Schweninger. Puffin, 1990.

Oliver Pig worries about his first day of kindergarten, but he soon finds school is not so scary after all. (transitional)

Wemberly Worried by Kevin Henkes. Greenwillow, 2000.

Wemberly worries about everything, but she is especially worried about her first day of school. (transitional and for reading aloud)

Timothy Goes to School by Rosemary Wells. Viking, 2000.

Timothy eagerly starts school, but his attitude changes when he meets Claude, the boy who thinks he is the best at everything. Fortunately, Timothy also meets Violet, who becomes a true friend. (transitional and for reading aloud)

When the Wind Blows

Who Took the Farmer's Hat? by Joan Nodset. Illus. by Fritz Siebel. Harper-Collins, 1963.

The wind carries off the farmer's hat, which eventually becomes a nest for baby birds. (emergent to transitional)

Farmer Brown Goes Round and Round by Teri Sloat. Illus. by Nadine Bernard Westcott. DK Ink, 1999.

A twister picks up Farmer Brown and his animals and twirls them around. When they finally land back in the barnyard, things are mixed up. The pigs are mooing, the cows oinking, and the sheep start laying eggs! (transitional and for reading aloud)

The Wind Blew by Pat Hutchins. Simon & Schuster, 1974.

The wind blows so hard, it picks up scarves, umbrellas, and letters and mixes them about. (transitional and for reading aloud)

Author and Illustrator Study

Catch Me If You Can! by Bernard Most. Harcourt, 1999.

The biggest dinosaur of all frightens everyone except one little dinosaur—who calls him Grandpa. (emergent to transitional)

ABC T-Rex by Bernard Most. Harcourt, 2000.

A young dinosaur eats his way through the alphabet. (emergent)

How Big Were the Dinosaurs? by Bernard Most. Harcourt, 1995.

In this nonfiction book, the author shows how the dinosaurs measured up to a variety of familiar objects, such as school buses and supermarket aisles. (transitional)

Author and Illustrator Study with a Poetry Connection

Sharing Danny's Dad by Angela Shelf Medearis. Illus. by Jan Spivey Gilchrist. Celebration Press, 1993.

A boy's father must go to work, so Danny shares his Dad for the day. (emergent)

Annie's Gifts by Angela Shelf Medearis. Illus. by Anna Rich. Just Us Books, 1994.

Annie wants so much to play a musical instrument, just like everyone else in her family. She tries hard, but without success, so she seeks other ways of finding her gifts. (proficient and for reading aloud)

For the Love of the Game: Michael Jordan and Me by Eloise Greenfield. Illus. by Jan Spivey Gilchrist. HarperCollins, 1995.

Children approach the "game of life" the way Michael Jordan plays basketball. Artist Jan Spivey Gilchrist creates memorable images and expressive faces in this book, and the others she illustrates. (proficient and for reading aloud)

In Daddy's Arms I Am Tall: African Americans Celebrating Fathers. Illus. by Javaka Steptoe. Lee & Low, 1997.

Sumptuous collages illustrate poems celebrating fathers. (proficient and for reading aloud)

Gifts of Love

A Kiss for Little Bear by Else Holmelund Minarik. Illus. by Maurice Sendak. HarperCollins, 1968.

Little Bear asks Hen to take a picture to grandmother, who likes it so much she sends a kiss back to him by way of many friends. (transitional)

Ask Mr. Bear by Marjorie Flack. Simon & Schuster, 1932.

Danny asks his friends the animals to give him something for his mother's birthday. Nothing seems right until he meets Mr. Bear, who suggests a big bear hug. (transitional and for reading aloud)

A Birthday Basket for Tía by Pat Mora. Illus. by Cecily Lang. Simon & Schuster, 1992.

Cecelia and her cat Chica gather a basket of very special gifts to give her great aunt for her ninetieth birthday. (proficient and for reading aloud)

Artistic Partners

Old Grizzly by Joy Cowley. Illus. by Jan van der Voo. Sunshine Books. The Wright Group, 1987.

Old Grizzly watches a parade go by and feels left out because everyone else is having fun. (emergent)

Parade by Donald Crews. Greenwillow, 1983.

Artist Crews turns a parade into a visual feast. (transitional, but best for looking at the splendid illustrations)

Unique Voices

Henry and Mudge and the Happy Cat by Cynthia Rylant. Illus. by Suçie Stevenson. Simon & Schuster, 1990.

When a cat appears on the doorstep, Henry and Mudge and Henry's parents take care of it until the owner appears. (transitional).

I Am the Dog/I Am the Cat by Donald Hall. Illus. by Barry Moser. Dial, 1994.

In their own voices, the Dog and the Cat take turns explaining their points of view. (proficient and for reading aloud)

I Am the Cat by Alice Schertle. Illus. by Mark Buehner. Lothrop, 1999.

Sophisticated poems and paintings with hidden pictures make this an intriguing collection. (proficient and for reading aloud)

It's About Dogs by Tony Johnston. Illus. by Ted Rand. Harcourt, 2000.

The poems and paintings in this collection bring out some of the many aspects of dogs. (proficient and for reading aloud)

Nonfiction/Fiction Connection

Polar Bears by Marcia Freeman. Capstone Press, 1999.

This brief text provides an easy-to-read introduction to polar bears. (emergent)

Polar Bears by Sarah Palmer. Rourke, 1989.

This clearly written, informative text describes many aspects of polar bear life. (transitional)

Ice Bear and Little Fox by Jonathan London. Illus. by Daniel San Souci. Dutton, 1998.

Striking paintings and a poetic text follow the adventures of a young polar bear. (proficient and for reading aloud)

The Polar Bear Son: An Inuit Tale retold and illustrated by Lydia Dabcovich. Clarion, 1997.

An old woman raises a polar bear as a son. (proficient and for reading aloud)

APPENDIX B
Picture Books for Emergent Readers

There are many wonderful picture books that are just right for emergent readers. I have listed just a few. Check your school and public library collections for these books, and ask the librarian to recommend others just like them. Some books have been re-issued and the original publication dates may be different from the dates listed below.

Ahlberg, Janet and Allan. 1988. *Each Peach Pear Plum.* New York: Viking.

Aliki. 1987. *We Are Best Friends.* New York: Morrow.

Axtell, David. 1999. *We're Going on a Lion Hunt.* New York: Holt.

Asch, Frank. 1981. *Just Like Daddy.* New York: Simon & Schuster.

Baker, Keith. 1999. *Quack and Count.* San Diego: Harcourt.

———. 1994. *The Big Fat Hen.* San Diego: Harcourt.

———. 1990. *Who Is the Beast?* San Diego: Harcourt.

Barton, Byron. 1981. *Building a House.* New York: Greenwillow.

———. 1995. *Buzz Buzz Buzz.* New York: Simon & Schuster.

———. 1989. *Dinosaurs, Dinosaurs.* New York: HarperCollins.

———. 1993. *The Little Red Hen.* New York: HarperCollins.

———. 1991. *The Three Bears.* New York: HarperCollins.

Bennett, David. 1990. *One Cow Moo Moo.* Illus. by Andy Cooke. New York: Holt.

Berenstain, Stan and Jan. 1971. *Bears in the Night.* New York: Random House.

Brown, Margaret Wise. 1947. *Goodnight Moon.* New York: HarperCollins.

Brown, Ruth. 1981. *A Dark Dark Tale.* New York: Dial.

Browne, Anthony. 1997. *I Like Books.* New York: Random House.

————. 1989. *Things I Like.* New York: Random House.

Butler, Dorothy. 1989. *My Brown Bear Barney.* Illus. by Elizabeth Fuller. New York: Greenwillow.

————. 2001. *My Brown Bear Barney at the Party.* Illus. by Elizabeth Fuller. New York: Greenwillow.

Cabrera, Jane. 1999. *Over in the Meadow.* New York: Holiday House.

Campbell, Rod. 1986. *Dear Zoo.* New York: Simon & Schuster.

Carle, Eric. 1997. *From Head to Toe.* New York: HarperCollins.

————. 1987. *Have You Seen My Cat?* New York: Simon & Schuster.

————. 1993. *Today is Monday.* New York: Philomel.

————. 1984. *The Very Busy Spider.* New York: Philomel.

————. 1970. *The Very Hungry Caterpillar.* New York: Philomel.

Carter, David. 1988. *How Many Bugs in a Box?* New York: Simon & Schuster.

Catalanotto, Peter. 1989. *Dylan's Day Out.* New York: Orchard.

Charlip, Remy. 1993. *Fortunately.* New York: Simon & Schuster.

Christelow, Eileen. 1989. *Five Little Monkeys Jumping on the Bed.* New York: Clarion.

Crews, Donald. 1986. *Flying.* New York: Greenwillow.

————. 1986. *Ten Black Dots.* New York: Greenwillow.

Cuyler, Margery. 2000. *Roadsigns: A Harey Race with a Tortoise.* Illus. by Steve Haskamp. Delray Beach, FL: Winslow Press.

Dorros, Aruthur. 1992. *Alligator Shoes.* New York: Dutton

Ehlert, Lois. 1992. *Planting a Rainbow.* San Diego: Harcourt.

————. 1995. *Snowballs.* San Diego: Harcourt.

Elting, Mary & Michael Folsome. 1980. *Q is for Duck: An Alphabet Guessing Game.* Illus. by Jack Kent. New York: Clarion.

Flack, Marjorie. 1997. *Angus and the Cat.* New York: Farrar, Straus and Giroux

Fleming, Denise. 1993. *In the Small Small Pond.* New York: Holt.

————. 1991. *In the Tall Tall Grass.* New York: Holt.

————. 1997. *Time to Sleep.* New York: Holt.

Fox, Mem. 1987. *Hattie and the Fox.* Illus. by Patricia Mullins. New York: Simon & Schuster.

Galdone, Paul. 1988. *Cat Goes Fiddle-i-fee.* New York: Clarion.

————. 1979. *Henny Penny.* Boston: Houghton Mifflin.

Gelman, Rita. 1993. *More Spaghetti, I Say!* Illus. by Mort Gerberg. New York: Scholastic.

Gershator, Phillis and David. 1998. *Greetings, Sun.* Illus. by Synthia St. James. New York: DK Ink.

Ginsburg, Mirra. 1982. *Across the Stream*. Illus. by Nancy Tafuri. New York: Greenwillow.

———. 1972. *The Chick and the Duckling*. Illus. by Jose Aruego and Ariane Dewey. New York: Simon & Schuster.

———. 1987. *Good Morning Chick*. Illus. by Byron Barton. New York: Greenwillow.

Guarino, Deborah. *Is Your Mama a Llama?* Illus. by Steven Kellogg. New York: Scholastic.

Hayes, Sarah. 1994. *This is the Bear*. Illus. by Helen Craig. Cambridge, MA: Candlewick.

Hill, Eric. 1980. *Where's Spot?* New York: Putnam.

Hoberman, Mary Ann, adapter. 2000. *The Eeensy Weensy Spider*. Illus. by Nadine Bernard Westcott. Boston: Little Brown.

Hoberman, Mary Ann. 2000. *The Two Sillies*. Illus. by Lynn Cravath. San Diego: Harcourt.

Hort, Lenny. 2000. *The Seals on the Bus*. Illus. by G. Brian Karas. New York: Holt.

Huck, Charlotte. 1998. *A Creepy Countdown*. Illus. by Jos. A. Smith. New York: Greenwillow.

Hudson, Cheryl and Bernette Ford. 1990. *Bright Eyes, Brown Skin*. Illus. by George Ford. Orange, NJ: Just Us Books.

Hutchins, Pat. 1986. *The Doorbell Rang*. New York: Greenwillow.

———. 1973. *Goodnight Owl*. New York: Viking Penguin.

———. 1991. *Happy Birthday Sam*. New York: Greenwillow.

———. 1999. *It's My Birthday*. New York: Greenwillow.

———. 1968. *Rosie's Walk*. New York: Simon & Schuster

———. 1991. *Tidy Titch*. New York: Greenwillow.

———. 1971. *Titch*. New York: Simon & Schuster.

———. 1990. *What Game Shall We Play?* New York: Greenwillow.

———. 1988. *Where's the Baby?* New York: Greenwillow.

———. 1983. *You'll Soon Grow Into Them, Titch*. New York: Greenwillow.

Jonas, Ann. 1984. *The Quilt*. New York: Greenwillow.

———. 1985. *The Trek*. New York: Greenwillow.

———. 1982. *Two Bear Cubs*. New York: Greenwillow.

Joyce, William. 1985. *George Shrinks*. New York: HarperCollins.

Jorgensen, Gail. 1994. *Crocodile Beat*. New York: Simon & Schuster.

Kalan, Robert. 1981. *Jump, Frog, Jump!* Illus. by Byron Barton. New York: Greenwillow.

———. 1987. *Rain*. Illus. by Donald Crews. New York: Greenwillow.

Kovalski, Maryann. 1990. *The Wheels on the Bus*. Boston: Little, Brown

Kraus, Robert. 1987. *Come Out and Play, Little Mouse.* Illus. by Jose Aruego and Ariane Dewey. New York: Greenwillow.

———. 1994. *Leo the Late Bloomer.* New York: HarperCollins.

———. 1986. *Where Are you Going, Little Mouse?* Illus. by Jose Aruego and Ariane Dewey. New York: Greenwillow.

Krauss, Ruth. 1945. *The Carrot Seed.* Illus. by Crockett Johnson. New York: HarperCollins.

Johnson, Crockett. 1977. *Harold and the Purple Crayon.* New York: Harper-Collins.

Jones, Carol. 1998. *Old MacDonald Had a Farm.* Boston: Houghton Mifflin.

Langstaff, John. 1974. *Oh, A-Hunting We Will Go.* Illus. by Nancy Winslow Parker. New York: Atheneum.

Lindgren, Barbro. 1982. *Sam's Cookie.* Illus. by Eva Eriksson. New York: Morrow.

———. 1982. *Sam's Teddy Bear.* Illus. by Eva Eriksson. New York: Morrow.

———. 1983. *Sam's Ball.* Illus. by Eva Eriksson. New York: Morrow.

———. 1983. *Sam's Lamp.* Illus. by Eva Eriksson. New York: Morrow.

———. 1986. *Sam's Wagon.* Illus. by Eva Eriksson. New York: Morrow.

London, Jonathan. 2000. *Snuggle Wuggle.* Illus. by Michael Rex. San Diego: Harcourt.

———. 1999. *Wiggle Waggle.* Illus. by Michael Rex. San Diego: Harcourt.

Long, Erlene. 1984. *Gone Fishing.* Illus. by Richard Brown. Boston: Houghton Mifflin.

Maris, Ron. 1982. *My Book.* New York: Penguin.

Martin, Bill. 1999. *A Beasty Story.* Illus. by Steven Kellogg. San Diego: Harcourt.

———. 1984. *Brown Bear, Brown Bear, What Do You See?* Illus. by Eric Carle. New York: Holt.

———. 1992. *Polar Bear, Polar Bear, What Do You Hear?* Illus. by Eric Carle. New York: Holt.

Martin, Bill and John Archambault. 1989. *Chicka Chicka Boom Boom.* Illus. by Lois Ehlert. New York: Simon & Schuster.

Mayer, Mercer. 1985. *All By Myself.* New York: Golden Press.

———. 1968. *There's a Nightmare in My Closet.* New York: Dial.

McLeod, Emilie. 1986. *The Bear's Bicycle.* Boston: Little, Brown

McMillan, Bruce. 1988. *Growing Colors.* New York: Lothrop.

———. 1990. *Mary Had a Little Lamb.* New York: Scholastic.

McPhail, David. 1988. *The Bear's Toothache.* Boston: Little Brown.

———. 1984. *Fix-It.* New York: Dutton.

Morozumi, Atsuko. 1993. *One Gorilla.* New York: Farrar, Straus and Giroux.

Most, Bernard. 1999. *Z-Z-Zoink!* San Diego: Harcourt Brace.

Nodset, Joan. 1963. *Who Took the Farmer's Hat?* Illus. by Fritz Siebel. New York: HarperCollins.

Peek, Merle. 1988. *Mary Wore Her Red Dress and Henry Wore His Green Sneakers.* New York: Clarion.

———. 1981. *Roll Over.* New York: Clarion.

Price, Hope Lynn. 1999. *These Hands.* Illus. by Bryan Collier. New York: Hyperion.

Raffi. 1989. *Five Little Ducks.* Illus. by Jose Aruego and Ariane Dewey. New York: Crown.

———. 1998. *The Wheels on the Bus.* Illus. by Sylvie Kantorovitz. New York: Crown

Raschka, Chris. 2000. *Ring! Yo?* New York: DK Ink.

———. 1993. *Yo! Yes?* New York: Orchard.

Rice, Eve. 1993. *Benny Bakes a Cake.* New York: Greenwillow.

Robart, Rose. 1986. *The Cake That Mack Ate.* Illus. by Maryann Kovalski. Boston: Little Brown.

Rockwell, Anne. 1993. *Boats.* New York: Dutton.

———. 1992. *Cars.* New York: Dutton.

Roth, Susan. 1998. *Cinnamon's Day Out.* New York: Dial.

Root, Phyllis. 1998. *Turnover Tuesday.* Illus. by Helen Craig. Cambridge, MA: Candlewick.

Rosen, Michael. 1989. *We're Going on a Bear Hunt.* Illus. by Helen Oxenbury. New York: McElderry.

Serfozo, Mary. 1988. *Who Said Red?* Illus. by Keiko Narahashi. New York: McElderry.

Seuling, Barbara. 1976. *The Teeny Tiny Woman.* New York: Viking.

Seuss, Dr. 1960. *Green Eggs and Ham.* New York: Random House.

———. 1963. *Hop on Pop.* New York: Random House.

Shannon, David. 1999. *David Goes to School.* New York: Scholastic.

Shaw, Charles. 1988. *It Looked Like Spilt Milk.* New York: HarperCollins.

Shaw, Nancy. 1986. *Sheep in a Jeep.* Illus. by Margot Apple. Boston: Houghton Mifflin.

Stadler, John. 1984. *Hooray for Snail!* New York: HarperCollins.

Stickland, Paul and Henrietta. 1994. *Dinosaur Roar!* New York: Dutton.

Stinson, Kathy. 1988. *Red is Best.* Illus. by Robin Baird Lewis. Toronto: Annick Press.

Swinburne, Stephen. 2000. *What's Opposite?* Honesdale, PA: Boyds Mills Press.

Tafuri, Nancy. 1984. *Have You Seen My Duckling?* New York: Greenwillow.

—. 1988. *Spots, Feathers, and Curly Tails.* New York: Greenwillow.

—. 1986. *Who's Counting?* New York: Greenwillow.

Titherington, Jeanne. 1990. *Pumpkin Pumpkin.* New York: Morrow.

Walsh, Ellen Stoll. 1996. *Hop Jump.* San Diego: Harcourt.

Ward, Cindy. 1988. *Cookie's Week.* Illus. by Tomie dePaola. New York: Putnam.

Wells, Rosemary. 1999. *Noisy Nora.* New York: Dial.

Westcott, Nadine Bernard. 1988. *I Know an Old Lady Who Swallowed a Fly.* Boston: Little Brown.

—. 1992. *Peanut Butter and Jelly: A Play Rhyme.* New York: Dutton.

—. 1990. *The Lady with the Alligator Purse.* Boston: Little Brown.

Wildsmith, Brian. 1982. *The Cat on the Mat.* New York: Oxford University Press.

Williams, Sue. 1990. *I Went Walking.* Illus. by Julie Vivas. San Diego: Harcourt.

Wood, Audrey. 1990. *The Little Mouse, the Red Ripe Strawberry, and the Big Hungry Bear.* Illus. by Don Wood. Child's Play.

—. 1984. *The Napping House.* Illus. by Don Wood. San Diego: Harcourt.

—. 1990. *Quick as a Cricket.* Illus. by Don Wood. Child's Play.

Young, Ed. 1992. *Seven Blind Mice.* New York: Philomel.

INDEX

213